WISDOM
IS A TREE OF
LIFE

A COMMENTARY ON THE BOOK OF PROVERBS

DAVID MELIN

WESTBOW
PRESS®
A DIVISION OF THOMAS NELSON
& ZONDERVAN

WestBow Press books may be ordered through booksellers or by contacting:

WestBow Press
A Division of Thomas Nelson & Zondervan
1663 Liberty Drive
Bloomington, IN 47403
www.westbowpress.com
844-714-3454

ISBN: 978-1-6642-0558-1 (sc)
ISBN: 978-1-6642-0559-8 (hc)
ISBN: 978-1-6642-0557-4 (e)

Library of Congress Control Number: 2020917626

Print information available on the last page.

WestBow Press rev. date: 11/17/2020

CONTENTS

Preface 1

Outline 3

A Study of Proverbs 5

- Learn and Then Live 7
- The Fear of the LORD 11
- Birds of a Feather Flock Together .16
- A Woman Scorned 20
- The Wisdom Hunter 23
- With Strings Attached 27
- A Beatitude to Wisdom 31
- Sweet Dreams 36
- Grandfather Knows Best 39
- Mind Your Step 43
- Preventing Heart Disease 47
- Biblical Sex Education 51
- I Am in Your Debt 55
- Aesop the Plagiarist 58
- Dirty Rotten Scoundrels 62
- God's Black List 66
- The Seventh Commandment 70
- The Moral of the Story 74
- The Tale of Two Women 78
- One Woman Who Will Tell Her Age 82
- Two Dinner Invitations 85
- Parental Pain or Pleasure 89
- Riches and Righteousness 91
- Desires and Destinies 93

- The Reward of Diligence 94
- The Blessed Life 96
- A Good Reputation 98
- The Talk of Fools 100
- Integrity 102
- The Fountain of Life 103
- Love Covers All 105
- Wise and Foolish Talk 107
- Wealth and Poverty 109
- The Wages of the Wicked. 111
- The Path of Life 113
- Slanderous Lies. 114
- Watch Your Mouth. 116
- The Power of the Tongue 118
- Wealth Enhancement 120
- The Pursuit of Pleasure. 122
- A Firm Foundation. 124
- The Sluggard 126
- The Fear of the LORD. 128
- The Way of the LORD. 130
- The LORD'S Land 132
- An Abomination to the LORD 134
- Pride. 136
- The Rewards of Righteousness. 137
- Warnings for the Wicked 139
- The Words of the Wicked. 141
- That Makes No Sense 143
- We the People. 145
- Honor. 147
- Cruel Intentions 149
- Be Sure Your Sin Will Find You Out 151
- Beautiful Women. 152
- Generosity 154
- Consequences. 156
- Family Inheritance 158
- A Fruitful Life 160
- Discipline. 162
- Divine Favor. 164
- What Were You Thinking?. 166

- Insight for Living 168
- Better Than 170
- In the Eye of the Beholder 172
- The Fool and the Prudent. 174
- Honesty is the Best Policy 176
- The Plot Thickens 178
- High Anxiety 180
- Shame on You. 182
- Wealth Management 183
- Strife. 185
- A Word of Advice 187
- Healthy Words 189
- The Life of a Fool 190
- Poverty. 192
- A Work Ethic 194
- Human Emotions. 196
- The Simple 198
- Patience 200
- Wisdom 202
- The Scoffer. 203
- Divine Omniscience 205
- Royal Proverbs 207
- Honesty 209
- The Wicked 211
- The Family 213
- Bribery 215
- Injustice 217
- Friendship 219
- Deep Waters 221
- Disputes 222
- The Fool. 224
- Royal Proverbs 226
- An Introduction to the 30 Sayings (22:17–21) 228
- Don't Exploit the Poor (22:22–23) 230
- Don't Associate with the Angry Man (22:24–25) 230
- Don't Make Rash Vows (22:26–27) 231
- Don't Steal from Others (22:28). 231
- Don't Be Lazy (22:29) 232
- Don't Eat Too Much (23:1–3) 232

- Don't Accumulate Wealth (23:4–5) 233
- Don't R.S.V.P. (23:6–8) 234
- Don't Talk to Fools (23:9) 234
- Don't Rob the Poor (23:10–11)...........................235
- Be a Good Listener (23:12)..............................235
- Don't Spoil Your Children (23:13–14) 235
- Make Your Parents Happy (23:15–16) 236
- Don't Envy the Wicked (23:17–18)....................... 236
- Live a Disciplined Life (23:19–21) 237
- Listen to Your Parents (23:22–25) 238
- Avoid Immorality (23:26–28)............................ 238
- Don't Abuse Alcohol (23:29–35) 239
- Don't Envy Evil Men (24:1–2) 240
- The Wise Builder (24:3–4)..............................241
- Brains Enhance Brawn (24:5–6) 242
- The Silent Fool (24:7)................................. 242
- The Schemer, the Sinner, and the Scoffer (24:8–9)...... 243
- High Anxiety (24:10) 243
- Get Involved (24:11–12) 244
- Pass the Honey (24:13–14).............................245
- The Righteous Will Rise (24:15–16) 245
- Don't Gloat (24:17–18)................................ 246
- Don't Worry about Others (24:19–20) 246
- Don't Rebel (24:21–22) 247
- Don't Play Favorites (24:23–25) 247
- Tell the Truth (24:26)................................ 248
- Do Your Homework (24:27)............................. 249
- Don't Lie (24:28) 249
- Don't Retaliate (24:29)...............................250
- Don't Be Lazy (24:30–34) 250
- The Proverbs of Solomon (25:1–29:27)..................251
- The Words of Agur (30:1–33)........................... 298
- The Words of King Lemuel (31:1–9) 307
- The Ideal Woman (31:10–31) 309
- The Ideal Woman: Her Rhetorical Rarity (31:10)........311
- The Ideal Woman: Her Impact on Her Husband (31:11–12, 23)....311
- The Ideal Woman: Her Impact on Her Family (31:13–27)........312
- The Ideal Woman: Words of Praise (31:28-30)...................314

Proverbs Index. **317**

PREFACE

In the fall of 2002, I traveled for the first time to the city of Kremenchuk, located on the banks of the Dnieper River in central Ukraine, to teach at the Kremenchuk Evangelical Seminary. I had been invited by its founder, Pastor Alexander Vasilyevich Zigalenko, to teach the book of Acts to a group of thirteen Ukrainian Baptist pastors. The initial teaching trip was a very gratifying experience for the students and teacher alike, and I was invited back to teach the following year. My congregation, Rush City Baptist Church, was very supportive of this ministry and they financed an annual teaching trip to Ukraine. The annual teaching trip has now doubled in frequency so that I teach once in the spring and the second time in the fall. I have now made 25 trips to Ukraine to teach at the seminary. My church also enjoys a sister church experience with the Rakovka Evangelical Church in Kremenchuk.

The following year, 2003, I taught the course Wisdom Literature, which is an introduction to the wisdom books of Psalms and Proverbs. When I took my students to their library to find a commentary in Russian on these two books, I realized there was very little in the Russian language by way of commentaries. My first attempt at writing a commentary resulted in the book "Meditations on the Psalter," a 750–page commentary covering the 150 Psalms and the book was published in Russian in the country of Ukraine. This project from start to finish was an eight-year endeavor. I wrote the book in English and it was translated into Russian by my good friend and translator, Bogdan Pais, who lives in the city of Cherkassy.

Based on the positive response from my Ukrainian audience, I determined to write a second commentary on the book of Proverbs. Beginning with my class notes, I began to read the main English commentaries on the book of Proverbs (Allen P. Ross, Tremper Longman, Bruce Waltke, Duane A. Garrett, Roland E. Murphy, David A. Hubbard, Derek Kidner, C.H. Toy) and began to write additional notes. Through the process of reading and writing for

1

three years, I was able to complete the commentary on Proverbs and had it translated into Russian for my Ukrainian audience. The book has been published in Russian and has been well-received as well.

Even though the commentary was originally written for the Russian-speaking church, the biblical truths of wisdom are relevant for an English-speaking audience as well. While I am a professor of Bible Exposition in Ukraine, I am first and foremost a pastor of a local church in Minnesota and my practical pastoral perspective is reflected in the nature of the commentary. While I will comment on some matters of Hebrew language and poetry, I focus more attention on the theological and cultural issues in play when the original wisdom material was first written. And, because biblical wisdom is timeless, the truths for the original audience are relevant for today's believer as well.

OUTLINE

I.   A Study of Proverbs.

II.   The Purpose Statement (1:1–6).

III.   The Theme of the Book (1:7).

IV.   The Long Addresses (1:8–9:18).
      A.   Birds of a Feather Flock Together (1:8–19).
      B.   A Woman Scorned (1:20–33).
      C.   The Wisdom Hunter (2:1–22).
      D.   With Strings Attached (3:1–12).
      E.   A Beatitude to Wisdom (3:13–20).
      F.   Sweet Dreams (3:21–35).
      G.   Grandfather Knows Best (4:1–9).
      H.   Mind Your Step (4:10–19).
      I.   Preventing Heart Disease (4:20–27).
      J.   Biblical Sex Education (5:1–23).
      K.   I Am in Your Debt (6:1–5).
      L.   Aesop the Plagiarist (6:6–11).
      M.   Dirty Rotten Scoundrels (6:12–15).
      N.   God's Black List (6:16–19).
      O.   The Seventh Commandment (6:20–35).
      P.   The Moral of the Story (7:1–27).
      Q.   The Tale of Two Women (8:1–21).
      R.   One Woman Who Will Tell Her Age (8:22–36).
      S.   Two Dinner Invitations (9:1–18).

V.   The Individual Proverbs of Solomon (10:1–22:16).

VI.   The Words of the Wise (22:17–24:22).

VII.   More Sayings of the Wise (24:23–34).

VIII.   Hezekiah's Collection of the Proverbs of Solomon (25:1–29:27).

IX.   The Words of Agur (30:1–33).

X.   The Words of Lemuel (31:1–9).

XI.   The Ideal Woman (31:10–31).

A STUDY OF PROVERBS

Introduction

Proverbs are used in most cultures to convey values. A well-known Middle Eastern proverb states, "The enemy of my enemy is my friend." There is a proverb from Nigeria that says, "He who sleeps with puppies catches fleas." An ancient Latin proverb advises, "If there is no wind, row." There is a French proverb that states, "One meets his destiny often on the road one takes to avoid it." Thomas Paine was an American philosopher and writer who lived during the Revolutionary War. He wrote, "Virtue is not hereditary." Another famous American who lived during that time was Benjamin Franklin, and he said, "Fish and visitors stink in three days." And, there is a Russian proverb that says, "If your heart is not clear, the day will be foggy."

Proverbs are concise, memorable statements of truth. They are fascinating sayings because they show the ordinary to be extraordinary.

> One pretends to be rich, yet has nothing; another pretends
> to be poor, yet has great wealth. (Proverbs 13:7)

The unique phrasing of proverbs hit home to the reader with great impact.

> Like a gold ring in a pig's snout is a beautiful woman without
> discretion. (Proverbs 11:22)

Proverbs convey their truth with a touch of humor.

Whoever meddles in a quarrel not his own is like one who takes a passing dog by the ears. (Proverbs 26:17)

And, proverbs are timeless expressions of truth proven over and over again by experience.

Wealth gained hastily will dwindle, but whoever gathers little by little will increase it. (Proverbs 13:11)

C. Hassell Bullock in his book *An Introduction to the Old Testament Poetic Books* writes,

Many persons who have become overwhelmed by a theoretical approach to Christianity have been able to get a "handle" on the faith by reading the book of Proverbs. For this book represents the commonsense approach to life and faith. It touches the shared concerns of all who are given the gift of life and struggle with how to live it. For those who are recipients of the fits of faith, this book distills the theological substance of Old Testament religion into its practical essence.

Interpretation

The following four hermeneutical (hermeneutics is defined as the art and science of biblical interpretation) rules are useful in helping the biblical student interpret the proverbs more accurately. The first rule is to think of proverbs as stating broad principles about life, and not as offering the reader binding promises from God. If the advice of the proverb is followed, and all other things being equal, blessings are likely to follow. However, the student is not guaranteed success. A good illustration of this rule concerns the training of children.

Broad not Binding

Train up a child in the way he should go; even when he is old he will not depart from it. (Proverbs 22:6)

The second rule encourages the student to consider the context of the proverbs. Proverbs must be read and balanced with other statements of wisdom, and compared with the rest of the scriptures.

Be not one of those who give pledges, who put up security
for debts. (Proverbs 22:26)

The third rule says that proverbs have limits. Proverbs are worded to be memorable, not to be precisely accurate.

If a ruler listens to falsehood, all his officials will be wicked.
(Proverbs 29:12)

The fourth rule requires the student to translate the proverb into a modern equivalent so that it is understood.

Do not move the ancient landmark that your fathers have
set. (Proverbs 22:28)

To understand this warning about stealing, one needs to be familiar with the Mosaic Law.

You shall not move your neighbor's landmark, which the
men of old have set, in the inheritance that you will hold in
the land that the LORD your God is giving you to possess.
(Deuteronomy 19:14)

"Learn and Then Live"
PROVERBS 1:1–6

Introduction

The superscription attributes the book of Proverbs to Solomon ("son of David, king of Israel"), but some sections of the book were written by other wisdom writers for younger members of the royal household (the men of Hezekiah in 25:1; Agur in 30:1; Lemuel in 31:1). Most scholars believe the material written by Solomon actually begins in chapter 10. The material was then compiled by a teacher who wanted to encourage his students to develop skill in two areas, namely, skillful living and skillful thinking.

Proverbs were written to develop skillful living (1:2a, 3–5). The first purpose statement says, "To know wisdom and instruction." Allen P. Ross writes that the Hebrew verb *yada* "encompasses an intellectual and experiential acquisition of wisdom and discipline." It is similar to the combination of formal schooling and learning on the job. The wisdom writer wanted his students to know two valuable commodities, namely, wisdom and instruction. The basic meaning of the word "wisdom" (*hokmah*) in all contexts is skill. For example, the word describes the skill of the Tabernacle craftsmen.

> And behold, I have appointed with him Oholiab, the son of Ahisamach, of the tribe of Dan. And I have given to all able men ability, that they may make all that I have commanded you. (Exodus 31:6).

The word was also used to describe the wits of seasoned sailors. "They reeled and staggered like drunken men and were at their wits' end" (Psalm 107:27). The word was also used to speak of the administrative justice of Solomon.

> And all Israel heard of the judgment that the king had rendered, and they stood in awe of the king, because they perceived that the wisdom of God was in him to do justice. (1 Kings 3:28)

And finally, it was used to describe the wise advice of a counselor. Consider this interesting Old Testament narrative.

> Then the woman went to all the people in her wisdom. And they cut off the head of Sheba the son of Bichri and threw it out to Joab. So he blew the trumpet, and they dispersed from the city, every man to his home. And Joab returned to Jerusalem to the king. (2 Samuel 20:22)

In the book of Proverbs, "wisdom" signifies skillful living, which is the ability to make wise decisions and to live successfully according to the moral standards of God's Word. A person with this wisdom has "expertise" in godly living. It is the combination of moral and spiritual intelligence.

The second term, "instruction" (*musar*) comes from the Hebrew verb "to admonish" or "to correct." The word denotes the training or discipline of the moral nature, involving verbal and corporal correction. It expresses the sometimes-painful process of acquiring wisdom as the student learns to fear the Lord.

Verse 3 develops the first purpose statement. "To receive instruction in wise dealing, in righteousness, justice, and equity." If the student will receive discipline, he will learn to behave wisely. This concept is illustrated by the behavior of Abigail toward David when she intercepted him on the way to kill her foolish husband, Nabal (1 Samuel 25). "Wise dealing" (*haskel*) is demonstrated when the individual does what is righteous, just, and equitable. The term "righteous" (*sedeq*) is from the verb "to be straight" which basically means conformity to a standard. For the believer, it means meeting God's standards in every area of life.

> These are the generations of Noah. Noah was a righteous man, blameless in his generation. Noah walked with God. (Genesis 6:9)

The term "justice" (*mispat*) describes that which is proper or fitting. Proverbs will develop a life that will have a sense of respectability in making wise decisions. And, the term "equity" (*mesarim*) describes that which is pleasing or acceptable. The book will instruct us in how to live a life that is pleasing, first to God, then to others, and also to ourselves.

Next, there is the application of the first purpose statement. Proverbs are intended "to give prudence to the simple, knowledge and discretion to the youth—Let the wise hear and increase in learning, and the one who understands obtain guidance" (1:4–5). The book of Proverbs will benefit a wide variety of people on the spiritual spectrum. The "simple" (*peti*) refers to a person who is naïve and inexperienced. That person is not an idiot, nor one who cannot comprehend. Nor is this individual a fool who despises wisdom. Instead, these are individuals whose exposure to life and wisdom has been limited. Because of this inexperience, they are gullible and easily influenced.

> The simple believes everything, but the prudent gives thought to his steps. (Proverbs 14:15)

The simple individual needs "prudence" (*orma*) which is the positive aspect of shrewdness which is the ability to foresee evil and avoid it.

> I, wisdom, dwell with prudence, and I find knowledge and discretion. (Proverbs 8:12)

The second category of individual who will benefit from proverbs is the "youth" (*na'ar*), the immature young person who needs "knowledge and discretion," this when taken together, describes the perceptive ability to develop a plan of attack to avoid making foolish decisions in the early stages of life.

The third category of individual who will benefit from proverbs is on the other end of the spiritual spectrum. The "wise" (*hakam*) individual cannot be kept from this book for he knows that continuing education is a lifelong process. The apostle Paul reflected this wise mindset when he wrote later in life.

> That I may know him and the power of his resurrection, and may share his sufferings, becoming like him in his death. (Philippians 3:10)

"Learning" is the comprehension of the truth and the ability to communicate it to others. The "one who understands" can obtain "guidance" from this book so they will continue in the right direction.

The book of Proverbs was also written to develop skillful thinking. The second purpose statement is found in the second half of verse 2 that says, "To understand words of insight." And then verse 6 states, "to understand a proverb and a saying, the words of the wise and their riddles." The word "understand" is the ability to distinguish between things, to compare, to form evaluations, to be discerning. This term was illustrated by Solomon's ability to discern between the claims of the two prostitutes who were mothers (1 Kings 3:16–28). The wisdom writer wanted his students to be discerning in two areas.

The first area is identified by the phrase "words of the wise." Proverbs will train people to discern lessons about life, such as distinguishing permanent values from immediate gratification. More will be said about this in the following chapters of the book.

The second area is identified by the word "proverb" which is the master category in which the following terms can be placed. A proverb (*mashal*) is a statement that seeks to reveal the true nature of one thing by comparing it to something else. Allen Ross defines a proverb "as an object lesson based on or using some comparison or analogy." Another term in this category is "a saying" (*melisa*) which is a puzzling saying that is intended to be ambiguous. Two other terms are "words of the wise" (practical instruction), and "riddles" (teasing questions that are clear enough to give clues to their solution, but also cryptic). One such riddle was given by Samson to his wedding guests.

> Out of the eater came something to eat. Out of the strong came something sweet. (Judges 14:14)

Consider this perspective on proverbs in general.

> The secondary purpose of Proverbs is to introduce the reader to a style of teaching that provokes his thoughts, getting under his skin by thrusts of wit, paradox, common sense, and teaching symbolism. (Derek Kidner)

"The Fear of the LORD"

PROVERBS 1:7

Introduction

"The fear of the LORD is the beginning of knowledge; fools despise wisdom and instruction." This statement is the theme of wisdom literature throughout the Old Testament. It is the climax of a poem on wisdom in the book of Job.

> Behold, the fear of the Lord, that is wisdom, and to turn away from evil is understanding. (Job 28:28)

It is the conclusion to an acrostic psalm listing the attributes of God.

> The fear of the Lord is the beginning of wisdom; all those who practice it have a good understanding. (Psalm 111:10)

It is the summation of the book of Ecclesiastes.

> The end of the matter; all has been heard. Fear God and keep his commandments, for this is the whole duty of man. (Ecclesiastes 12:13)

Contrast between the wise + the fool

This theme sets the tone for the entire book of Proverbs. The ten discourses in Proverbs 1:8–9:18 appear to be a development of this theme. And, the contrast between the wise and the fool, which begins in this verse, continues throughout the book.

The phrase "the fear of the LORD" occurs fourteen times in the book of Proverbs (1:7, 29; 2:5; 8:13; 9:10; 10:27; 14:26–27; 15:16, 33; 16:6; 19:23; 22:4; 23:17). The verbal form "fear the LORD" occurs four times in the book (3:7; 14:2; 24:21; 31:30).

The wise person is one who fears the LORD (1:7a). The term "fear" can describe a variety of feelings. Fear described the intimidation the nation of Israel felt toward the Canaanites who already inhabited the land (Deuteronomy 1:29). It also described the terror the sailors felt during the storm as Jonah was trying to flee from God (Jonah 1:10). It was also used to describe the awe the people felt toward Solomon for his wisdom.

> And all Israel heard of the judgment that the king had rendered, and they stood in awe of the king, because they perceived that the wisdom of God was in him to do justice. (1 Kings 3:28)

The term can also speak of respect.

> Every one of you shall revere his mother and his father, and you shall keep my Sabbaths: I am the LORD your God. (Leviticus 19:3)

Allen Ross writes, "With the LORD as the object, fear captures both aspects of shrinking back in fear and drawing close in awe." A great example of this dual response took place at Mount Sinai.

> When the people saw the thunder and lightning and heard the trumpet and saw the mountain in smoke, they trembled with fear. They stayed at a distance and said to Moses, "Speak to us yourself and we will listen. But do not have God speak to us or we will die." Moses said to the people, "Do not be afraid. God has come to test you, so that the fear of God will be with you to keep you from sinning." The people remained at a distance, while Moses approached the thick darkness where God was. (Exodus 20:18–21)

Consider the following perspective on fearing God.

> "Fear" is best understood as "reverent obedience." Although it includes worship, it does not end there. It radiates out from our adoration and devotion to our everyday conduct that sees each moment as the Lord's time, each relationship as the Lord's opportunity, each duty as the Lord's command, and each blessing as the Lord's gift. It is a new way of looking at life and seeing what it is meant to be when viewed from God's perspective. (David A. Hubbard)

Notice other definitions of "the fear of the LORD" found in the book of Proverbs.

> The fear of the LORD is hatred of evil. Pride and arrogance and the way of evil and perverted speech I hate. (Proverbs 8:13)

> The fear of the LORD is the beginning of wisdom, and the knowledge of the Holy One is insight. (Proverbs 9:10)

> The fear of the LORD is instruction in wisdom, and humility comes before honor. (Proverbs 15:33)

> By steadfast love and faithfulness iniquity is atoned for, and by the fear of the LORD one turns away from evil. (Proverbs 16:6)

The term "beginning" (*re'sit*) describes that which is foundational, the necessary starting point. Derek Kidner writes of, "the first or controlling principle, rather than a stage which one leaves behind."

> What the alphabet is to reading, notes to reading music, and numerals to mathematics, the fear of the LORD is to attaining the revealed knowledge of this book. (Bruce Waltke)

Having a reverential awe of the LORD and living in a subservient position to His Word is the first step in living a wise life. While it is possible to have knowledge or expertise in certain areas of life, apart from having an intimate knowledge of God, it is impossible to fully comprehend life when the Author of life is not known and revered. The word "knowledge" is a general term for knowledge, particularly that which is of a personal, experiential nature. It is a synonym for wisdom.

The New Testament authors made the same observation about individuals who claimed to be wise, but did not have a knowledge of God. The apostle Paul spoke of individuals who only had a superficial knowledge of God, but who lacked the reverential fear that leads to intimate knowledge.

> For although they knew God, they did not honor him as God or give thanks to him, but they became futile in their thinking, and their foolish hearts were darkened. Claiming to be wise, they became fools. (Romans 1:21–22)

He said much the same thing about the unsaved Gentiles to the church in Ephesus.

> They are darkened in their understanding, alienated from the life of God because of the ignorance that is in them, due to their hardness of heart. (Ephesians 4:18)

The wisdom writer next describes the foolish person (1:7b). There are three Hebrew words that are translated "fool" in the book of Proverbs. One kind of "fool" (kesil) is mentally dull and unteachable. This individual is simpleminded and obstinate.

> The heart of him who has understanding seeks knowledge, but the mouths of fools feed on folly (Proverbs 15:14)

This term occurs more frequently in Proverbs than the other two words (48 times). Another kind of "fool" (nabal) is one who does not comprehend spiritual truths. This word is used only three times in the book of Proverbs.

> Fine speech is not becoming to a fool; still less is false speech to a prince. (Proverbs 17:7)

The third kind of "fool" (ewil) which is the term used here, is conceited and disrespectful, as well as mentally dull. This person is crude and hardened in their ways. This word is used nineteen times in Proverbs. The emphasis is more on moral deficiency than on mental capacity. In Proverbs this kind of "fool" lacks discernment.

> The lips of the righteous feed many, but fools die for lack of sense. (Proverbs 10:21)

The fool does not gain knowledge.

> The wise lay up knowledge, but the mouth of a fool brings ruin near. (Proverbs 10:14)

The fool does not grasp wisdom.

> Wisdom is too high for a fool; in the gate he does not open his mouth. (Proverbs 24:7)

The fool thinks he is smart when he is not.

> Answer a fool according to his folly, lest he be wise in his own eyes. (Proverbs 26:5)

The fool is quarrelsome.

> It is an honor for a man to keep aloof from strife, but every fool will be quarreling. (Proverbs 20:3)

The fool rejects correction.

> A fool despises his father's instruction, but whoever heeds reproof is prudent. (Proverbs 15:5)

To "despise" (*buz*) means "to hold in contempt, to treat as insignificant." It is used seven other times in Proverbs (6:30; 11:12; 13:13; 14:21; 23:9, 22; 30:17). Fools are unteachable precisely because they are wise in their own eyes, and view God and biblical wisdom with disdain. We have defined "wisdom" as the ability to live life skillfully, the ability to make wise choices. The second term "discipline" describes the training of the moral nature, involving verbal and corporal correction,

Wisdom - live life skillfully and make wise choices
Discipline - moral nature;

Conclusion

I was introduced to the book of Proverbs by Dr. Edward Glenny when I was in seminary. He paraphrased Proverbs 1:7 as, "A right relationship with the Lord is the foundation of all skillful living, but the morally deficient think that the Lord's will and discipline are unimportant."

"Birds of a Feather Flock Together"
PROVERBS 1:8–19

Introduction

Following the purpose statement (proverbs were written to develop skillful living; 1:2-6) and the theme of the book (a right relationship with God is the foundation to all skillful living; 1:7), this first major section elaborates on the theme in a series of addresses. The student is encouraged to consider, to compare, and then to choose between the ways of foolishness and the ways of wisdom. This lengthy section (1:8–9:18) serves as the introduction to the collection of concise sayings contained in the next section of the book. Its purpose is to whet the appetite of the reader and to prepare the mind for the individual sayings to come. The wisdom writers provide statement after statement to demonstrate the superiority of wisdom over any other course of life. Their statements focus generally on a productive and meaningful existence. This section runs in cycles: (1) the purpose of Proverbs is to give wisdom (1:1–7), but foolishness may interrupt this purpose (1:8–33); (2) there are advantages to seeking wisdom (2:1–4:27), but foolishness may prevent one from seeking it (5:1–6:19); and (3) there are advantages to finding wisdom (6:20–9:12), but foolishness may prevent this too (9:13–18).

This section begins with the admonition of the father.

> Hear, my son, your father's instruction, and forsake not your mother's teaching, for they are a graceful garland for your head and pendants for your neck. (Proverbs 1: 8–9)

According to this verse, the primary educators of children are the parents. This perspective is reflected in the statutes of the Mosaic Law.

You shall teach them diligently to your children, and shall talk of them when you sit in your house, and when you walk by the way, and when you lie down, and when you rise. (Deuteronomy 6:7)

The same responsibility is placed on Christian parents in the New Testament by the apostle Paul.

Fathers, do not provoke your children to anger, but bring them up in the discipline and instruction of the Lord. (Ephesians 6:4)

The father asks his son to give him his attention. Young people who heed their parents' counsel are promised an ornamental "garland" for the head and a "chain" about the neck. Following parental instruction will give young people a life that is attractive and productive. The implied contrast is that disobedience and rebellion lead to dishonor and ruin. The rebellious young person views parental boundaries as chains of bondage that are intended to limit the fun, rather than as chains of beauty that will limit the failures.

Observations

Notice the challenge parents are faced with when it comes to giving direction for their children's lives: (1) It is a competition between family and friends; (2) It is a competition between parents and peers; (3) It is friends offering excitement, versus parents who offer an education.

Next is the attraction of the wicked.

My son, if sinners entice you, do not consent. If they say, "Come with us, let us lie in wait for blood; let us ambush the innocent without reason; like Sheol let us swallow them alive, and whole, like those who go down to the pit; we shall find all precious goods, we shall fill our houses with plunder; throw in your lot among us; we will all have one purse. (Proverbs 1:10–14)

The basic idea of the Hebrew verb "entice" is "to be open, spacious, or wide." This verb belongs to the same word family of the noun translated "simple" (1:4). The word might relate to the immature or simple young person who is open to all kinds of enticement, not having developed a discriminating judgment as to what is right and wrong. Notice what bad companions offer a young person who lacks discernment. "Come with us" offers acceptance (1:11a). "Let us ambush the innocent without reason" offers adventure (1:11b). "Let us swallow them alive" offers power (1:12). "We shall find all precious goods" offers prosperity (1:13). "We will all have one purse" offers security (1:14).

The wisdom writer closes out the section by detailing the destruction of the wicked.

> My son, do not walk in the way with them; hold back your foot from their paths, for their feet run to evil, and they make haste to shed blood. For in vain is a net spread in the sight of any bird, but these men lie in wait for their own blood; they set an ambush for their own lives. Such are the ways of everyone who is greedy for unjust gain; it takes away the life of its possessors. (Proverbs 1:15–19)

The appeal of the wicked, which is so attractive initially, is presented by the father in its full scope. A foolish person is dazzled by the prospects of acquiring wealth easily and being gratified quickly by the immediate. But a wise person views the long-term consequences of sin and foolishness. The father urges his son not to become involved with these people for it will begin an irreversible course of action that leads to sin and sorrow. The sad truth that the unsuspecting youth does not see is that these so-called friends are also offering something that none of them can see, namely, the promise of self-destruction. Notice the sad irony: those who boast, "let us ambush the innocent without reason" (1:11) will "set an ambush for their own lives" (1:18).

The reference to "birds" allows the father to make the analogy that even birds are smart enough to avoid a trap if they see it being set. Here is an interesting alternative interpretation of the statement.

> "In the eyes of a bird, the net is spread [with grain] for no reason." If taken this way the meaning would be, the bird does not see any connection between the net and what is scattered on it; it just sees food that is free for the taking. In the process it is trapped and killed. In the same way, the gang

cannot see the connection between their acts of robbery and the fate that entraps them. (Duane Garrett)

The father describes the poetic justice of their future. Those who "lie in wait" to attack others will be caught in their own trap. "Unjust gain" cannot be enjoyed. Crime does not pay. Thieves who take the money of others will find that it takes their own lives. The apostle Paul offered a similar warning.

Do not be deceived: God is not mocked, for whatever one sows, that will he also reap. (Galatians 6:7)

Conclusion

For the young adults who are the focus of these opening addresses, as they stand on the threshold of adulthood, they are susceptible to two primary temptations, namely, easy money and casual sex. The father knows of these temptations and so he addresses them in this section and the one to follow. Sin, while it often appears exciting and initially appealing, always leaves the participant with a self-inflicted wound. Satan understands our need for social acceptance, and therefore makes the appeal to join in sin to be a part of peer pressure. The book of Numbers provides an apt caption for this passage.

But if you will not do so, behold, you have sinned against the LORD, and be sure your sin will find you out. (Numbers 32:23)

A life of discipline, while it is never easy and is initially boring, is the only resource to provide a young person with a life that is both attractive and productive.

Application

Here are some practical suggestions for parents who have younger children. Successfully rearing wise children requires early intervention. Don't wait until your children are older to give them your time and advice. When your children are young, talk to them about God. When your children are older, talk to God about them. It requires two parents who are equally committed to biblical truth, to their marriage, and to their children's discipline. Be aware of who your children are spending time with. Check out the home life of your children's friends. Know what they are doing when away from home. Develop a friendship with your children's friends. Be aware that your actions will always speak louder to your children than your advice. Save your "no's" for the really important issues and be more flexible with the minor ones. Be a consistent parent. Remind your children that a household is not a democracy. Be loving parents who allow their children to feel the negative consequences of sin.

"A Woman Scorned"
PROVERBS 1:20–33

Introduction

Having warned his son of the false allurements of the wicked (Hubbard calls the section of 1:10–14, "the siren song of the wicked"), namely, companionship, adventure, wealth, and security, the father now personifies Wisdom as a woman who desires to attract simple and naïve young people to her way of life. This personified character will reappear in chapters 8 and 9. Longman says of this character, "she is the personification of Yahweh's wisdom and thus stands for God himself." Notice three features about this particular address. The tense of the address is past tense ("I have called and you refused to listen"). The invitation had been offered and had been rejected by the naïve young men ("because you have ignored all my counsel and would have none of my reproof"). Now, it is too late (1:24–25). Because of their rejection, the tone of the address is negative and condemning. Wisdom is no longer inviting the audience to listen. She is hurling her condemnation at them because they would not listen. Finally, the terminology of the address is sarcastic and almost chilling (1:26). Wisdom acts as though is too late so that the young and naïve she is appealing to will take her seriously.

The section begins with Wisdom's rejection of fools.

> Wisdom cries aloud in the street, in the markets she raises her voice; at the head of the noisy streets she cries out; at the entrance of the city gates she speaks: How long, O simple ones, will you love being simple? How long will scoffers delight in their scoffing and fools hate knowledge? If you

turn at my reproof, behold, I will pour out my spirit to you;
I will make my words known to you." (Proverbs 1:20–23)

While the appeal of the wicked is normally given in secret, the appeal of
Wisdom is quite public. The image of this section is that of a town crier who
walks the streets of the village shouting public announcements and words of
warning. Notice the verbs that describe Wisdom's public appeal: (1) "Wisdom
cries aloud"; (2) "she raises her voice"; (3) "she cries out"; and (4) "she speaks."
Notice also the location of this invitation, which implies that the offer of Wisdom
was a public invitation that was readily available for anyone who would accept:
(1) "in the street"; (2) "in the markets"; (3) "at the head of the noisy streets"; and
(4) "at the entrance of the city gates." Consider this perspective on Wisdom.

Wisdom is not some hidden treasure that has to be dug from
the depths of the earth or the sole possession of the lonely
sage sitting atop a mountain. To the contrary, Wisdom
roams the streets looking for someone to instruct. The ways
of right and wrong, as presented in the word of God are open
for all to read and follow. (Duane A. Garrett)

Using rhetorical questions, Wisdom rebukes three different types of people
who refused to forsake their sinful ways (1:22). There seems to be a progression in
the confirmed condition of those who are rebuked, as indicated by the emotional
responses of each group. First, "simple ones" are naïve and untaught people who
"love being simple. They are not stupid people who cannot comprehend. Instead,
they are young people whose exposure to life and wisdom has been limited.
Because of their inexperience, they are gullible and easily influenced. Second,
"scoffers" are proud people who refuse to accept instruction from either God or
from others. They have progressed to the point that they find "delight in their
scoffing" of wisdom by ridiculing the lifestyle of the wise.

Blessed is the man who walks not in the counsel of the
wicked, nor stands in the way of sinners, nor sits in the seat
of scoffers. (Psalm 1:1)

Finally, "fools" are now confirmed in their nature to the point that they
actually "hate knowledge." They are stubborn, lazy, and shortsighted people
who reject the instruction of others (1:7).

Having identified her audience, Wisdom now makes her offer, implying that it is not too late for the gullible youth. Wisdom demands that they recognize the dangerous path they are on, and that they "turn at her reproof." The verb "turn" (*sub*) speaks of an individual who is going one way, but who then turns and goes in the opposite direction. This physical change of direction becomes an important word picture in the Old Testament for the theological concept of spiritual repentance. When genuine repentance is demonstrated, the reward is the possession of Wisdom's "spirit" (*ruah*). This leads to a greater understanding of her "words" of wisdom, two concepts that take on greater import in the Bible.

The next section addresses the fools' rejection of Wisdom (1:24–25, 29–30). Using the conditional term "because," notice the various responses to Wisdom's offer: (1) "Because I have called and you refused to listen, have stretched out my hand and no one has heeded"; (2) "because you have ignored all my counsel and would have none of my reproof"; (3) "Because they hated knowledge and did not choose the fear of the LORD"; and (4) "would have none of my counsel and despised all my reproof."

The warning of the dangers of repeatedly rejecting Wisdom's offer is similar to the prophet Isaiah and his warning to the nation of Judah.

> I was ready to be sought by those who did not ask for me; I was ready to be found by those who did not seek me. I said, "Here am I, here am I," to a nation that was not called by my name. I spread out my hands all the day to a rebellious people, who walk in a way that is not good, following their own devices. (Isaiah 65:1-2)

In this chapter the prophet rehearses the dominant themes that have been discussed throughout the prophecy of Isaiah. God reminds the nation of His sovereign choice to make them His special people, and their insulting response to His gracious selection. God was continually reaching out to these people, and they repeatedly rejected His overtures because they were too busy pursuing their own sinful interests.

Next are the consequences of rejecting Wisdom. "I also will laugh at your calamity; I will mock when terror strikes you, when terror strikes you like a storm and your calamity comes like a whirlwind, when distress and anguish come upon you. Then they will call upon me, but I will not answer; they will seek me diligently but will not find me. Therefore they shall eat the fruit of their way, and have their fill of their own devices" (1:26–28, 31).

The consequences of rejecting Wisdom's offer fall into two categories. First, there is the personal reaction. Wisdom's reactions are sarcasm (1:26) and silence (1:28). Because Wisdom has been continually rejected, she will laugh at the calamity of those who have rejected her. Allen Ross writes, "The figure of laughing reveals the absurdity of choosing a foolish life and being totally unprepared for disaster."

> The wicked plots against the righteous and gnashes his teeth at them; but the Lord laughs at the wicked, for he sees that his day is coming. (Psalm 37:12–13)

Then there are the natural consequences of rejecting Wisdom. The natural consequences are described as a "storm" and a "whirlwind" (1:27). It is also described as food that does not nourish or satisfy (1:31). The expression "they will eat the fruit of their ways" is an Old Testament equivalent to Paul's statement, "Do not be deceived: God is not mocked, for whatever one sows, that will he also reap" (Galatians 6:7).

The address concludes with an antithetical summary.

> For the simple are killed by their turning away, and the complacency of fools destroys them; but whoever listens to me will dwell secure and will be at ease, without dread of disaster. (Proverbs 1:32–33)

The address is encapsulated in the final two verses. Ignoring Wisdom will result in self-destruction caused by "complacency," while heeding Wisdom will guarantee genuine security and serenity. Complacency is just as dangerous as rejection, for it is a delayed no.

"The Wisdom Hunter"
PROVERBS 2:1–22

Introduction

Because life is full of dangerous landmines for the unsuspecting youth, the acquisition of wisdom is the key to survival. Two major temptations for a young person are highlighted: wicked men who offer power and easy money, and the promiscuous woman who offers passion and easy sex. The father urges his son to make the acquisition of wisdom his primary pursuit.

> The "alphabetic" poem is a single sentence consisting of 22 verses, matching the number of letters in the Hebrew alphabet, probably to suggest its completeness. (Bruce Waltke)

The section begins with the determination necessary for the acquisition of wisdom.

> My son, if you receive my words and treasure up my commandments with you, making your ear attentive to wisdom and inclining your heart to understanding; yes, if you call out for insight and raise your voice for understanding, if you seek it like silver and search for it as for hidden treasures. (Proverbs 2:1–4)

The entire person must be dedicated to the serious pursuit of wisdom. First, notice the verbs that emphasize the hands and the heart (2:1). The verb "receive" means "to accept" or "to lay hold of." While the teacher can offer wise advice, it is up to the student to accept it. The second verb "treasure up" means "to hide" something of great value for future use. The verb conveys the image of storing up a great treasure on account of its value to the individual. Biblical wisdom is stored up, not as a collection of facts, but as truths to be applied to one's life. Also, because the learner is young, the wisdom may not be readily apparent, so the student will need to store up the teachings for future use.

Next notice the verbs that emphasize the ears and the heart (2:2). In the expression "making your ear attentive" the verb describes the activity of hearing, with the emphasis on paying close attention. The physical act of eavesdropping is a good word picture for the verb. In the second expression "inclining your heart" the verb means "to extend, to stretch out." Then, there are verbs that emphasize the mouth (2:3). The two verbs "call out" and "raise your voice" create a word picture of searching for someone who is lost by calling out their name. Because biblical wisdom does not always come easily, the student must make a greater effort to possess it.

Finally, there are verbs that emphasize the eyes (2:4). The first verb "seek" means "to seek after, to search for, to inquire about." The basic meaning speaks of a person's earnest seeking after something that is of great value. The intention is that it is an object to be found or acquired. Job had a great commentary on the effort to find wisdom by comparing it to the search for precious metals.

> Man puts his hand to the flinty rock and overturns mountains by the roots. He cuts out channels in the rocks, and his eye sees every precious thing. He dams up the streams so that they do not trickle, and the thing that is hidden he brings out to light. (Job 28:9–11)

Consider these observations. The "if" statements reveal that every young person has important life choices to make. These choices will determine the success or failure of life. Success is not automatic, nor is failure accidental. Successful living is based on the choices a person makes regarding the pursuit of wisdom found in God's Word. The choices cannot be avoided, nor can they be combined with both options. The choices are key because they reflect and determine the character that will go with that young person the remainder of life. And the effort that one puts into the acquisition of biblical wisdom will be reflected by the impact that biblical wisdom has on the person's life.

Next, there is the discovery of the wisdom.

> Then you will understand the fear of the LORD and find the knowledge of God. For the LORD gives wisdom; from his mouth come knowledge and understanding; he stores up sound wisdom for the upright; he is a shield to those who walk in integrity, guarding the paths of justice and watching over the way of his saints. Then you will understand righteousness and justice and equity, every good path; for wisdom will come into your heart, and knowledge will be pleasant to your soul; discretion will watch over you, understanding will guard you." (Proverbs 2:5-11)

The "if" clauses are followed by several "then" clauses that demonstrate result. This stresses the importance of choice. The acquisition of wisdom comes after a deliberate decision. In the remaining verses we see the integral connection between wisdom and a relationship with the LORD.

The first benefit of wisdom is the discernment of God's will (2:5-8). Earlier "the fear of the LORD" was defined as a Hebrew expression that described an Old Testament saint who had an intimate relationship with God (1:7). The phrase expresses a reverential submission to God's will as revealed through His Word. Although the search for wisdom demands effort on the part of the student (2:1–4), the teacher reminds him that it is the "LORD who gives wisdom" (2:6). James says the same thing in the New Testament.

> If any of you lacks wisdom, let him ask God, who gives generously to all without reproach, and it will be given him. (James 1:5)

The student who single-mindedly pursues wisdom will receive success and safety ("shield"). Individuals who choose not to pursue wisdom are putting their lives at risk.

The second benefit of wisdom is the discernment of man's ways (2:9–11). Wisdom will both protect and preserve the young person. The student will develop the intellectual capacity and moral insight to discern what is "right and just and fair," namely, "every good path," which describes the journey of life. And the learning process will be a "pleasant" experience for the student.

The next section provides two case studies in the application of wisdom (2:12–19). First, wisdom is a protection from perverse men.

> Delivering you from the way of evil, from men of perverted speech, who forsake the paths of uprightness to walk in the ways of darkness, who rejoice in doing evil and delight in the perverseness of evil, men whose paths are crooked, and who are devious in their ways. (Proverbs 2:12–15)

Evil people can be detected by how they talk ("perverted speech"), by how they walk ("whose paths are crooked"), and by what they take pleasure in ("rejoice in doing evil").

Second, wisdom is a protection from the promiscuous woman.

> So you will be delivered from the forbidden woman, from the adulteress with her smooth words, who forsakes the companion of her youth and forgets the covenant of her God; for her house sinks down to death, and her paths to

the departed; none who go to her come back, nor do they regain the paths of life. (Proverbs 2:16–19)

Notice the different ways a young man can detect a promiscuous woman. She flatters the unsuspecting young man with her words (7:14–20). She forsakes her husband and her vows before God. And, she is fatal to her victims. The address concludes with a summary statement.

So you will walk in the way of the good and keep to the paths of the righteous. For the upright will inhabit the land, and those with integrity will remain in it, but the wicked will be cut off from the land, and the treacherous will be rooted out of it. (Proverbs 2:20–22)

Choices reflect character. Choices determine consequences. The choices are either righteousness or wickedness. The consequences are either life or death.

Failure to heed wisdom's call leads either to premature death or to a life so void of happiness as to be a living death in which none of the God-given blessings of the earth is available to lend any joy or meaning to life. (David Hubbard)

"With Strings Attached"
PROVERBS 3:1-12

Introduction   *3rd in series of 10*   *Responsibility = Reward*
Irresponsibility = I Key Consequences

This is the third in a series of ten exhortations given by the father to his son. While the first addresses were more negative in tone, this one is a positive motivational speech. These verses follow an alternating pattern with the odd verses giving the responsibilities of life, and the even verses stating the rewards of wise living. The first two series address the son's relationship to people, with the next four series addressing his relationship to God.
The father begins with the son's obligations to others.

My son, do not forget my teaching, but let your heart keep my commandments, for length of days and years of life and peace they will add to you. Let not steadfast love and faithfulness forsake you; bind them around your neck; write them on the tablet of your heart. So you will find favor and good success in the sight of God and man. (Proverbs 3:1–4)

The father first promises the son that obedience to his teaching will bring longevity (3:1–2). The verb "forget" can also mean "to ignore." Forgetfulness is not always due to a lapse in memory. Sometimes forgetfulness occurs when an individual chooses to ignore something not felt to be important. This is supported by the second verb "keep" that implies the action of obedience. So, instead of forgetting, the son could choose to not remember his father's teaching (*torah*). The parents must fulfill their God-given task of teaching their children about God's Word.

And these words that I command you today shall be on your heart. You shall teach them diligently to your children, and shall talk of them when you sit in your house, and when you walk by the way, and when you lie down, and when you rise. You shall bind them as a sign on your hand, and they shall be as frontlets between your eyes. You shall write them on the doorposts of your house and on your gates. (Deuteronomy 6:6–9)

And then the children need to see that their parents have taken personal ownership of God's Word ("my commands"). This is based on the belief that the father's teaching comes from the Pentateuch. A "prolonged" life was an Old Testament sign of God's blessing and it was often associated with obedience to one's parents.

Honor your father and your mother, that your days may be long in the land that the LORD your God is giving you. (Exodus 20:12)

A prolonged life is more than just years and wealth (quantity). A prolonged life includes "peace" which signifies a life of substance and significance (quality).

The father next promises his son that the performance of his obligations will bring him credibility with God and man (3:3–4). The combination of "steadfast love and faithfulness" describes the very nature of God in His covenant relationship with Israel.

The LORD passed before him and proclaimed, "The LORD, the LORD, a God merciful and gracious, slow to anger, and abounding in steadfast love and faithfulness, keeping steadfast love for thousands, forgiving iniquity and transgression and sin, but who will by no means clear the guilty, visiting the iniquity of the fathers on the children and the children's children, to the third and the fourth generation." (Exodus 34:6–7)

These two covenant terms also describe what Israel's commitment should be to God and what their obligation ought to be to one another. The former term "steadfast love" (*hesed*) speaks of fidelity shown toward others. The latter word "faithfulness" (*'emet*) is the quality of being dependable. God's people are to be known for their consideration of others and for their consistency. The verb "forsake" describes the abandonment of virtuous qualities. The next two phrases figuratively describe the effort that is necessary to make these teachings a part of the student's nature. They speak of the external adornment ("bind them around your neck") and the internal attitude ("write them on the tablet of your heart"). A considerate and consistent person will have credibility with God and with people (2 Corinthians 8:21). In the next section the father speaks of the son's obligations to God.

Do it right

Trust in the LORD with all your heart, and do not lean on your own understanding. In all your ways acknowledge him, and he will make straight your paths. Be not wise in your own eyes; fear the LORD, and turn away from evil. It will be healing to your flesh and refreshment to your bones. Honor the LORD with your wealth and with the firstfruits of all your produce; then your barns will be filled with plenty, and your vats will be bursting with wine. My son, do not despise the LORD's discipline or be weary of his reproof, for the LORD reproves him whom he loves, as a father the son in whom he delights. (Proverbs 3:5–12)

The father promises the son that dependence on God will bring serenity to life (3:5–6). The verb "trust" means "to rely on" or "to feel secure." It describes complete security in God alone. We are to trust God: (a) entirely ("with all your heart"); (b) exclusively ("do not lean on your own understanding"); and (c) extensively ("in all your ways acknowledge him"). Both the will ("heart") and the mind ("understanding") are to be submitted to God. When we rely completely on God we are promised "straight paths" instead of rocky roads. Consider this interesting observation about the pursuit of wisdom.

> The acquisition of wisdom and competence was stressed by none as highly as by the teachers; but they also knew that wherever it gives a man a sense of security or where it tempts him into boasting, wisdom has already cancelled itself out. (Von Rad)

Next the father promises his son that reverence for God will bring <u>vitality</u> to life (3:7–8). The reverential fear of God will protect the individual from two common problems, namely, pride ("wise in your own eyes") and sin ("turn away from evil"). This combination of fearing God and shunning evil was the description of the Old Testament character Job.

> There was a man in the land of Uz whose name was Job, and that man was blameless and upright, one who feared God and turned away from evil. (Job 1:1)

The words "flesh" and "bones" are holistic terms, not just physical ones. They describe an overall spiritual soundness of body and mind, rather than just physical health.

Then the father promises his son that a preference for the LORD will bring <u>prosperity</u> to life (3:9–10). This "honor" is not a matter of words, for the father provides tangible ways for his son to show respect to God. In Israel, honoring God with the "first fruits of all your produce" was a way of expressing gratitude to Him for His provision, and expressing faith in Him for the rest of the harvest.

> When you come into the land that the LORD your God is giving you for an inheritance and have taken possession of it and live in it, you shall take some of the first of all the fruit of the ground, which you harvest from your land that the LORD your God is giving you, and you shall put it in a basket, and you shall go to the place that the LORD your God will choose, to make his name to dwell there. And you shall go to the priest who is in office at that time and say to

him, I declare today to the LORD your God that I have come into the land that the LORD swore to our fathers to give us. (Deuteronomy 26:1–3)

Please note that there are several financial principles that I have gleaned from the writings of Ron Blue and other financial advisors who write from a biblical perspective. God owns it all. God has the right to whatever He wants whenever He wants it. It is all His, because an owner has rights, and I, as a steward, have only responsibilities. Every spending decision is a spiritual decision. You cannot fake stewardship. Your checkbook reveals your priorities. God uses money and material possessions as a tool to be properly invested, as a test to determine your character, and as a testimony. The amount is not important, but how you handle what you have been entrusted is what is important.

Finally, the father tells his son that the acceptance of divine discipline will bring maturity to life (3:11–12). The verb "despise" means "to reject" or "to take lightly." The second verb "be weary" means "to be grieved" or "to loathe." Believers are not to resent God's discipline of their lives for it is evidence of His love for them. The Bible has numerous passages that describe the proper response to divine discipline. These verses are quoted by the writer of the book of Hebrews in a lengthy passage on discipline (12:4–11). Even though Job's advisor Eliphaz was wrong about the cause of his suffering, he was right when he spoke about the blessing of divine discipline.

> Behold, blessed is the one whom God reproves; therefore despise not the discipline of the Almighty. For he wounds, but he binds up; he shatters, but his hands heal. (Job 5:17–18)

"A Beatitude to Wisdom"
PROVERBS 3:13–20

Introduction

Having urged his son to fulfill his responsibilities in life, both to others and to God, the father continues the third address by describing the value of wisdom. Wisdom is evaluated from two perspectives: first, from a human viewpoint, and then from God's. The acquisition of wisdom is the most valuable commodity an individual can possess for it puts the person in a right relationship with God. And the presence of wisdom will affect every aspect of that individual's life.

The section begins with a practical argument for wisdom. Using the form of a beatitude ("Blessed is the one"), the father urges his son to pursue the acquisition of wisdom by stressing the practical rewards that result in its possession. The emphasis is on the direct connection between wise conduct and the blessed life.

> Blessed is the one who finds wisdom, and the one who gets understanding, for the gain from her is better than gain from silver and her profit better than gold. She is more precious than jewels, and nothing you desire can compare with her. Long life is in her right hand; in her left hand are riches and honor. Her ways are ways of pleasantness, and all her paths are peace. She is a tree of life to those who lay hold of her; those who hold her fast are called blessed. (Proverbs 3:13–18)

The father first speaks of the value of wisdom as seen in the effort to obtain it (3:13, 18). Notice the set of synonymous verbs used to describe the effort required to obtain wisdom. The person who "finds" wisdom does so after an extended time of deliberate seeking. Wisdom is not something accidentally stumbled upon. Job asked about the finding of wisdom in one of his addresses. And then, a few verses later he began to answer his own question. Job then completed the answer.

> But where shall wisdom be found? And where is the place of understanding? God understands the way to it, and he knows its place. Behold, the fear of the Lord, that is wisdom, and to turn away from evil is understanding. (Job 28:12, 23, 28)

The second verb "gain" reminds me of an athletic motto: "No pain, no gain." Once wisdom has been found, the individual needs to "hold her fast" so he will not lose his possession later on (3:18). The only way to maintain this valuable commodity is to "lay hold" of wisdom with a secure grasp. We must not only exert much effort to obtain wisdom, but we must also exert equal effort to maintain wisdom as well.

The father next says that the value of wisdom is seen in its effect upon the lives of those who have obtained it. First, the possession of wisdom will provide one's life with pleasure (3:13, 18). In order for a person to be "blessed," that is, truly happy, one must first trust God completely. Notice other wisdom sayings that promote the blessed or happy life.

> Whoever gives heed to instruction prospers, and blessed is he who trusts in the LORD. (Proverbs 16:20)

> Where there is no revelation, the people cast off restraint; but blessed is he who keeps the law. (Proverbs 29:18)

> He who despises his neighbor sins, but blessed is he who is kind to the needy. (Proverbs 14:21)

> Blessed is the man who does not walk in the counsel of the wicked or stand in the way of sinners or sit in the seat of mockers. (Psalm 1:1)

The father next tells his son that wisdom will provide his life with prosperity (3:14–15). Because wisdom brings genuine happiness that even financial wealth cannot supply, wisdom's eternal value far exceeds the temporal worth of precious metals. In another Wisdom Book, the Preacher warned of the risks of only pursuing earthly riches.

> Whoever loves money never has money enough; whoever loves wealth is never satisfied with his income. This too is meaningless. As goods increase, so do those who consume them. And what benefit are they to the owner except to feast his eyes on them? The sleep of a laborer is sweet, whether he eats little or much, but the abundance of a rich man permits him no sleep. (Ecclesiastes 5:10–12)

On the other hand, the wealth of biblical wisdom cannot contaminate the soul. And so, while the father is not denigrating wealth, he is promoting the pursuit of wisdom.

In the next section wisdom is personified (3:16, 18). Wisdom is personified as a woman who offers her treasures with both hands extended to the searching young person. In her right hand she offers a "long life" and in her left hand she offers "riches and honor." The Egyptians had a goddess of justice named Ma'at who carried the sign for life in one hand and a scepter, a symbol of riches and honor, in the other hand. In the United States the Statue of Liberty offers a light to those immigrants who are searching for freedom and opportunity. The father then changed the simile to describe Wisdom as a tree. In the Middle East a tree was a picture of life and vitality. Its leaves provided the weary traveler with shade and its fruit provided nourishment. This may also be a reference to the Genesis account where Adam and Eve were banished from the Garden of Eden and the Tree of Life because their disobedience broke their right relationship with God (Genesis 3:22–24). And what is interesting is the matter of the pursuit of wisdom in the narrative.

> So when the woman saw that the tree was good for food, and that it was a delight to the eyes, and that the tree was to be desired to make one wise, she took of its fruit and ate, and she also gave some to her husband who was with her, and he ate. (Genesis 3:6)

Finally, the father tells his son that wisdom will provide his life with peace (3:17). Besides giving a long life, wisdom also guarantees a quality life. Long life with no thought for its quality could be a curse rather than a blessing.

> Do not be overawed when a man grows rich, when the splendor of his house increases; for he will take nothing with him when he dies, his splendor will not descend with him. Though while he lived he counted himself blessed— and men praise you when you prosper—he will join the generation of his fathers, who will never see the light of life. A man who has riches without understanding is like the beasts that perish. (Psalm 49:16–20)

The father closes his address with a theological argument for wisdom.

> The LORD by wisdom founded the earth; by understanding he established the heavens; by his knowledge the deeps broke open, and the clouds drop down the dew. (Proverbs 3:19–20)

The commodities of "wisdom, understanding and knowledge" were used by God in the creation of the universe. If God used these qualities to create life, then people need God's wisdom to enjoy life.

Conclusion

Solomon is the poster boy for this section. When he came to the throne of Israel as a young man, following his father David's death, God came to him in a dream and made him an amazing offer.

> At Gibeon the LORD appeared to Solomon in a dream by night, and God said, "Ask what I shall give you." (1 Kings 3:5)

And Solomon made a wise choice.

> Give your servant therefore an understanding mind to govern your people, that I may discern between good and evil, for who is able to govern this your great people? (1 Kings 3:9)

And notice God's response to Solomon's choice.

> It pleased the Lord that Solomon had asked this. And God said to him, "Because you have asked this, and have not asked for yourself long life or riches or the life of your enemies, but have asked for yourself understanding to discern what is right, behold, I now do according to your word. Behold, I give you a wise and discerning mind, so that none like you has been before you and none like you shall arise after you. I give you also what you have not asked, both riches and honor, so that no other king shall compare with you, all your days. And if you will walk in my ways, keeping my statutes and my commandments, as your father David walked, then I will lengthen your days." (3:10–14)

Unfortunately, this narrative does not have a happy ending for later in life Solomon failed to hold fast to wisdom (1 Kings 11).

"Sweet Dreams"

PROVERBS 3:21-35

Introduction

The father exhorts his son to develop "sound wisdom" and to exercise "discretion" in his life. If the son will develop these related qualities, two benefits will result: they will prosper his own life (3:21–26) and they will produce better relationships with other people (3:27–35).

The section begins with the father's assessment of wise living.

> My son, do not lose sight of these—keep sound wisdom and discretion, and they will be life for your soul and adornment for your neck. Then you will walk on your way securely, and your foot will not stumble. If you lie down, you will not be afraid; when you lie down, your sleep will be sweet. Do not be afraid of sudden terror or of the ruin of the wicked, when it comes, for the Lord will be your confidence and will keep your foot from being caught. (Proverbs 3:21–26)

The combination of "sound wisdom and discretion" addresses the practical nature of wisdom. These two related qualities speak of being resourceful and shrewd in a good sense. Wisdom is not just the accumulation of information and facts. It is the application of that information so that sound decisions are made and discretion is exercised. Positively, practical wisdom is to be kept, and negatively, it is not to be lost sight of. The verbs address the concentration and long-term commitment needed when it comes to the acquisition and application of wisdom. In an earlier address the father told his son that wisdom guards those individuals who seek it. "Discretion will watch over you, understanding will guard you" (2:11). Now, he tells his son that those who seek wisdom will guard it (3:21). So, if the son will guard the Lord's wisdom, the Lord will guard his life.

Notice the rewards the father promises his son if he will treasure the biblical wisdom being offered. First, he will experience the beauty of an attractive life (3:22). A life that is characterized by wise living is attractive to others. The phrase "adornment for your neck" expresses the opinion that other people will have about his life if it is characterized by "sound wisdom and discretion." While it is most important what God thinks about our lives, it also matters what other people think about us as well. The apostle Paul included this in his qualifications for church leaders.

> Moreover, he must be well thought of by outsiders, so that he may not fall into disgrace, into a snare of the devil. (1 Timothy 3:7)

Second, the son will enjoy the security that comes from living wisely (3:23, 25, 26). These verses do not guarantee a trouble-free life, but they promise a safe environment that reduces the risk. They simply state the fact that the exercise of "sound wisdom and discretion" will not expose the individual to unnecessary risks. Individuals who make foolish decisions actually bring trouble on themselves. Verse 26 reminds the son of the presence of God in his life. If he will fulfill his obligations to live wisely, as defined by scripture, God promises to fulfill His covenant obligations to the son.

Third, the son will experience the serenity that comes from having a clear conscience (3:24). When individuals lie down to sleep, they are most susceptible to the attacks of others. One's mind is free to roam the problems of the day and the potential threats of the future. This verse addresses the attending peace of mind that comes to the individual who has made wise choices. Consider the words of the psalmist.

> In peace I will both lie down and sleep; for you alone, O LORD, make me dwell in safety. (Psalm 4:8)

Because of the psalmist's confidence in God, he could lie down and sleep in peace because he knew that his safekeeping was in God's hands. In the New Testament, the apostle Paul gave these instructions.

> Rejoice in the Lord always; again I will say, rejoice. Let your reasonableness be known to everyone. The Lord is at hand; do not be anxious about anything, but in everything by prayer and supplication with thanksgiving let your requests be made known to God. And the peace of God, which surpasses all understanding, will guard your hearts and your minds in Christ Jesus. (Philippians 4:4–7)

Because of justification, each believer has "peace with God" (Romans 5:1). But, the "peace of God" comes as a result of a close walk with God. This peaceful state of mind is beyond the human ability to comprehend while it guards believers' emotions and thoughts.

In the next section the father gives the application of sound judgment.

> Do not withhold good from those to whom it is due, when it is in your power to do it. Do not say to your neighbor, "Go, and come again, tomorrow I will give it"—when you have it with you. Do not plan evil against your neighbor, who dwells trustingly beside you. Do not contend with a man for no reason, when he has done you no harm. Do not envy a man of violence and do not choose any of his ways, for the devious person is an abomination to the LORD, but the upright are in his confidence. The LORD's curse is on the house of the wicked, but he blesses the dwelling of the righteous. Toward the scorners he is scornful, but to the humble he gives favor. The wise will inherit honor, but fools get disgrace. (Proverbs 3:27–35)

The father now gives his son some concrete examples of when he needs to apply "sound wisdom and discretion" in his life. This section addresses the topic of how the son should relate to others. First, the father tells his son to fulfill his obligations to his neighbors, referring specifically to other members of the covenant community of Israelites (3:27–28). Later in the New Testament, Jesus would tell a famous parable to expand the definition that a neighbor is any human being that you come into contact with (Luke 10:25–37).

What do the following verses have in common?

> We who are strong have an obligation to bear with the failings of the weak, and not to please ourselves. (Romans 15:1)

> In the same way husbands should love their wives as their own bodies. He who loves his wife loves himself. (Ephesians 5:28)

> Since all these things are thus to be dissolved, what sort of people ought you to be in lives of holiness and godliness. (2 Peter 3:11)

Beloved, if God so loved us, we also ought to love one another. (1 John 4:11)

Therefore we ought to support people like these, that we may be fellow workers for the truth. (3 John 8) *This is life — Prov. 3:27-35*

These verses speak of believers' obligations to other people in their lives. We are to keep our promises, honor confidences, do our work well, pay our bills, be a good neighbor, look for opportunities to get involved in people's lives, and lend a helping hand.

Second, the father tells his son not to attack his neighbor (3:29–30). The narrative of Jezebel's attack against Naboth comes to mind (1 Kings 21). Her husband, King Ahab, coveted the vineyard of Naboth which was near his palace, but Naboth would not sell the king his inheritance. So, Jezebel had several individuals bring false charges against Naboth, which resulted in his death.

Third, the father instructs his son not to emulate the wicked (3:31–35). There is often an attraction to people who use power to get what they want. The father lists four reasons why his son should not envy the wicked. First, because God finds dishonest people particularly offensive, but He enjoys a close relationship with the righteous (3:32). Second, God will ultimately punish the wicked and everything they hold precious, but He will bless the home of the righteous (3:33). Third, God hates arrogance and those individuals who mock His wisdom, but He responds graciously to the humble person (3:34). And fourth, God will bestow honor on those who live wisely, but He will put fools to shame (3:35).

"Grandfather Knows Best"
PROVERBS 4:1-9

Introduction

The father's greatest concern for his sons was that they would make the pursuit of wisdom their top priority in life. In an attempt to impress on them the importance of this pursuit, he recalled his own childhood and the exhortations he received from his father, their grandfather.

The father's instructions to his children.

Hear, O sons, a father's instruction, and be attentive, that you may gain insight, for I give you good precepts; do not forsake my teaching. (Proverbs 4:1–2)

Notice the sense of urgency in the father's voice as he exhorts his children to heed what he has to say. If his children will pay attention to what he has to say, they will gain a valuable commodity, namely, the moral "instruction" (*musar*) that will serve them well throughout their lives. The father's choice of verbs reveals an awareness of the human tendency for children to disregard the advice of their parents.

This disregard for parental advice is caused by a variety of factors. A key factor that causes children to disregard the instruction of their parents is their sinful nature that naturally rebels against authority. The following proverb expresses the problem succinctly.

Folly is bound up in the heart of a child, but the rod of discipline drives it far from him. (22:15)

There is the pressure by the youth's peer group to listen to them, and thus, disregard the parents. This peer pressure was expressed in the opening address of Proverbs (1:10–14). Another factor that hinders listening is the belief that the parents do not know what their children are going through. Another factor is the lack of communication between parents and children. The Mosaic Law addressed this possibility.

And these words that I command you today shall be on your heart. "You shall teach them diligently to your children, and shall talk of them when you sit in your house, and when you walk by the way, and when you lie down, and when you rise. (Deuteronomy 6:6–7)

Another danger is found in uninvolved parents who fail to address the issues in their children's lives. The high priest Eli is the poster child for this type of parent. God spoke of this when He talked to the young Samuel.

And I declare to him that I am about to punish his house forever, for the iniquity that he knew, because his sons were blaspheming God, and he did not restrain them. (1 Samuel 3:13)

Another factor, common today, is the Christian family that is busy with too many activities.

Notice the four synonymous terms that describe the educational process God intends to take place in a Christian home. "Instruction" is the body of biblical knowledge that is to be taught and modeled by the parents. This instruction is then to be learned and valued by the children. While teaching can result in learning, only the consistent modeling of biblical wisdom by the parents will cause the children to value what they see their parents value. "Insight" is the acquisition of wisdom that leads to discernment on the part of the children as they are exposed to more of life's choices. "Good precepts" are the parents' voice of experience that young people need to heed. "Teaching" focuses on the source of instruction that takes place in the home. For the writer of Proverbs, the source of teaching was the Old Testament Torah that provided the foundation of a Jewish parent's education of their children.

The father's recollection of his own childhood.

> When I was a son with my father, tender, the only one in the sight of my mother, he taught me and said to me. (Proverbs 4:3–4a)

In order to impress on his sons the importance of what he is saying, the father begins to recount the experiences of his own childhood when he was still young and impressionable. The education handed down from his parents, his children's grandparents, had shaped his life and had proven reliable. These words take on added significance because this was a shared experience.

The psalmist reminded his readers of their covenantal obligations to God and their educational obligations to the next generation.

> He established a testimony in Jacob and appointed a law in Israel, which he commanded our fathers to teach to their children, that the next generation might know them, the children yet unborn, and arise and tell them to their children, so that they should set their hope in God and not forget the works of God, but keep his commandments. (Psalm 78:5–7)

The New Testament example of this generational instruction was modeled for young Timothy by the maternal side of his family.

I am reminded of your sincere faith, a faith that dwelt first in your grandmother Lois and your mother Eunice and now, I am sure, dwells in you as well. (2 Timothy 1:3)

And then, later in the letter, Paul continued to talk about Timothy's homelife.

But as for you, continue in what you have learned and have firmly believed, knowing from whom you learned it and how from childhood you have been acquainted with the sacred writings, which are able to make you wise for salvation through faith in Christ Jesus. (2 Timothy 3:14–15)

The grandfather's instruction to the father is provided.

Let your heart hold fast my words; keep my commandments, and live. Get wisdom; get insight; do not forget, and do not turn away from the words of my mouth. Do not forsake her, and she will keep you; love her, and she will guard you. The beginning of wisdom is this: Get wisdom, and whatever you get, get insight. Prize her highly, and she will exalt you; she will honor you if you embrace her. She will place on your head a graceful garland; she will bestow on you a beautiful crown. (Proverbs 4:4b–9)

The father's advice in the first section will only be effective if the children know that their father listened to the instruction of his father which is given in the second section. Notice the various commands that demand either an attitude or an action. The verb "hold fast" means "to grasp securely." The basic meaning of the verb "get" is "to buy" and it is often used in the context of the financial acquisition of property.

Buy truth, and do not sell it; buy wisdom, instruction, and understanding. (Proverbs 23:23)

The grandfather viewed wisdom as the most valuable commodity his son could acquire. Therefore, every ounce of energy should be expended to acquire it. Notice the fourfold repetition of the verb "get" in verses 5 and 7.

The success of a person's life is determined by what one chooses to "get" and failure is determined by what one chooses to "forget."

Notice also the love affair the young person must have with wisdom. The father's personification of wisdom is to describe her as the bride a son is to have and to hold from this day forth, and that his cherished treatment of this woman will bring him a full life, security, and honor.

Application

The Christian home is the primary training ground for children. While the church and the school serve important roles, the parents have the most profound responsibility and greatest opportunity to provide moral education for their children. There are 168 hours in a week. Approximately 40 hours are spent in school, 4 hours at church, 56 hours sleeping. That leaves 68 hours a week for parents to invest in their children's spiritual education. Parents need to view each situation as a potential teaching opportunity.

Biblical wisdom is a godly inheritance that can be passed from generation to generation. Parents need to remember that they are setting the tone, not only for their children's relationship with God, but with their grandchildren's relationship with God as well. This passage also demonstrates the truth that "rules without relationship equals rebellion." The father's affection for his children is demonstrated by the sense of urgency in his voice.

"Mind Your Step"
PROVERBS 4:10–19

Introduction

Once again, the wisdom writer presents his son with a very clear choice between right ("the way of wisdom") and wrong ("the path of the wicked"). The choice the young man makes will be determined by the counsel he chooses to follow. But the father warns that the choice will be accompanied by unavoidable consequences as well.

The father first describes the way of wisdom to his son.

> Hear, my son, and accept my words, that the years of your
> life may be many. I have taught you the way of wisdom; I

have led you in the paths of uprightness. When you walk, your step will not be hampered, and if you run, you will not stumble. Keep hold of instruction; do not let go; guard her, for she is your life. (Proverbs 4:10–13)

The wisdom writer appeals to his son, not only to listen to his advice, but also to demonstrate that he is listening by his obedience. The motivation is, if the son will listen to his father's wise counsel, he is promised a long and productive life, which is a common theme in Proverbs. Notice two earlier promises of longevity that are connected to obedience.

My son, do not forget my teaching, but let your heart keep my commandments, for length of days and years of life and peace they will add to you. (Proverbs 3:1–2)

Blessed is the one who finds wisdom, and the one who gets understanding, for the gain from her is better than gain from silver and her profit better than gold. She is more precious than jewels, and nothing you desire can compare with her. Long life is in her right hand; in her left hand are riches and honor. (Proverbs 3:13–16)

The promise of a long life was first found in the fifth commandment of the Decalogue.

Honor your father and your mother, that your days may be long in the land that the LORD your God is giving you. (Exodus 20:12)

Notice two ways his father provided his son with guidance. First, guidance was given by exhortation ("I have taught you the way of wisdom"). So, the son had the benefit of his father's words. Second, guidance was given by example ("I have led you in the paths of uprightness"). The father backed up his words by his own walk. The father fulfilled his parental responsibilities by providing the correct direction for his son's life. Now, it was up to the son to make the proper choices. This does not imply that the father was the perfect parent. But it does mean that, as a parent, he had performed a commendable job of teaching his children about life and how God's Word gives direction to life's choices.

If the son will follow his father's advice and make the correct choices, he will be able to avoid detours ("paths of uprightness"), delays ("your step will not be hampered"), and dangers ("you will not stumble"). The expression "paths of uprightness" is translated "straight paths" in other versions. The Hebrew term refers to that which is narrow, confining, or restricting. In Christian circles, we are familiar with the expression "the straight and narrow." Proverbs would rather describe it as "the straight and clear." Notice the irony of the parent/child relationship: if children resist the biblical advice of their godly parents because they feel it is too confining, the liberated children will find that getting their freedom can prove to be very restricting. This was the painful lesson the younger son learned in the parable of the prodigal son (Luke 15:11–32).

Speaking in terms of discovering a rare treasure, the son is told to "Keep hold of instruction; do not let go; guard her, for she is your life" (4:13). Biblical wisdom is such a rare and valuable treasure, that once it is discovered, it should never leave one's grasp.

Next, the father describes the path of the wicked in vivid terms so that his son sees the alternative for the evil that it really is. Using a series of six terse commands, the father repeatedly warns his son to avoid contact with the company of the wicked.

> Do not enter the path of the wicked, and do not walk in the way of the evil. Avoid it; do not go on it; turn away from it and pass on. For they cannot sleep unless they have done wrong; they are robbed of sleep unless they have made someone stumble. For they eat the bread of wickedness and drink the wine of violence. (Proverbs 4:14–17)

A sense of urgency is indicated by the arrangement of the six imperatives. The father warns his son to not even begin walking down that path, not out of rebellion, or even out of curiosity, for when you realize the danger you are in, you may not be able to turn back. The wisdom writer urged his son to avoid the wicked because their lifestyle is addictive, and ultimately enslaving. The wicked are so preoccupied with taking advantage of others that they eat, drink, and sleep wickedness. The irony is, though, that while the wicked delight in causing others to fall, they are the ones who will ultimately stumble (4:19).

The psalmist talked about this type of person as well.

Transgression speaks to the wicked deep in his heart; there is no fear of God before his eyes. For he flatters himself in his own eyes that his iniquity cannot be found out and hated. The words of his mouth are trouble and deceit; he has ceased to act wisely and do good. He plots trouble while on his bed; he sets himself in a way that is not good; he does not reject evil. (Psalm 36:1–4)

In the opening stanza, the psalmist portrayed human depravity at its very worst. The thoughts of sin speak to the individual from deep within the heart. Because sin has blinded the eyes, the wicked individual has no sense of the fear of the LORD. The apostle Paul quoted this phrase at the end of a lengthy series of quotations in his description of human depravity (Romans 3:10–18).

The father then contrasts the two ways for his son.

But the path of the righteous is like the light of dawn, which shines brighter and brighter until full day. The way of the wicked is like deep darkness; they do not know over what they stumble. (Proverbs 4:18–19)

Bringing his argument to a close, the father once more illustrates the sharp contrast between the two directions in life, using the imagery of light and darkness. The father encourages his son to heed his advice with the incentive that if he will make the correct choices now in his youth, the direction of his life will become clearer and more illuminated as he goes throughout his life. Just as the first rays of early morning sunlight gradually increase to the full light of noonday, so too will making correct choices in one's youth provide greater clarity to life as the young person gets older.

By contrast, the father warns his son that the way of wickedness is characterized by the darkness of nighttime that causes people to stumble. The wrong choices in one's youth will lead to increased darkness and greater chances of personal injury. The writer of Ecclesiastes made a similar observation.

Then I saw that there is more gain in wisdom than in folly, as there is more gain in light than in darkness. The wise person has his eyes in his head, but the fool walks in darkness. (2:13–14a)

Application

Since 2002 I have traveled every fall to the city of Kremenchuk in southern Ukraine to teach at a seminary and to spend time with our sister church. I travel from Minneapolis and have a three-hour layover in Amsterdam before I fly on to Kiev. As I walk through the large Schiphol airport in Amsterdam to stretch my legs after a long flight, I encounter moving walkways. And as you approach the end of the walkway you hear an automated voice saying over and over, "Mind your step, mind your step." That is what the wisdom writer is telling us.

"Preventing Heart Disease"
PROVERBS 4:20–27

Introduction

I came across the following description of the human heart in a magazine years ago.

> Everyone knows that the heart is a vital organ. However, when you get right down to it, the heart is just a pump. A complex and important one, yes, but still just a pump. As with all other pumps it can become clogged, break down, and need repair. This is why it is critical that we know how the heart works. The heart is a hollow, cone-shaped muscle located between the lungs and behind the sternum. It is 5 inches long, 3.5 inches wide, and 2.5 inches from front to back, and is roughly the size of your fist. The average weight of the heart in a female is 9 ounces and, in the male, is 10.5 ounces. The heart is divided into four chambers (right and left atrium and ventricle). Each chamber has a sort of one-way valve at its exit that prevents blood from flowing backwards. When each chamber contracts, the valve at its exit opens. When it is finished contracting, the valve closes so blood does not flow backwards. The right and left sides of the heart have separate functions. The right side of the heart collects oxygen-poor blood from the body and pumps

it to the lungs where it picks up oxygen and releases carbon dioxide. The left side of the heart then collects oxygen rich blood from the lungs and pumps it to the body so that the cells throughout your body have the oxygen they need to function properly. The average heartbeat is 72 times per minute. In the course of one day it beats over 100,000 times. In one year the heart beats almost 38 million times, and by the time you are 70 years old, on average, it beats 2.5 billion times. An average heart pumps 2.4 ounces per heartbeat. Therefore, an average heart pumps 1.3 gallons per minute. In other words, it pumps 1,900 gallons per day, almost 700,000 gallons per year, or 48 million gallons by the time someone is 70 years old. (Reader's Digest)

Once again, the father seeks to attract his son's undivided attention to heed his words of wisdom. But this time, in addition to the usual references to the ears and eyes, the father goes to the "heart" of the matter when he addresses the condition of his son's heart. The section begins with an admonition from the father to his son.

My son, be attentive to my words; incline your ear to my sayings. Let them not escape from your sight; keep them within your heart. For they are life to those who find them, and healing to all their flesh. Keep your heart with all vigilance, for from it flow the springs of life. (Proverbs 4:20–23)

Hubbard calls this section "the anatomy of discipleship" for the father speaks of the son's ears, eyes, heart, tongue, and feet.

In the Old Testament, in a general sense, the term "heart" (*leb*) was used to describe the innermost part of an object.

God is our refuge and strength, a very present help in trouble. Therefore, we will not fear though the earth gives way, though the mountains be moved into the heart of the sea. (Psalm 46:1–2)

In the prescientific world of the Old Testament the heart was viewed as the central bodily organ, the seat of one's physical life. But like other anthropological terms in the Old Testament, the word "heart" was frequently used in a psychological sense, as the center of a person's inner personal life. The heart is the source of motives, the seat of the passions, the center of the thought processes, and the spring of conscience.

Intellectually, the heart is where thinking takes place.

> Let the words of my mouth and the meditation of my heart
> be acceptable in your sight, O Lord, my rock and my
> redeemer. (Psalm 19:14)

Having seriously considered God's Word in the second stanza of the psalm, the psalmist concluded his psalm by considering his words and thoughts, and God's evaluation of them. He prayed that the words of his mouth and the thoughts of his heart would be acceptable offerings to God.

Emotionally, the heart is where a person's feelings originate.

> The Lord is near to the brokenhearted and saves the crushed
> in spirit. (Psalm 34:18)

The superscription to this psalm cites a narrative in 1 Samuel 21:10–15 when David fled from Saul to the territory of the Philistines. But in this foreign land he feigned madness so they would not harm him. David praised the LORD for his deliverance, and he enjoined others to extol His greatness as well. When he was in a tight spot and he cried out for deliverance, the LORD heard and responded to his plea.

Volitionally, the heart is where the decisions are made. The historian described the contributions of the Israelites for the tabernacle after the need was presented to the people and Moses asked for generous hearts.

> And they came, everyone whose heart stirred him, and
> everyone whose spirit moved him, and brought the Lord's
> contribution to be used for the tent of meeting, and for all
> its service, and for the holy garments. (Exodus 35:21)

The father concludes the section with some points of application. Using various parts of the human body, the father uses the remainder of the exhortation to apply his admonition to guard one's heart.

> Put away from you crooked speech, and put devious talk far from you. Let your eyes look directly forward, and your gaze be straight before you. Ponder the path of your feet; then all your ways will be sure. Do not swerve to the right or to the left; turn your foot away from evil. (Proverbs 4:24–27)

The father warns his son concerning the dangers of an uncontrolled tongue and tells him to remove perverse talk from his life. Types of speech that qualify as "crooked speech" include swearing, lying, gossip, grumbling, boasting, slander, crude jokes, ridicule, sarcasm, criticism, and idle talk. The apostle Paul wrote about the tongue in his letter to the Ephesian church. He first began with the prohibition: "Let no corrupting talk come out of your mouths." The term "corrupting" is used elsewhere in scripture to speak of rotten fish (Matthew 13:48) and spoiled fruit (Luke 6:43). Our words should not harm the persons addressed or the persons talked about. The prohibition is followed by the correction: "but only such as is good for building up, as fits the occasion." There are no such things as neutral words; either they build others up or tear them down. Believers should weigh their words carefully because someday they will have to give an account of them to God (Matthew 12:36). Paul concluded the section with the motivation: "that it may give grace to those who hear." The Bible places great value on timely talk.

The father tells his son to develop tunnel vision so he will not be distracted from the path. There are many things in life that appear attractive initially that eventually can become a distraction.

> I will ponder the way that is blameless. Oh when will you come to me? I will walk with integrity of heart within my house; I will not set before my eyes anything that is worthless. I hate the work of those who fall away; it shall not cling to me. (Psalm 101:2–3)

Because the eyes of God and people were watching him, the psalmist was careful what he set before his eyes.

> The discerning sets his face toward wisdom, but the eyes of a fool are on the ends of the earth. (Proverbs 17:24)

And, connected to the son's focus on the straight and narrow are his feet which will not stray from the path.

Conclusion

To prevent heart disease doctors tell us to get regular exercise and to eat a healthy diet. To prevent spiritual heart disease, the wisdom writer advises us to guard our hearts for everything in life emanates from the heart. Jesus said the same thing to his disciples.

> What comes out of a person is what defiles him. For from within, out of the heart of man, come evil thoughts, sexual immorality, theft, murder, adultery, coveting, wickedness, deceit, sensuality, envy, slander, pride, foolishness. All these evil things come from within, and they defile a person. (Mark 7:20–23)

"Biblical Sex Education"
PROVERBS 5:1-23

Introduction

In their book "Intimate Allies," Dan Allender and Tremper Longman write concerning the connection between sensuality and spirituality.

> In many ways, sexuality is a barometer of the weather of a marriage relationship. When areas of spiritual and relational intimacy are lacking or troubled, then sexual intimacy as God designed it will be affected as well. (Allendar and Longman)

The authors go on to advocate a biblical approach to sexual intimacy

> Certainly the scripture does not advocate or permit an unbridled sensuality, but it encourages a delight in sensual intimacy within the bounds of marriage. Indeed, the oneness that married couples experience in the act of sexual intercourse becomes a biblical symbol for the oneness we experience in our deeply intimate relationship with God. (Allendar and Longman)

Notice the balanced approach of the father as he talks to his sons about God's design for sexual intimacy.

The father begins with the deception of sexual immorality.

> My son, be attentive to my wisdom; incline your ear to my understanding, that you may keep discretion, and your lips may guard knowledge. For the lips of a forbidden woman drip honey, and her speech is smoother than oil, but in the end she is bitter as wormwood, sharp as a two-edged sword. Her feet go down to death; her steps follow the path to Sheol; she does not ponder the path of life; her ways wander, and she does not know it. (Proverbs 5:1–6)

The father asks his son to concentrate on what he is saying since he is addressing the very important topic of sexual purity. If he will listen attentively, the son will receive discretion and knowledge that will assist him in making the correct moral decisions. The father proceeds to warn his son about the dangers of the immoral (*zara*) woman. Her deceptive, seductive speech is sweet like "honey" and "smoother than oil." But what seems attractive at first proves to be bitter (*mara*) and deadly later. The exciting, but brief night of immorality is followed by the painful and permanent morning of reality. The direction of an immoral woman's life leads to death, and those who associate with her will meet a similar fate.

Next the father details the dangers of sexual immorality.

> And now, O sons, listen to me, and do not depart from the words of my mouth. Keep your way far from her, and do not go near the door of her house, lest you give your honor to others and your years to the merciless, lest strangers take their fill of your strength, and your labors go to the house of a foreigner, and at the end of your life you groan, when your flesh and body are consumed, and you say, "How I hated discipline, and my heart despised reproof! I did not listen to the voice of my teachers or incline my ear to my instructors. I am at the brink of utter ruin in the assembled congregation. (Proverbs 5:7–14)

Notice the high cost of immorality. Immorality leads to dishonor within the community (5:9a). There is also the possibility of sexually transmitted diseases (5:9b, 11). The best years of life can be sacrificed because of immorality. Immorality leads to financial destitution (5:10; 6:26). There is also the distress of regret (5:11–14). Falling prey to lust brings remorse when a person recognizes too late that they did not listen to instruction. This section reflects the "if only" despair of making the wrong moral choices.

The father then switches his strategy to describe to his son the delight that comes from marital intimacy.

> Drink water from your own cistern, flowing water from your own well. Should your springs be scattered abroad, streams of water in the streets? Let them be for yourself alone, and not for strangers with you. Let your fountain be blessed, and rejoice in the wife of your youth, a lovely deer, a graceful doe. Let her breasts fill you at all times with delight; be intoxicated always in her love. (Proverbs 5:15–19)

Using highly suggestive and figurative language, the father urges his son to find his contentment and delight within the marriage relationship. Marriage is to provide sexual contentment (5:15). In the dry climate of Palestine cisterns were hewn from rock and then plastered to store water collected during the rainy season for use in the dry season. By finding his sexual satisfaction in his marriage, the son would be able to avoid sexual temptation outside of marriage. Marriage is to provide physical descendants (5:16–17). The father uses a graphic figure of speech to warn his son not to be just a sperm donor with strange women. Sexual desires should be controlled and channeled in one's marriage. Marriage is to provide sexual enjoyment (5:18–20). The father illustrates a healthy sexual relationship between a husband and wife with several strong verbs. The verb "rejoice" denotes a joyful disposition when sex takes place in a God-honoring environment. The verb "satisfy" literally means "to drink to the full." And the verb "intoxicate" speaks of being "captivated" in a good way, rather than the prison of regret.

The father closes the section with a reminder for his son of the destructive nature of sexual immorality.

> Why should you be intoxicated, my son, with a forbidden woman and embrace the bosom of an adulteress? For a man's ways are before the eyes of the Lord, and he ponders all his paths. The iniquities of the wicked ensnare him, and he is

held fast in the cords of his sin. He dies for lack of discipline, and because of his great folly he is led astray. (Proverbs 5:20–23)

The father gives his son three motivations to pursue sexual purity. First, he cannot avoid God's scrutiny (5:21). Second, he cannot avoid sin's captivity (5:22). Third, he cannot avoid sin's penalty (5:23).

If the young man is not captivated by his wife, but becomes captivated with a stranger in sinful acts, then his own iniquities will captivate him; and he will be led to ruin. (Allen Ross)

Application

Consider a biblical view of sex. First, sex is a God-given activity.

So God created man in his own image, in the image of God he created him; male and female he created them. And God blessed them. And God said to them, "Be fruitful and multiply and fill the earth and subdue it." (Genesis 1:27–28a)

Second, sex is to be a marital activity.

Let marriage be held in honor among all, and let the marriage bed be undefiled, for God will judge the sexually immoral and adulterous. (Hebrews 13:4)

Third, sex is to be a giving activity.

Now concerning the matters about which you wrote: "It is good for a man not to have sexual relations with a woman." But because of the temptation to sexual immorality, each man should have his own wife and each woman her own husband. The husband should give to his wife her conjugal rights, and likewise the wife to her husband. For the wife does not have authority over her own body, but the husband does. Likewise, the husband does not have authority over his own body, but the wife does. (1 Corinthians 7:1–4)

Fourth, sex is to be a continuous activity.

> Do not deprive one another, except perhaps by agreement for a limited time, that you may devote yourselves to prayer; but then come together again, so that Satan may not tempt you because of your lack of self-control. (1 Corinthians 7:5)

Fifth, sex is to be a pleasant activity.

> Let your fountain be blessed, and rejoice in the wife of your youth, a lovely deer, a graceful doe. Let her breasts fill you at all times with delight; be intoxicated always in her love. (Proverbs 5:18–19)

"I Am in Your Debt"
PROVERBS 6:1-5

Introduction

At the beginning of this chapter in which the father addresses a variety of important topics for his son to consider, the matter of financial debt and the rash decisions that often lead to debt, is first on the list. The father wants his son to realize that while getting into debt is as easy as sliding down a hill, getting out of debt is as hard as climbing up a steep mountain.

The father first details for his son the consequences of underwriting the bad investment of other people.

My son, if you have put up security for your neighbor, have given your pledge for a stranger, if you are snared in the words of your mouth, caught in the words of your mouth. (Proverbs 6:1–2)

In Israel, lending money was intended as a means of helping a fellow countryman get out of debt, not as a moneymaking transaction as it is today. The Mosaic Law forbade the charging of interest to a fellow Israelite.

> If your brother becomes poor and cannot maintain himself with you, you shall support him as though he were a stranger and a sojourner, and he shall live with you. Take no interest from him or profit, but fear your God, that your brother may

live beside you. You shall not lend him your money at interest, nor give him your food for profit. (Leviticus 25:35–37)

The Mosaic Law instructed that interest could be applied to a loan to non-Israelites, but even then, unreasonably high interest rates were illegal (Deuteronomy 23:19). Exorbitant interest often resulted in injustice that the law sought to prevent.

Now the wife of one of the sons of the prophets cried to Elisha, "Your servant my husband is dead, and you know that your servant feared the LORD, but the creditor has come to take my two children to be his slaves." (2 Kings 4:1)

The warning in this passage is not against borrowing or lending, or against being generous. Instead, the father is advising his young son not to make rash financial decisions that foolishly commit him to the equally unwise financial decisions of others because it will result in debt. The expression "put up security" describes the act of underwriting the financial debt of another person. So, the father is warning his son not to pledge himself as a guarantee for another person's debts.

The expression "given your pledge" literally reads "to strike the palm" and is similar to a handshake deal that was honored in our past. It means to strike hands with someone, signifying your pledge as collateral in a business arrangement. In our culture, it is equivalent to signing on the dotted line.

Warnings against pledging security for the debts of others are found frequently in the book of Proverbs.

Whoever puts up security for a stranger will surely suffer harm, but he who hates striking hands in pledge is secure. (Proverbs 11:15)

One who lacks sense gives a pledge and puts up security in the presence of his neighbor. (Proverbs 17:18)

Using very vivid language, the father describes the uncomfortable feeling that comes from making a rash decision to cover someone else's debts. Being "snared" refers to the setting of a trap to catch some prey, often in the context of trapping a bird. The second use of being "snared" is used figuratively of the entrapment in the context of becoming a prisoner of war in a military conflict. These words indicate that by accepting responsibility for someone else's high interest debt, it would place the co-signer in a financial position over which one has no control.

The father then describes the tactics his son should use to extricate himself from his pledge.

> Then do this, my son, and save yourself, for you have come into the hand of your neighbor: go, hasten, and plead urgently with your neighbor. Give your eyes no sleep and your eyelids no slumber; save yourself like a gazelle from the hand of the hunter, like a bird from the hand of the fowler. (Proverbs 6:3–5)

The father's concern that his son would make unwise financial decisions for which he would be held liable causes him to use quite intense language to express the urgency of rectifying the matter. The father tells his son to use two tactics in order to free himself from the trap of a bad financial agreement.

The first tactic is to humble himself (6:3). The expression "save yourself" is strong wording that has the literal idea of allowing oneself to be trampled on. This is a strong statement considering the importance of loss of face in the Middle East. The father tells his son that although swallowing his pride will leave a bad taste in his mouth, it is better than eating his losses. The second tactic is to harass your neighbor (6:3). The expression "plead urgently" occurs only four times in the Old Testament and signifies storming at or against something. The father tells his son to persistently pester or annoy his friend in every effort to be released from one's pledge. It denotes a boisterous attitude. This urgency is illustrated in verses 4–5. Nothing should stand in the way of getting out of this financial obligation. Not even one night was to pass before the situation should be rectified. Just as a gazelle or a bird, if trapped, would immediately begin struggling for its life, so a person snared by a foolish financial decision should frantically fight to be free of it.

Conclusion

When it comes to the matter of debt, I have benefitted greatly from the financial advice of author Ron Blue in his book "Master Your Money." Consider his biblical perspective on debt and the key points of his arguments against debt. First, Ron Blue writes that debt is not a sin. The Bible discourages the use of debt, but does not prohibit it. Second, debt is never the real problem; it is only symptomatic of the real problem, such as greed, self-indulgence, impatience, poor self-image, depression, lack of self-discipline, or a desire to impress others. I recall a lady who sought my counsel because she was deep in debt without her husband's knowledge. He traveled a lot for work and she coped with the loneliness by spending money. Blue writes that the primary danger of debt is that compounding works against you rather than for you. The second economic danger of debt is that debt becomes a trap. Getting into debt takes no effort, but getting out can be difficult. The third economic danger of debt is that it always mortgages the future. When you are in debt, you are limited in what you can do. The spiritual dangers of debt are twofold. First, borrowing always presumes upon the future. Jesus made this point with his followers when he was addressing the cost of discipleship.

> For which of you, desiring to build a tower, does not first sit down and count the cost, whether he has enough to complete it? (Luke 14:28)

Second, borrowing may deny God an opportunity to work. Who needs God to provide one's needs when lenders are available? Before you take on debt Ron Blue says to ask yourself four questions: Does it make economic sense? Do my spouse and I have unity about taking on this debt? Do I have spiritual peace of mind to enter into this debt? What personal goals am I meeting with this debt that can be met in no other way?

"Aesop the Plagiarist"
PROVERBS 6:6–11

Introduction

Aesop, a Greek slave, who lived from about 620–560 B.C., wrote many popular fables. One of his best-known fables was entitled "The Grasshopper and the Ant." There are many versions of the ancient fable and this is one of them.

> The Grasshopper having sung all the summer long, found herself lacking food when the North Wind began its song.

Not a single little piece of fly or grub did she have to eat. She went complaining of hunger to the Ant's home, her neighbor, begging there for a loan of some grain to keep herself alive till the next season did arrive. "I shall pay you," she said, "Before next August, on my word as an animal. I'll pay both interest and principal." The Ant was not so inclined: this not being one of her faults. "What did you do all summer?" Said she to the grasshopper. "Night and day I sang. I hope that does not displease you." "You sang? I will not look askance. But now my neighbor it's time to dance."

The sage, writing many centuries before Aesop, cited the work ethic of the ant to warn his readers against the dangers of laziness. The sage began with the identification of the sluggard.

Go to the ant, O sluggard; consider her ways, and be wise. How long will you lie there, O sluggard? When will you arise from your sleep? (Proverbs 6:6, 9)

The Hebrew term for 'sluggard' ('asel) occurs fourteen times in the book of Proverbs and nowhere else in the Old Testament. While the main emphasis of this section is on the topic of physical laziness, the remainder of Proverbs indicates it is due to a greater problem.

Notice the failures of the sluggard throughout the book of Proverbs. The sluggard is contrasted with the righteous person who lives a godly life. The sluggard is compared to the person who lacks purpose and ambition. The sluggard is compared to the person who lacks discernment.

The way of a sluggard is like a hedge of thorns, but the path of the upright is a level highway. (Proverb 15:19)

Slothfulness casts into a deep sleep, and an idle person will suffer hunger. (Proverb 19:15)

The desire of the sluggard kills him, for his hands refuse to labor. All day long he craves and craves, but the righteous gives and does not hold back. (Proverbs 21:25–26)

> I passed by the field of a sluggard, by the vineyard of a man lacking sense, and behold, it was all overgrown with thorns; the ground was covered with nettles, and its stone wall was broken down. Then I saw and considered it; I looked and received instruction. A little sleep, a little slumber, a little folding of the hands to rest, and poverty will come upon you like a robber, and want like an armed man. (Proverbs 24:30–34)

The individual who refuses to accept the God-given responsibility to labor in order to provide for one's physical needs ultimately has a spiritual problem. In the Old Testament, the Mosaic Law commanded all able-bodied people to work in order to support themselves.

> Six days shall work be done, but on the seventh day is a Sabbath of solemn rest, a holy convocation. You shall do no work. It is a Sabbath to the LORD in all your dwelling places. (Leviticus 23:3)

This principle was continued in the New Testament with the instructions of the apostle Paul to the various churches.

> Let the thief no longer steal, but rather let him labor, doing honest work with his own hands, so that he may have something to share with anyone in need. (Ephesians 4:28)

> For even when we were with you, we would give you this command: If anyone is not willing to work, let him not eat. (2 Thessalonians 3:10)

The sage then gives an illustration of the sluggard.

> Go to the ant, O sluggard; consider her ways, and be wise. Without having any chief, officer, or ruler, she prepares her bread in summer and gathers her food in harvest. How long will you lie there, O sluggard? When will you arise from your sleep? A little sleep, a little slumber, a little folding of the hands to rest, and poverty will come upon you like a robber, and want like an armed man. (Proverbs 6:6–11)

Based on the sage's observation of ants, he did not perceive any organization within an ant colony. What is interesting is that scientists who study ants have discerned some patterns of self-organization and cooperation within the colony of ants. But from the author's prescientific world, as he observed how an ant conducts its life, the writer gives two character traits that the sluggard does not possess (6:6–8). First, the sluggard is not self-motivated (6:6–8a). The person who only works when he is commanded to do so does not possess wisdom. When I was young, I remember my father saying that even if his children were not talented, they would not be lazy. Second, the sluggard does not plan for the future, but only lives for the present (6:8b).

Rebuking the sluggard, the sage asks how long the lazy one will continue to lay in bed while work is waiting to be done. Verse 10 has the father mimicking the sluggard's reply. "A little sleep, a little slumber, a little folding of the hands to rest." The sluggard, rather than directly refusing to work, simply procrastinates, asking for a few more moments of rest. I had a roommate in college who dealt with the stress of not doing his homework by simply taking a nap. For when he was asleep, he did not have to think about the work he was putting off.

Notice further descriptions of the sluggard throughout the book of Proverbs. The sluggard is a source of aggravation and embarrassment to those who depend on him.

> Like vinegar to the teeth and smoke to the eyes, so is the sluggard to those who send him. (Proverbs 10:26)

The sluggard has big dreams and expectations, but never realizes any of them.

> The soul of the sluggard craves and gets nothing, while the soul of the diligent is richly supplied. (Proverbs 13:4)

> The desire of the sluggard kills him, for his hands refuse to labor. (Proverbs 21:25)

The sluggard lacks diligence and is easily hindered by obstacles along the way.

> The way of a sluggard is like a hedge of thorns, but the path of the upright is a level highway. (Proverbs 15:19)

Not only will the sluggard refuse to begin a project, the lazy individual will not finish anything either. This humorous portrayal is certainly an exaggeration.

> The sluggard buries his hand in the dish and will not even bring it back to his mouth. (Proverbs 19:24)

The sluggard also has an excuse for inactivity, no matter how flimsy.

> The sluggard says, "There is a lion outside! I shall be killed in the streets!" (Proverbs 22:13)

The sluggard is filled with self-conceit, believing he or she has life all figured out. The sluggard has the opinion that he or she is wiser than those who are trying to help with good advice.

> The sluggard is wiser in his own eyes than seven men who can answer sensibly. (Proverbs 26:16)

The sage concludes this section with some words of instruction to the sluggard (6:6-11). The sage says that sluggards can learn their lessons only one of two ways. First, the sluggard can learn the lesson by example (6:6–8). The sage challenges the lazy, irresponsible person to learn from the example of the ant. Ants, known for being industrious, are commended for their initiative. As the sage observed them, he could not detect any leadership, yet they were able to store up their food for the winter. Second, the sluggard can learn the lesson by experience (6:9–11). If sluggards will not learn from the examples of others, they will eventually learn their lessons the hard way through life's painful realities.

"Dirty Rotten Scoundrels"

PROVERBS 6:12–15

Introduction

By describing the person who is deceptive and contentious, the author urges his readers to avoid this type of behavior and to avoid associating with this type of person. A right relationship with God will be demonstrated by a right relationship with others. If a person's vertical relationship with God is in order, then the horizontal relationship with other people will be in order as well. To walk in wisdom requires a person to avoid people who are walking in foolishness. The author wants the youth of the nation of Israel to be constructive members of society by avoiding these destructive people and by not emulating their behavior.

The author begins with a description of the dirty rotten scoundrel.

> A worthless person, a wicked man, goes about with crooked speech, winks with his eyes, signals with his feet, points with his finger, with perverted heart devises evil, continually sowing discord. (Proverbs 6:12–14)

Notice first the description of the scoundrel's evil character (6:12a). The individual is described as being both a "worthless person" ('adam beliyya'al) and a "wicked man." A survey of the biblical uses of the first term, which literally reads, "a worthless man," reveals an individual who has violated God's Law, and as a result, has violated the rights of others. The Mosaic Law warned about an unworthy thought.

> Take care lest there be an unworthy thought in your heart and you say, "The seventh year, the year of release is near," and your eye look grudgingly on your poor brother, and you give him nothing, and he cry to the LORD against you, and you be guilty of sin. (Deuteronomy 15:9)

In this context of the Sabbatical year that required the cancellation of debts throughout the nation of Israel, a worthless person would be guilty of not showing generosity toward a fellow Israelite in need.

And then, we have this description of the nation of Israel that demonstrated its worthless nature during the period of the judges. The narrative tells the story of the Levite and his concubine who stopped overnight in the village of Gibeah instead of the Jebusite village, later known as Jerusalem.

> As they were making their hearts merry, behold, the men of the city, worthless fellows, surrounded the house, beating on the door. And they said to the old man, the master of the

house, "Bring out the man who came into your house, that we may know him." (Judge 19:22)

This desired mistreatment of the Levite was due in part to the attitude that existed in the country during the period of the judges. The spirit of the age was summed up in the following statement.

In those days there was no king in Israel. Everyone did what was right in his own eyes. (Judges 17:6)

Again, speaking of the period of the judges, the term "worthless" was used to describe the sons of Eli the high priest (1 Samuel 2:12). The second phrase of the verse explains why the historian described the sons of Eli as "worthless men." The subsequent description of their behavior toward the worshipers who came to the tabernacle in Shiloh demonstrated their contempt toward God (2:12–17, 22).

Later on, during the reign of King Ahab over the northern kingdom of Israel, we have this description of worthless individuals in the narrative where Jezebel stole the vineyard from Naboth by having him killed.

Proclaim a fast, and set Naboth at the head of the people. And set two worthless men opposite him, and let them bring a charge against him, saying, "You have cursed God and the king." Then take him out and stone him to death. (1 Kings 21:9–10)

This worthless and wicked character is an individual who, first of all, has no reverence for the things of God, and who, as a result, has no respect for the rights and feelings of others. Returning to the book of Proverbs, a later proverb speaks of the worthless man.

A worthless man plots evil, and his speech is like a scorching fire. (Proverbs 16:27)

As we see from these passages, the worthless individual of Proverbs 6:12 violated the religious and social institutions of the day. Thus, the two terms describe an individual who is worthless because he or she is wicked.

Next, we have the description of the scoundrel's conduct (6:12b–14). The scoundrel "goes about with crooked speech, winks with his eyes, signals with his feet, points with his finger, with perverted heart devises evil, continually sowing discord." The sage names many parts of the human body to demonstrate that wickedness affects the entire individual.

The worthless and wicked individual has an uncontrollable tongue (6:12b). "Crooked speech" describes communication that is perverse and twisted. Therefore, "crooked speech" includes profanity, boasting, lying, flattery, crude jokes, ridicule, gossip, sarcasm, cynicism, grumbling, criticism, and idle talk. In an earlier section of the book of Proverbs the father advised his son.

> Put away from you crooked speech, and put devious talk far
> from you. (4:24)

In the New Testament James also identified a worthless individual by his speech.

> If anyone thinks he is religious and does not bridle his tongue
> but deceives his heart, this person's religion is worthless.
> (1:26)

A person with an uncontrolled tongue reveals a worthless religion. It is worthless or without value in the sense that the individual has not substantially changed behavior. The person may have accepted Christ as Savior, but Christ has not been made the Lord of life. This religion is also worthless in the sense that it does not benefit others. Instead of building up other believers, an uncontrolled tongue causes a lot of damage. And, around unbelievers, an uncontrolled tongue actually contradicts the new life in Christ that is being proclaimed.

The worthless and wicked individual uses sinister sign language (6:13). By winking with the eyes and gesturing in some way with the feet and fingers this worthless individual signals an evil message to fellow conspirators. While winking often conveys merriment, in this context it communicates wickedness.

> Whoever winks the eye causes trouble, and a babbling fool
> will come to ruin. (Proverbs 10:10)

Whoever winks his eyes plans dishonest things; he who purses his lips brings evil to pass. (Proverbs 16:30)

The worthless and wicked individual feigns outward sincerity while inwardly planning further wickedness (6:14). "Discord" is caused by hatred, an uncontrolled temper, perversity, greed, and anger. Note the following proverbs that describe the causes of discord.

Hatred stirs up strife, but love covers all offenses. (10:12)

A hot-tempered man stirs up strife, but he who is slow to anger quiets contention. (15:18)

A dishonest man spreads strife, and a whisperer separates close friends. (16:28)

A greedy man stirs up strife, but the one who trusts in the Lord will be enriched. (28:25)

A man of wrath stirs up strife, and one given to anger causes much transgression (29:22)

The section concludes with the destruction of the dirty rotten scoundrel (6:15). "Therefore calamity will come upon him suddenly; in a moment he will be broken beyond healing." Individuals who spend time plotting the downfall of others will experience their own downfall, unexpectedly and quickly. The downfall will be caused by natural consequences or by divine intervention. This is also known as the doctrine of divine retribution.

"God's Black List"
PROVERBS 6:16–19

Introduction

Having warned readers about the scoundrel by describing his sinful traits (6:12–15), the wisdom writer provides a list of sinful traits that God finds particularly offensive. The nature of this numerical list is not exhaustive, but it is a good starting point.

> There are six things that the LORD hates, seven that are an abomination to him: haughty eyes, a lying tongue, and hands that shed innocent blood, a heart that devises wicked plans, feet that make haste to run to evil, a false witness who breathes out lies, and one who sows discord among brothers. (Proverbs 6:16-19)

The author warns readers that God hates the attitudes and activities of the scoundrel. He uses two emotionally charged terms to describe God's revulsion toward the sinful behavior of the scoundrel. The verb "hate" describes an emotional attitude toward persons and things that are opposed, detested, despised, and with which one wishes to have no contact or relationship. God has nothing to do with these sinful behaviors, and He will not be in a relationship with an individual who is characterized by them. The second term "abomination" is used most often to describe activities that are particularly offensive to God. Notice other Old Testament passages that use the term "abomination."

> Sexual perversions – You shall not lie with a male as with a woman; it is an abomination. And you shall not lie with any animal and so make yourself unclean with it, neither shall any woman give herself to an animal to lie with it: it is perversion. (Leviticus 18:22–23)

> Idolatry – The carved images of their gods you shall burn with fire. You shall not covet the silver or the gold that is on them or take it for yourselves, lest you be ensnared by it, for it is an abomination to the LORD your God. (Deuteronomy 7:25)

> Human sacrifice – You shall not worship the LORD your God in that way, for every abominable thing that the LORD hates they have done for their gods, for they even burn their sons and their daughters in the fire to their gods. (Deuteronomy 12:31)

Occultism – When you come into the land that the LORD your God is giving you, you shall not learn to follow the abominable practices of those nations. There shall not be found among you anyone who burns his son or his daughter as an offering, anyone who practices divination or tells fortunes or interprets omens, or a sorcerer or a charmer or a medium or a necromancer or one who inquires of the dead, for whoever does these things is an abomination to the LORD. And because of these abominations the LORD your God is driving them out before you. (Deuteronomy 18:9–12)

The "six . . . seven" pattern, known as a numerical ladder, is used elsewhere in scripture. This poetic arrangement provides a specific, though not exhaustive list. Notice other examples of this pattern in other poetic sections of the Old Testament.

He will deliver you from six troubles; in seven no evil shall touch you. (Job 5:19)

Three things are too wonderful for me; four I do not understand: the way of an eagle in the sky, the way of a serpent on a rock, the way of a ship on the high seas, and the way of a man with a virgin. (Proverbs 30:18–19)

Thus says the Lord: "For three transgressions of Gaza, and for four, I will not revoke the punishment, because they carried into exile a whole people to deliver them up to Edom." (Amos 1:6)

Highlighting various members of the human body, the wisdom writer lists seven attitudes or actions that demonstrate an evil person's denial of God's presence in one's life. In Matthew 5 we have Jesus' list of virtues known as the Beatitudes. In Proverbs, we have the wisdom writer's list of seven vices that we will call the Bad Attitudes.

The first vice God hates is haughty eyes (6:17a) because human pride ignores the majestic transcendence of God. The adjective "haughty" comes from a verb that means "to be high or to be lofty." Used in a negative sense, it describes the arrogant look of a person who no longer feels they need God or believes they are better than other people. God will not tolerate anyone who thinks so highly of self. Notice other Old Testament passages that speak of the sin of arrogance using the imagery of uplifted eyes or an uplifted heart. Moses warned the next generation of Israelites who were about to inherit the land of Canaan.

> Then your heart be lifted up, and you forget the LORD your God, who brought you out of the land of Egypt, out of the house of slavery. (Deuteronomy 8:14)

Prayer of Pharisee and tax collector

> O LORD, my heart is not lifted up; my eyes are not raised too high; I do not occupy myself with things too great and too marvelous for me. (Psalm 131:1)

The second vice God hates is a lying tongue (6:17b) which is literally "a tongue of deception." God hates deception for the damage this vice does to relationships.

> Be not silent, O God of my praise! For wicked and deceitful mouths are opened against me, speaking against me with lying tongues. (Psalm 109:2)

The apostle Peter quoted from this psalm when he addressed the betrayal of Judas (Acts 1:20; Psalm 109:8). A lying tongue includes stretching the truth, deception, insincere flattery, misleading statements, and letting others jump to conclusions.

The third vice God hates is deadly hands (6:17c). God prohibited the shedding of human blood because mankind is made in the image of God (Genesis 9:6). But shedding "innocent blood" was an even greater crime as seen during the evil reign of Manasseh (2 Kings 21:16; 24:1–4). Even David was prohibited from building the temple because he had shed much blood during his reign (1 Chronicles 22:8).

The fourth vice God hates is a devising heart (6:18a). The verb "devise" comes from a verb that means "to plow" (for example, a field in preparation for planting). From this literal usage came the figurative meaning "to prepare or to plan."

> Do not plan evil against your neighbor, who dwells trustingly beside you. (Proverbs 3:29)

The plotting of Absalom against Amnon to avenge the rape of his sister Tamar is a good illustration of this vice (2 Samuel 13:22–29).

The fifth vice God hates is when are feet are quick to go after evil (6:18b). Isaiah spoke of such evil people who are quick to pursue evil plans.

> Their feet run to evil, and they are swift to shed innocent blood; their thoughts are thoughts of iniquity; desolation and destruction are in their highways. (59:7)

The sixth vice God hates is dishonest words (6:19a). There are several biblical examples of this particular vice of being a lying witness to harm others. In the Old Testament, Jezebel hired scoundrels to falsely accuse Naboth so Ahab could steal his vineyard (1 Kings 21:7–14). In the New Testament, Stephen was falsely accused of blasphemy (Acts 6:8–14).

The seventh vice God hates is divisive words (6:19b) because they damage close and intimate relationships between people who are related either physically or emotionally. Because the twelve tribes of Israel descended from one father, they were all considered brothers.

"The Seventh Commandment"
PROVERBS 6:20–35

Introduction

While the act of sex is a gift from God, it is only to be enjoyed within the confines of the marital union between a man and a woman. When God created Eve and introduced her to Adam, He established the standard for sexual purity and intimacy.

> Therefore a man shall leave his father and his mother and hold fast to his wife, and they shall become one flesh. (Genesis 2:24)

The New Testament author agreed with this position.

> Let marriage be held in honor among all, and let the marriage bed be undefiled, for God will judge the sexually immoral and adulterous. (Hebrews 13:4)

As a father, the wisdom writer was concerned about the moral character of his son. In this section the sage moves from the general to the specific to warn his son about the high cost of adultery.

The section begins with a general exhortation for the son to heed his parents' instruction.

The whole of Proverbs

> My son, keep your father's commandment, and forsake not your mother's teaching. Bind them on your heart always; tie them around your neck. When you walk, they will lead you; when you lie down, they will watch over you; and when you awake, they will talk with you. For the commandment is a lamp and the teaching a light, and the reproofs of discipline are the way of life. (Proverbs 6:20–23)

There are several concepts in the section that are signs of a good home life. Both parents need to be actively involved in the process of rearing their children (6:20). The father and the mother need to be in agreement with the overall approach to their child's instruction and discipline. And when the parents have fulfilled their obligation, the child is also responsible to match the commitment level of their parents. Proper behavior must not only be demonstrated by the external conduct of the child, but it must also reflect the internal character (6:21). Effective training must become a way of life for the young person (6:22). The foundation of effective education in the home must come from the Word of God (6:23). Balanced childrearing consists of positive guidance and negative discipline (6:23). And, sex education is a topic best taught at home (6:24).

The father returns to his oft-repeated theme that exhorts his son to attend to and to retain the instruction that he has received at home. He believes that a good home life, with both parents actively involved in the education of the children, will go a long way to prevent the youth from falling into immorality. The terminology is very similar to what is found in the Mosaic Law.

> You shall teach them diligently to your children, and shall talk of them when you sit in your house, and when you walk by the way, and when you lie down, and when you rise. (Deuteronomy 6:7)

The father now moves from the general exhortations to heed parental instruction to the specific application of sexuality (6:24–30). On his mind is the concern he has for the moral standards of his son. The father knows his son will be exposed to many sexual temptations and opportunities, and so he relates several facts about immorality.

First, the father admits that immorality is initially attractive to a young person. The parental advice is intended "To preserve you from the evil woman, from the smooth tongue of the adulteress. Do not desire her beauty in your heart, and do not let her capture you with her eyelashes" (6:24–25). The woman is described as being "evil" because she is a married woman who is being unfaithful to her husband with tempting words to an unsuspecting young man. She strokes his ego by telling him what he wants to hear. Earlier in the book the father issued a similar warning to his son.

> For the lips of a forbidden woman drip honey, and her speech is smoother than oil. (5:3)

The young man is flattered because he has found a beautiful woman who is interested in him.

> With much seductive speech she persuades him; with her smooth talk she compels him. (Proverbs 7:21)

In addition to her flattering words, the unsuspecting young man is captivated by the immoral woman's physical beauty (6:25). The last chapter of Proverbs issues a strong warning about the dangers of physical beauty where moral character is lacking.

> Charm is deceitful, and beauty is vain, but a woman who fears the LORD is to be praised. (Proverbs 31:30)

That which began as a seemingly harmless and flirtatious look has developed into a dangerous heart condition. Perhaps the wisdom writer had in mind the experience of King David and his adultery with Bathsheba, the wife of Uriah.

> It happened, late one afternoon, when David arose from his couch and was walking on the roof of the king's house, that he saw from the roof a woman bathing; and the woman was very beautiful. And David sent and inquired about the

woman. And one said, "Is not this Bathsheba, the daughter of Eliam, the wife of Uriah the Hittite?" (2 Samuel 11:2–3)

According to Jesus, to lust mentally after a woman is equivalent to the physical act of immorality.

You have heard that it was said, 'You shall not commit adultery.' But I say to you that everyone who looks at a woman with lustful intent has already committed adultery with her in his heart." (Matthew 5:27–28)

The second lesson the father wants his son to learn is that immorality is expensive.

For the price of a prostitute is only a loaf of bread, but a married woman hunts down a precious life. Can a man carry fire next to his chest and his clothes not be burned? Or can one walk on hot coals and his feet not be scorched? So is he who goes in to his neighbor's wife; none who touches her will go unpunished. People do not despise a thief if he steals to satisfy his appetite when he is hungry, but if he is caught, he will pay sevenfold; he will give all the goods of his house. He who commits adultery lacks sense; he who does it destroys himself. He will get wounds and dishonor, and his disgrace will not be wiped away. For jealousy makes a man furious, and he will not spare when he takes revenge. He will accept no compensation; he will refuse though you multiply gifts. (Proverbs 6:26–35)

The father totals up the high cost of immorality for his son. He warns that immorality will cost him his income (6:26–29). Immorality can reduce a person to utter poverty "for the price of a prostitute is only a loaf of bread, but a married woman hunts down a precious life" (6:26). While both acts of immorality are wrong, a relationship with a married woman is more complicated because there is an angry husband who has been wronged and who is seeking compensation. The father uses the imagery of fire to warn his son that adultery cannot go unpunished. Fire is fitting because the sexual urge is likened to burning by the apostle Paul (1 Corinthians 7:9). In modern terminology, the person who engages in adultery is like an individual who plays with fire and who gets burned.

The father also warns his son that immorality will cost him his integrity (6:30–34). People may sympathize with a thief if he or she steals in order to avoid starvation. However, the thief had to make full restitution. The thief's punishment, though difficult, is less severe than that of the adulterer. One who steals another man's spouse finds no forgiveness and leniency. There is no restitution for immorality because the stolen object cannot be returned. The father closes this section by telling his son that adultery reveals his ignorance. "He who commits adultery lacks sense" (6:32a). The ignorant young man persists in immorality even though he knows the painful and costly consequences. Committing immorality is equivalent to committing suicide for "he who does it destroys himself" (6:32b).

"The Moral of the Story"
PROVERBS 7:1-27

Introduction

Throughout the opening chapters of the book of Proverbs, the father has repeatedly warned his son about the dangers of immorality (2:16–19; 5:1–23; 6:20–35). Now, using the device of a vivid story, in very graphic terms he dramatizes the deceptiveness and the dangers of immorality.

The father begins his story with a prologue that urges the son to pay close attention to the tale.

> My son, keep my words and treasure up my commandments with you; keep my commandments and live; keep my teaching as the apple of your eye; bind them on your fingers; write them on the tablet of your heart. Say to wisdom, "You are my sister," and call insight your intimate friend, to keep you from the forbidden woman, from the adulteress with her smooth words. (Proverbs 7:1–5)

The father begins with his oft-repeated exhortation for his son to accept, to appreciate, and to apply the instruction he receives from his parents. Notice the five verbs in the opening section. The first verb "to treasure" means to hide something on account of its value. The second verb "keep" means "to pay careful attention to" the commandments the father has been teaching his son throughout his childhood and now into early adulthood. The father repeats the verb "keep" and adds the expression "the apple of your eye." The expression literally reads "the little man of the eye," named for the miniature portrait of the individual who looks into someone's eye and who is reflected from it. The Mosaic Law, like the pupil of the eye, is a precious thing that is to be guarded with the utmost care. The expression was first used by Moses as he described God's care of the nation of Israel.

> He found him in a desert land, and in the howling waste of the wilderness; he encircled him, he cared for him, he kept him as the apple of his eye. (Deuteronomy 32:10)

The expression is also used in Psalm 17:8 as the psalmist asked for God's safekeeping.

The third verb "bind" speaks of tying things together. Previously the son was exhorted to bind his father's teachings around his neck.

> Let not steadfast love and faithfulness forsake you; bind them around your neck; write them on the tablet of your heart. (Proverbs 3:3)

Now he is to bind the teachings like rings on his fingers. This is an allusion to the book of Deuteronomy and the teaching of the Mosaic Law to the next generation.

> And these words that I command you today shall be on your heart. You shall teach them diligently to your children, and shall talk of them when you sit in your house, and when you walk by the way, and when you lie down, and when you rise. You shall bind them as a sign on your hand, and they shall be as frontlets between your eyes. You shall write them on the doorposts of your house and on your gates. (Deuteronomy 6:6–9)

The fourth verb "write," together with the previous verb, imply the instruction of the parents is to become a part of the young man's nature as he writes out his own copy of the instructions. The fifth verb "say" is the declaration the young man is to make that indicates he has learned from his father's instruction. In Old Testament times, one's "sister" was considered an intimate relative. Therefore, "sister" was sometimes used as a synonym for one's wife.

> You have captivated my heart, my sister, my bride; you have captivated my heart with one glance of your eyes, with one jewel of your necklace. How beautiful is your love, my sister, my bride! How much better is your love than wine, and the fragrance of your oils than any spice! (Song of Solomon 4:9–10)

Intimacy with the proper woman (7:4) will keep a young man from immorality with the promiscuous woman (7:5).

Now the father presents the drama in vivid details (7:6–23). Perhaps recounting an actual experience or just using his imagination, the father describes the deadly encounter between a naïve young man and a cunning seductress.

The first character in the drama is the simpleton.

> For at the window of my house I have looked out through my lattice, and I have seen among the simple, I have perceived among the youths, a young man lacking sense, passing along the street near her corner, taking the road to her house in the twilight, in the evening, at the time of night and darkness. (Proverbs 7:6–9)

One evening, while looking through the blinds of his window, the father observed a group of naïve young men walking through the village. Out of this group his attention was drawn to one young man who appeared to be particularly gullible. The youth demonstrated his lack of commonsense by whom he was keeping company with ("among the simple"), where he went ("near her corner"), and when he went there ("at twilight"). The young man was simply wandering around his village aimlessly, but he wandered into the neighborhood of a woman who had an evil and immoral purpose to her life.

> If you want to avoid the devil, stay away from his neighborhood. If you suspect you might be vulnerable to a particular sin, take steps to avoid it. (Robert L. Alden)

The next character in the drama is the seductress.

> And behold, the woman meets him, dressed as a prostitute,
> wily of heart. She is loud and wayward; her feet do not stay
> at home; now in the street, now in the market, and at every
> corner she lies in wait. (Proverbs 7:10–12)

From the description, the woman dressed and talked like a prostitute,
but she informed the young man that she was married, and she never asked
for money. The father describes her as seductive ("dressed as a prostitute"),
secretive ("wily of heart"), aggressive ("she is loud"), and manipulative ("at
every corner she lies in wait").

Next, we have the action of the seduction.

> She seizes him and kisses him, and with bold face she says
> to him, "I had to offer sacrifices, and today I have paid
> my vows; so now I have come out to meet you, to seek
> you eagerly, and I have found you. I have spread my couch
> with coverings, colored linens from Egyptian linen; I have
> perfumed my bed with myrrh, aloes, and cinnamon. Come,
> let us take our fill of love till morning; let us delight ourselves
> with love. For my husband is not at home; he has gone on a
> long journey; he took a bag of money with him; at full moon
> he will come home. (Proverbs 7:13–20)

Notice the five tactics the immoral married woman used to seduce
this unsuspecting young man. Brashness ("she seizes him and kisses him"),
hypocrisy ("I had to offer sacrifices, and today I have paid my vows"), flattery
("to seek you eagerly, and I have found you"), sensuality ("let us take our fill
of love till morning"), and security ("my husband is not at home").

Then there is the sin of adultery.

> With much seductive speech she persuades him; with her
> smooth talk she compels him. All at once he follows her,
> as an ox goes to the slaughter, or as a stag is caught fast
> till an arrow pierces its liver; as a bird rushes into a snare;
> he does not know that it will cost him his life. (Proverbs
> 7:21–23)

Unable to resist her persuasive seduction, the foolish young man suddenly follows her to her house and into her bedroom. In descriptive terms the father pictures the deadly decision made by the young man. He is dumb like an unsuspecting ox being lead to the slaughter house, desperate like a deer caught in a noose until it is shot with an arrow (deer is from the Syriac, while the Hebrew reads "as an anklet for the discipline of a fool"), and doomed like a bird running toward a snare.

The story closes with this epilogue.

> And now, O sons, listen to me, and be attentive to the words of my mouth. Let not your heart turn aside to her ways; do not stray into her paths, for many a victim has she laid low, and all her slain are a mighty throng. Her house is the way to Sheol, going down to the chambers of death. (Proverbs 7:24–27)

"The Tale of Two Women"
PROVERBS 8:1–21

Introduction

The father personifies Wisdom as another prospective woman who is also hoping to attract the attention of his son. Wisdom announces her offer by presenting all young men with a very appealing proposal, in contrast with the immoral proposition of the married woman of the previous chapter. This material is similar to the address of 1:20–33 in which Wisdom proclaims her value.

The section begins with the public invitation that Wisdom offers to the young men of her community.

> Does not wisdom call? Does not understanding raise her voice? On the heights beside the way, at the crossroads she takes her stand; beside the gates in front of the town, at the entrance of the portals she cries aloud: "To you, O men, I call, and my cry is to the children of man. O simple ones, learn prudence; O fools, learn sense. (Proverbs 8:1–5)

Compare the invitations made by the two women in chapters 7 and 8, noting first the similarities. As to the relationship between the women and the young men, both women are strangers to their potential customers (7:5; 8:5). As for the location where their offers are announced, both women meet the young men in the marketplace and in the public thoroughfares (7:12; 8:1–3). Concerning the customers, both women make their appeal to young men who are characterized as simpletons (7:7; 8:5). And as for the sales pitch, both women make their offers sound appealing (7:14–20; 8:6–21).

However, notice the differences in the two women and their respective offers. Concerning the women's offers, the adulteress makes her offer in private (7:9), while Wisdom "cries aloud" with great fervency in public. Concerning the women's customers, the adulteress is available only to the simpleton (7:7), while Wisdom is available to the masses. Concerning the women's character, the adulteress speaks words of deceit (7:5), while Wisdom speaks words of integrity (8:6–9). And, concerning the women's offers, the adulteress can only offer temporary pleasure that will result in the death of the young man (7:18), while Wisdom can offer permanent prosperity that will enhance the life of the young men (8:18).

The larger section provides the motivation for gullible and inexperienced young men to pursue Wisdom (8:6–21). In order to attract the interest of the impressionable youth, Wisdom cites her four most endearing qualities.

> Hear, for I will speak noble things, and from my lips will
> come what is right, for my mouth will utter truth; wickedness
> is an abomination to my lips. All the words of my mouth are
> righteous; there is nothing twisted or crooked in them. They
> are all straight to him who understands, and right to those
> who find knowledge. (Proverbs 8:6–9)

Wisdom is depicted as a noble woman who is known for speaking the truth (8:6). The term "noble things" is actually a noun that is found almost fifty times in the Old Testament and it often used to denote a respected leader, whether governmental (king), military (general), or religious (high priest). Unlike the immoral married woman who was known for her vulgar words and despicable nature (7:13–20), Wisdom can offer virtues that are excellent and worthy of the interest of these young men. In fact, Wisdom is so committed to the truth that dishonesty is an abomination to her. The term "abomination" was first used in Proverbs 6:16–19 to describe the things that God hates. The offer to consider noble things is similar to Paul's advice to the Philippian church.

> Finally, brothers, whatever is true, whatever is honorable, whatever is just, whatever is pure, whatever is lovely, whatever is commendable, if there is any excellence, if there is anything worthy of praise, think about these things. (Philippians 4:8)

Wisdom is also portrayed as a dependable woman who can be counted on (8:7–9). Wisdom promises that her "mouth will utter truth" (8:7). The word "truth" describes that which is reliable, firm, or dependable. Contrast the adulteress who told the naïve young man the lies that he wanted to hear (7:15). Wisdom further states, "all the words of my mouth are righteous" (8:8). The term "righteous," contrasted with "twisted or crooked," describes words that are straight and accurate, rather than perverse and corrupt. Wisdom offers a straight path that is free from detours, rather than the misleading shortcuts that initially look appealing, but ultimately prove to be death traps. Wisdom offers the truth, no matter how painful it is, rather than deceptive, false flattery. Wisdom offers long-term, hard-earned prosperity, rather than immediate, but fleeting pleasure.

Wisdom will also prove to be valuable to the one who possesses her.

> Take my instruction instead of silver, and knowledge rather than choice gold, for wisdom is better than jewels, and all that you may desire cannot compare with her. I, wisdom, dwell with prudence, and I find knowledge and discretion. The fear of the LORD is hatred of evil. Pride and arrogance and the way of evil and perverted speech I hate. I have counsel and sound wisdom; I have insight; I have strength. By me kings reign, and rulers decree what is just; by me princes rule, and nobles, all who govern justly. (Proverbs 8:10–16)

The value of wisdom is found in its practical use. Wisdom ought to be valued more highly than material wealth, for the correct use of wisdom provides a person with the resources needed to gain and appreciate wealth. Or, stated negatively, wealth without wisdom will be squandered by fools (1 Timothy 6:9–10). The decision to choose wisdom over wealth was made by Solomon when he ascended the throne.

Since you have asked for this and not for long life or wealth for yourself, nor have asked for the death of your enemies but for discernment in administering justice, I will do what you have asked. I will give you a wise and discerning heart, so that there will never have been anyone like you, nor will there ever be. Moreover, I will give you what you have not asked for—both riches and honor—so that in your lifetime you will have no equal among kings. (1 Kings 3:11–13)

It appears that Wisdom has a roommate whose name is "Prudence," a Hebrew term that emphasizes the positive aspect of being shrewd. Positively, Wisdom and her roommate ("I, wisdom, dwell with prudence") provide her subjects with "knowledge and discretion," which is the ability to make wise choices. Negatively, wisdom prevents her subjects from the sins of pride, arrogance, and evil speech and behavior, which are the abominations that God finds particularly disgusting (Proverbs 6:16–19).

Wisdom is also portrayed as a woman who is available, in a good way, to the young men who pursue her.

I love those who love me, and those who seek me diligently find me. Riches and honor are with me, enduring wealth and righteousness. My fruit is better than gold, even fine gold, and my yield than choice silver. I walk in the way of righteousness, in the paths of justice, granting an inheritance to those who love me, and filling their treasuries. (Proverbs 8:17–21)

Wisdom, although available to all (8:4), is acquired only by those who love her and seek her. For those who seek after wisdom, not only do they find it, but they also find honor and wealth, with the emphasis on spiritual wealth, rather than material riches. James gave the same advice concerning the pursuit of wisdom.

If any of you lacks wisdom, let him ask God, who gives generously to all without reproach, and it will be given him. But let him ask in faith, with no doubting, for the one who doubts is like a wave of the sea that is driven and tossed by the wind. For that person must not suppose that he will receive anything from the Lord; he is a double-minded man, unstable in all his ways. (James 1:5–8)

"One Woman Who Will Tell Her Age"

PROVERBS 8:22–36

Introduction

In the opening section of this chapter, the father personified Wisdom as another prospective woman who hoped to attract the interest of his son (8:1–21). To make her appeal, Wisdom cited her four most endearing qualities, nobility, dependability, prosperity, and availability. Wisdom's many claims are credible because of her association with God in creation. She is able to enrich people's lives in the present because she was involved in the creation of the world in the past.

In the opening section, Wisdom cites her antiquity as the motivation for young men to pursue her. She describes her origin as taking place before the creation of the world.

> The LORD possessed me at the beginning of his work, the first of his acts of old. Ages ago I was set up, at the first, before the beginning of the earth. When there were no depths I was brought forth, when there were no springs abounding with water. Before the mountains had been shaped, before the hills, I was brought forth, before he had made the earth with its fields, or the first of the dust of the world. When he established the heavens, I was there; when he drew a circle on the face of the deep, when he made firm the skies above, when he established the fountains of the deep, when he assigned to the sea its limit, so that the waters might not transgress his command, when he marked out the foundations of the earth. (Proverbs 8:22–29)

Notice the three verbs Wisdom uses to describe her origin. The first verb "possessed" (*qana*) can mean either "to possess" or "to create." To acquire or possess is the common meaning of the word in the book of Proverbs (1:5; 4:5). One example of where the verb means to create is found in the Psalter.

> For you created my inmost being; you knit me together in my mother's womb. (Psalm 139:13)

The older translations chose the translation "to possess," for fear that it gave the impression that God lacked wisdom, and so created it before the world began. But, the synonymous verbs in the section convey the idea of the creation of Wisdom from the mind of God before He created the world.

The second verb "set up" means "to appoint" or "to install." God installed Wisdom into her office prior to the creation of the world, and therefore, her antiquity demands respect. The third verb "brought forth" originally means "to writhe in pain." From this meaning the verb acquired the additional sense of the writhing movements of labor contractions. Wisdom was given birth prior to any creative work of God. Wisdom existed before the creation of the world, and therefore was present when God created the universe. Wisdom existed before the waters were separated, making clouds and oceans (second day of creation; Genesis 1:6–8), and before the dry land appeared (third day of creation; Genesis 1:9–10). The same thoughts are basically repeated in verses 27–29.

Wisdom then describes her role in the process of God's creation as being constantly by His side.

> Then I was beside him, like a master workman, and I was daily his delight, rejoicing before him always, rejoicing in his inhabited world and delighting in the children of man. (Proverbs 8:30–31)

Wisdom is described as a craftsman at God's side when He created the world. This attribute of God, personified by an assistant in the creative work, poetically indicates that God was wise in what He created. The presence of Wisdom at the creation of the world is similar in expression to the presence of the Logos (a New Testament designation of Jesus) at the creation of the world.

> In the beginning was the Word, and the Word was with God, and the Word was God. He was in the beginning with God. All things were made through him, and without him was not anything made that was made. (John 1:1–3)

The apostle Paul wrote much the same thing to the believers in Colossae concerning the person of Jesus Christ.

> He is the image of the invisible God, the firstborn of all creation. For by him all things were created, in heaven and

on earth, visible and invisible, whether thrones or dominions or rulers or authorities—all things were created through him and for him. And he is before all things, and in him all things hold together. (Colossians 1:15–17)

As the "firstborn of all creation" Jesus Christ preceded the whole creation, he was the cause of creation, and he is sovereign over all creation. The following verses, using a series of prepositional phrases, argue against the interpretation that Christ was a created being. Christ is before all things both in time and in rank. Christ is not only the One through whom all things came to be, but also the One by whom they continue to exist.

The next section has the invitation of Wisdom to listen to her.

And now, O sons, listen to me: blessed are those who keep my ways. Hear instruction and be wise, and do not neglect it. Blessed is the one who listens to me, watching daily at my gates, waiting beside my doors. For whoever finds me finds life and obtains favor from the Lord, but he who fails to find me injures himself; all who hate me love death. (Proverbs 8:32–36)

Having added antiquity to her list of endearing qualities (recall nobility, dependability, prosperity, and availability), Wisdom makes a final appeal. Wisdom's threefold call to listen implies she is simply one of many voices clamoring for the attention of people. On any given day, the other voices of work, entertainment, education, recreation, money, success, peer pressure, stress, and family clamor for our attention. Taking a close look at verses 32–34 we see an interesting pattern develop. The words "listen" and "blessed" are used alternatively, indicating that God's blessing will follow one's obedience, not vice versa.

Besides the verbs for listen, several other verbs in verses 32–34 describe our responsibility toward obtaining wisdom. "Blessed are those who keep my ways" (8:32). The verb "keep" means "to pay close attention to." The acquisition of Wisdom demands the full attention of the student so that other things in life do not become a distraction. "Hear instruction and be wise, and do not neglect it" (8:33). The verb "neglect" means "to let go, to dismiss, to break loose from." Once Wisdom has been initially acquired, the student needs to maintain his continued focus on its presence in his life. "Blessed is the

watch for wisdom
wait for wisdom by your door
Satan crouches at your door

one who listens to me, watching daily at my gates" (8:34). The verb "watch" means "to give attention to." This attention to Wisdom is to be given on a daily basis. Much like devotions and prayer time, the emphasis on Wisdom is a daily commitment. And then there is the expression, "waiting beside my doors" (8:34). The verb translated "waiting" is the same verb as the first one. The picture is that of a young man who is waiting every day outside the door of a woman that he is interested in. In this instance, the woman is Wisdom, and the young man is pursuing her.

The individual who finds Wisdom will receive a life of quality, fulfillment, and satisfaction ("For whoever finds me finds life"). The one who finds wisdom will also receive divine favor ("And receives favor from the LORD"), a term that occurs fourteen times in Proverbs. The term "favor" means acceptance, goodwill, or approval. The individual who fails to find Wisdom will receive the very opposite, namely, a life of condemnation, ill will, and disapproval. The verb "fail" means "to miss the mark." Individuals who reject God's wisdom will bring harm to their lives. The Old Testament character Samson is an appropriate illustration of the negative warning. Even though God endowed him with great powers, because he did not resist sin and failed to obtain wisdom, he brought upon himself divine disfavor. Only in his death did he begin to realize the potential that God had in store for him.

"Two Dinner Invitations"
PROVERBS 9:1–18

Lady Wisdom
Woman Folly

Introduction

Chapter 9 forms the conclusion of the opening nine-chapter introduction to the book of Proverbs by repeating the major themes the father addressed with his son in the first eight chapters. In this closing address, both Lady Wisdom and Woman Folly will make their final appeals to the young men who are passing by their houses. Both personified women appeal to the same group of people. Young and inexperienced individuals need to pursue a life of wisdom, but they are also naturally attracted to folly. Both dinner invitations require a response on the part of the invited guests. The individual's response will prove to be a life and death decision.

In this final section the father repeats five truths that have been highlighted throughout the opening addresses. First, wisdom and folly compete for the allegiance of people and they demand a choice must be made. Second, the ultimate choice between wisdom and folly lies with each individual and it is an either/or, not a both/and decision. Third, the wisdom or foolishness of individuals will be measured by how they respond to correction. Fourth, behind wisdom lies God and His call to obedience to His Word. And fifth, to heed folly, while it may be fun at first, is to commit suicide.

The last address begins with a contrast in the preparations made by the two hostesses for their invited dinner guests. Notice first of all the preparations of Lady Wisdom.

> Wisdom has built her house; she has hewn her seven pillars. She has slaughtered her beasts; she has mixed her wine; she has also set her table. She has sent out her young women to call from the highest places in the town. (Proverbs 9:1–3)

Lady Wisdom's industrious nature is evidenced by three actions. She has built a large and spacious home that can accommodate many dinner guests (see Proverbs 14:1). The reference to the seven pillars might be symbolic of the completeness of her house. She has prepared a magnificent banquet that includes a sumptuous meal of the finest meats and wines available. In the ancient world, wine would be mixed with spices to enhance its flavor. The menu items of meat and wine represent the good teaching of wisdom that will be pleasant and profitable. Finally, Lady Wisdom has sent her maid servants out to invite the guests, much like the invitations in Jesus' parable of the wedding feast (Matthew 22:1–14).

Contrast the preparations of Lady Wisdom with the reputation and lack of preparation of the second hostess, Woman Folly.

> The woman Folly is loud; she is seductive and knows nothing. She sits at the door of her house; she takes a seat on the highest places of the town, calling to those who pass by, who are going straight on their way. (Proverbs 9:13–15)

Woman Folly's boisterous nature is evidenced by three traits. She says too much (the term "loud" is related to the idea of riotous), she knows too little (the emphasis is on moral ignorance, not intelligence), and she does very little to prepare for her guests. She is undisciplined, like her guests, and morally ignorant, which explains their natural attraction to accept her invitation. Unlike the other hostess who diligently prepared for the banquet, Woman Folly simply sits at the door of her house and calls out to the gullible youth who are passing by.

Consider next the invitations of the two hostesses (9:4–6, 15–18). First, there is the invitation of Lady Wisdom.

> Whoever is simple, let him turn in here!" To him who lacks sense she says, "Come, eat of my bread and drink of the wine I have mixed. Leave your simple ways, and live, and walk in the way of insight. (Proverbs 9:4–6)

And then there is the invitation of Woman Folly.

> Whoever is simple, let him turn in here!" And to him who lacks sense she says, "Stolen water is sweet, and bread eaten in secret is pleasant." But he does not know that the dead are there, that her guests are in the depths of Sheol." (Proverbs 9:15–18)

There is an initial similarity between the two invitations in that they are both directed toward the simpletons, the gullible youth who are lacking in understanding and in experience. But the remainder of the description reflects the differences in the invitations of the two women.

Lady Wisdom offers the youth who come to her banquet a meaningful life, but with no initial mention of pleasure. "Leave your simple ways and you will live; walk in the way of understanding" (9:6). The pleasure in life will ultimately come when a young person chooses to pursue a life of wisdom. But the choice must first be made to pursue the discipline of wisdom. On the other hand, Woman Folly offers her guests sensual pleasures, but with no mention of the negative consequences. "Stolen water is sweet; food eaten in secret is delicious! But little do they know that the dead are there, that her guests are in the depths of the grave" (9:17–18). The youth who enter the house of Woman Folly do not realize until it is too late that the other dinner guests are already dead, and they will soon follow. Lady Wisdom demands that people make some hard choices in how they live their lives. "Leave your simple ways and you will live" (9:6). On the other hand, Woman Folly appeals to the sinful desires of these naïve youth. "Stolen water is sweet; food eaten in secret is delicious!" (9:17). Lady Wisdom offers her guests long-term satisfaction in life (9:6), while Woman Folly can only offer immediate gratification (9:17). Lady Wisdom's offer of life is clearly conditioned by obedience (9:6), while Woman Folly's offer of death is purposefully obscured by disobedience (9:18).

The next section seems to be an interlude to the dinner parties.

> Whoever corrects a scoffer gets himself abuse, and he who reproves a wicked man incurs injury. Do not reprove a scoffer, or he will hate you; reprove a wise man, and he will love you. Give instruction to a wise man, and he will be still wiser; teach a righteous man, and he will increase in learning. The fear of the LORD is the beginning of wisdom, and the knowledge of the Holy One is insight. For by me your days will be multiplied, and years will be added to your life. If you are wise, you are wise for yourself; if you scoff, you alone will bear it. (Proverbs 9:7–12)

At first glance these six verses do not seem to fit the rest of the passage. Because they seem to interrupt the flow of the passage, some commentators have considered them a later insertion. And while that is possible, since the book of Proverbs was ultimately assembled by a final editor, a number of themes in the interlude can be found in the invitations. The father is focused on the gullible youth who are naturally attracted to folly, but who desperately need wisdom. But gullible youth who reject wisdom in favor of folly, can easily become scoffers, and ultimately, wicked people. And, therein lies the danger for the sage who is trying to educate these youth to choose wisdom. If wisdom is rejected, the youth will eventually turn on their teachers. On the other hand, if the youth choose the way of wisdom, they will learn to love their teacher and they will become wiser still. The decision of the youth will come down to an understanding of God's presence in their lives and whether it produces a proper reverential fear. If the youth choose wisdom, their days will be multiplied and meaningful. But if they choose folly, they will become scoffers who will live lives of ignorance.

The foolish person is described as a scoffer who mocks the truth and those who try to deliver it. The fool is further described as a wicked person who persists in sin despite the many warnings. And the fool is portrayed as a vindictive individual who not only hates correction, but who also abuses those who try to help the most by telling the truth. On the other hand, wise people love correction, and they have a continual desire for personal improvement. Verse 12 is a summary statement that declares the person who is wise will enjoy the rewards of wisdom, while the fool will bear the consequences of foolish decisions.

With the long addresses brought to a conclusion, the editor of the book of Proverbs now inserts the individual sayings of Solomon that begin in 10:1 and run to 22:16. Since the individual sayings are random, they have been grouped together based on similar topics.

Parental Pain or Pleasure

10:1 – "A wise son makes a glad father, but a foolish son is a sorrow to his mother."

This antithetical proverb states the truism that the choices made by children as they grow into adulthood have a huge impact on the emotional state of their parents. The proverb makes the assumption that the parents have raised their children with godly discipline to make wise decisions. And so, if the children reject their instruction and choose folly instead, the parents will be naturally sorrowful. For godly Christian parents, their greatest joys occur when their children choose to follow the Lord, and their greatest sorrows are experienced when even one child chooses to reject the biblical instruction they were given in their formative years. Because godly parents pour so much of their lives into their children, it is understandable why their joy or sorrow is determined by their children's choices. A later proverb in the collection is almost identical to this saying except it uses the verb "despise" instead of the noun "sorrow."

A wise son makes a glad father, but a foolish man despises his mother. (Proverbs 15:20)

A foolish child not only brings private sorrow into the life of his mother, but his intentional disregard of parental discipline shows his public disdain for his parents.

13:1 – "A wise son hears his father's instruction, but a scoffer does not listen to rebuke."

This antithetical proverb emphasizes the effort the father makes to bring discipline into the life of his child. The discipline comes in the form of verbal and physical correction. But if the child resists that discipline, he or she will become a scoffer, which is the worst aspect of a fool. If the child grows up with no respect for parental or divine authority, the child will become a mocker who ridicules the parents because, foolishly, the child thinks he or she is wiser than the parents. A later proverb is a worst-case scenario for parental abuse.

> He who does violence to his father and chases away his mother is a son who brings shame and reproach. (Proverbs 19:26)

Contempt for one's parents is a violation of the fifth commandment of the Decalogue.

> Honor your father and your mother, that your days may be long in the land that the LORD your God is giving you. (Exodus 20:12)

The apostle Paul repeated this theme in Ephesians 6:1.

17:21 – "He who sires a fool gets himself sorrow, and the father of a fool has no joy."

This proverb uses two common Hebrew nouns to describe the pain of fathering a fool. The first term *kesil* emphasizes the dull-witted nature of the fool, while the second term *nabal* focuses on the moral indifference to parental discipline. The indescribable joy that parents experience at the birth of a baby can be wiped away when the child grows into an adult who has chosen to become a fool.

17:25 – "A foolish son is a grief to his father and bitterness to her who bore him."

These five related proverbs demonstrate the huge impact godly and consistent parental discipline can have on the lives of children. This reality is intended to motivate parents not to neglect their parental responsibility when the children are young and impressionable. But the book of Proverbs also places a great burden on the children to receive this discipline. If parents have made a good faith effort to invest in their children's lives to bring them under the authority of Almighty God, the burden then falls to the children not to squander this godly legacy. The apostle John said it best in his third letter.

> I have no greater joy than to hear that my children are walking in the truth. (3 John 4)

Riches and Righteousness

10:2 – "Treasures gained by wickedness do not profit, but righteousness delivers from death."

This antithetical proverb warns that financial wealth that is gained through dishonest means will not profit the thief in the long run. Having said that, the proverb does not deny there is some financial advantage to being dishonest. The matter is clarified in the second half of the proverb when it brings up the topic of death. Many individuals have benefitted financially in this lifetime from dishonesty. But physical death is the great equalizer when it comes to financial matters.

> As he came from his mother's womb he shall go again, naked as he came, and shall take nothing for his toil that he may carry away in his hand. (Ecclesiastes 5:15)

While financial riches do not last beyond this lifetime, being righteousness does have permanency.

11:18 – "The wicked earns deceptive wages, but one who sows righteousness gets a sure reward."

This proverb acknowledges that both the wicked and the righteous will receive a monetary reward for how they live. But the saying warns the wicked that their wages are deceptive, in that they will not last. On the other hand, the righteous are likened to a farmer who sows the seed, and who is guaranteed a good crop. One of the Minor Prophets also speaks of sowing righteousness.

Sow for yourselves righteousness; reap steadfast love; break up your fallow ground, for it is the time to seek the LORD, that he may come and rain righteousness upon you. (Hosea 10:12)

This reminds us of the apostle Paul's proverb in his second letter to the church in Corinth.

Whoever sows sparingly will also reap sparingly, and whoever sows bountifully will also reap bountifully. (2 Corinthians 9:6)

14:24 – "The crown of the wise is their wealth, but the folly of fools brings folly."

Living a wise life has its own rewards. The imagery of a crown speaks of that which adorns a person's head. Wisdom literature does not always conceive of wealth in monetary terms. On the other hand, the unwise decisions of a fool with only bring more trouble into his or her life.

15:6 – "In the house of the righteous there is much treasure, but trouble befalls the income of the wicked."

The truth of this proverb is attested by the lives of many of the patriarchs. Beginning with Abraham, these men and their houses were financially blessed by God. That being said, wealth is not always an indication of God's favor. For that reason, the wisdom writer offered this saying.

Better is a little with righteousness than great revenues with injustice. (Proverbs 16:8)

But the second half of the proverb is always true. There is not enough money in the world to protect a wicked individual from trouble in the form of divine punishment. The narrative of Achan and his theft of the devoted things in Jericho and the subsequent judgment from God comes to mind (Joshua 7). The narrative also shows the negative impact his decision had on his household.

21:6 – "The getting of treasures by a lying tongue is a fleeting vapor and a snare of death."

This emblematic proverb uses the imagery of the wisp of a cloud to depict the momentary possession of treasures that were obtained through dishonesty. Jezebel's lies to have Naboth killed and his vineyard given to King Ahab is a biblical example of the temporary possession of something gained because of lies (1 Kings 21; 2 Kings 9:30–37). For this couple, the treasure disappeared into thin air.

Desires and Destinies

10:3 – "The LORD does not let the righteous go
hungry, but he thwarts the craving of the wicked."

This antithetical proverb is a summary of the covenant promises God made to the nation of Israel in the Mosaic Law. In the blessings and the curses spelled out in Deuteronomy 28, God promised the nation that He would reward righteousness and punish wickedness. And while we often think of hunger primarily in physical terms, the expression "the righteous" literally reads "the appetite (or soul, *nephesh*) of the righteous," which would include the inner feelings and longings as well. God promises to meet all the needs of those who pursue His righteousness. In contrast, the wicked, while they may have their physical needs met, will have their greedy cravings go unfulfilled throughout their lives. Because proverbs are general principles, and not promises, read the frustrations of Asaph in Psalm 73 which reflect the opposite reality of this proverb. Asaph asked the question, "Why do the wicked seem to prosper, while the righteous suffer?" The turning point was when Asaph stopped looking at the wicked and started looking more closely at God and when he considered the ultimate destiny of the wicked.

10:24 – "What the wicked dreads will come upon *Salvation*
him, but the desire of the righteous will be granted."

This proverb actually starts with the wicked and ends with the righteous. The wicked go through life plagued by a bad conscience for they know their conduct is wrong. But the wisdom writer warns them that they will get what they desperately want to avoid, while the righteous will get the desires of their heart granted. Even though God is not mentioned in the proverb, the wisdom writer wants his readers to understand that God is the agent in determining that people receive what they deserve.

*10:28 – "The hope of the righteous brings joy, but
the expectation of the wicked will perish."*

What a person hopes for implies they have not yet realized their expectations. But this proverb encourages the righteous that God will help them realize their expectations and that it will result in their joy. On the other hand, the wisdom writer warns the wicked that their plans will die with them.

*11:8 – "The righteous is delivered from trouble,
and the wicked walks into it instead."*

This proverb expresses confidence in God's justice system for the world. The wisdom writer believes that the righteous will ultimately walk away from trouble, while the wicked will actually walk into the trouble they are hoping to avoid, or what they want to inflict on others. The narrative of the book of Esther is an example of the principle of this proverb, at least for the second half of the proverb. While Esther and Mordecai are not portrayed in the narrative as Jews who were living righteous lives in exile, the unnamed character in the book, namely, God, delivered His people from trouble, while Haman walked into the trouble he was hoping to inflict on the Jews.

*11:23 – "The desire of the righteous ends only in
good, the expectation of the wicked in wrath."*

The idea of desire also implies it has not yet been realized by the righteous. But the wisdom writer encourages the righteous to remain faithful, because God will eventually bring about His good will in their lives. On the other hand, he warns the wicked that whatever they were expecting in life, they will only experience the wrath of God because their character and conduct contradict God's just nature.

The Reward of Diligence

*10:4 – "A slack hand causes poverty, but
the hand of the diligent makes rich."*

This antithetical proverb promotes a good work ethic for individuals, with a direct cause and effect for financial success in life. The classic statement on laziness was found earlier in Proverbs 6:6–11 when the father used the illustration of the ant to promote diligence for his son. Laziness is directly connected to poverty, and a good work ethic will lead to wealth. The wisdom writer focused on the hand to depict the careless labor of an individual who sees no benefit or honor in manual labor. See also Proverbs 18:9 and 12:24. The Mosaic Law had a welfare system for the poor in the nation of Israel, but it still required labor on the part of the needy to gather the food (Leviticus 19:9–10). The apostle Paul had strong words for believers who did not work for a living.

> For even when we were with you, we would give you this command: If anyone is not willing to work, let him not eat. For we hear that some among you walk in idleness, not busy at work, but busybodies. Now such persons we command and encourage in the Lord Jesus Christ to do their work quietly and to earn their own living. (2 Thessalonians 3:10–12)

10:5 – "He who gathers in summer is a prudent son, but he who sleeps in harvest is a son who brings shame."

The very next proverb also promotes a good work ethic, while it condemns laziness. The emphasis of this proverb is on the young person and his or her attitude toward work. In the agricultural society of Israel, the timing of work was connected to the growing season of the crops. A lazy son who chose to sleep while the family was engaged in the harvest would bring shame to the parents for raising a lazy child. This particular proverb makes a connection between being industrious and being intelligent.

12:27 – "Whoever is slothful will not roast his game, but the diligent man will get precious wealth."

This proverb reflects a culture of hunters and gatherers who have to go out and make the effort to find their food. A lazy person will never find game to roast because he or she will not make the necessary effort. See also Proverbs 19:15. Or, if the individual finds games, he or she is too lazy to roast it, and therefore, will have nothing to eat. But the diligent individual is promised financial success in life.

13:4 – "The soul of the sluggard craves and gets nothing,
while the soul of the diligent is richly supplied."

This proverb contrasts two types of "souls" or individuals, namely, the sluggard and the diligent. Both individuals have physical needs in life, but only one of them will have those needs realized. Daydreaming leaves the sluggard with nothing, but diligence will supply the needs of the laborer.

21:5 – "The plans of the diligent lead surely to abundance,
but everyone who is hasty comes only to poverty.

While the other proverbs contrasted diligence with laziness, this proverb focuses on another cause of poverty. In addition to a good work ethic, this proverb promotes the importance of planning before the individual engages in the work. You can either work fast or work smart. Taking the time to work smart will eventually lead to prosperity. On the other hand, the person who is impulsive is prone to make quick and rash decisions that will be financially harmful. Speaking of poverty, see Proverbs 14:23 and 20:13.

The Blessed Life

10:6 – "Blessings are on the head of the righteous,
but the mouth of the wicked conceals violence."

This antithetical proverb has two obvious contrasts: the righteous and the wicked, and the head and the mouth. And while we would expect a contrast with the idea of blessings (the noun is plural), the wisdom writer chose to emphasize the harm that is inflicted on others by the words of the wicked. The two thoughts might actually contrast if we thought of the blessings as words of blessing pronounced on the righteous. The idea of a reward for righteous living is found throughout the Old Testament. We find it promised by God to the nation of Israel in the blessings and curses of Deuteronomy 28.

> And all these blessings shall come upon you and overtake you, if you obey the voice of the LORD your God. (Deuteronomy 28:2)

We also find the promise of reward in Psalm 1.

> Blessed is the man who walks not in the counsel of the
> wicked, nor stands in the way of sinners, nor sits in the seat
> of scoffers; but his delight is in the law of the LORD, and on
> his law he meditates day and night (Psalm 1:1–2)

This psalm is a fitting introduction to the Psalter in that it summarizes the two ways open to mankind: righteousness or wickedness.

> *11:26 – "The people curse him who holds back grain,*
> *but a blessing is on the head of him who sells it."*

This proverb also speaks of a blessing on the head of an individual with an emphasis on the socially responsible merchant. A merchant could take advantage of those in need when he recognized that demand was high and he would withhold his supply to drive up the price. This proverb pronounced a blessing on the merchant who cared more about people, and less about profit. While the merchant would not make as much money in the short term, he would develop a good reputation, which, in the long run, would prove to be more valuable.

> *16:20 – "Whoever gives thought to the word will discover*
> *good, and blessed is he who trusts in the LORD."*

This proverb pronounces a blessing on the individual who lives out his faith by putting his complete confidence in the LORD. And, he proves his faith by his careful consideration of biblical instruction. The reference to the "word" can either speak of the individual's reading of the Word of God, or the biblical instruction that he receives from his teachers. The first half of the proverb advocates a thoughtful response to the word because it is how God communicates His will to His people. The individual who reveres God is promised a reward for that reverence. Having stated this, it is equally important to point out that the idea of reward should not be thought of solely in monetary terms.

> *22:9 – "Whoever has a bountiful eye will be*
> *blessed, for he shares his bread with the poor."*

While Proverbs 11:26 spoke of the merchant who willingly sold his supply to those in need, this proverb addresses the non-merchant who is willing to share his supply with those in need. A generous person is described as having a "bountiful eye" which literally reads "a good eye." This is in contrast with the wicked person who has an "evil eye" because he or she is covetous and miserly. A similar thought is expressed in another saying in the collection.

> Whoever despises his neighbor is a sinner, but blessed is he
> who is generous to the poor. (Proverbs 14:21)

A great illustration of generosity was the behavior of the stranger in the parable of the good Samaritan (Luke 10:33–35).

A Good Reputation

10:7 – "The memory of the righteous is a blessing,
but the name of the wicked will rot."

The collection of individual proverbs is full of sayings that address the benefits of living a righteous life. We have already examined three such sayings in this tenth chapter.

> Treasures gained by wickedness do not profit, but
> righteousness delivers from death. The LORD does not let
> the righteous go hungry, but he thwarts the craving of the
> wicked. Blessings are on the head of the righteous, but the
> mouth of the wicked conceals violence. (Proverbs 10:3,
> 4, 6)

Most of the promised blessings for living a righteous life concern this lifetime. But this proverb speaks of the singular blessing of living a righteous life long after the individual's life has come to an end. This antithetical proverb addresses the opposing reputations of the righteous and the wicked and the enduring nature of both reputations.

The authors of wisdom literature in the Old Testament were concerned about the memory of the righteous and whether it would endure. Speaking positively on the subject was the psalmist.

For the righteous will never be moved; he will be remembered forever. (Psalm 112:6)

One of the greatest blessings of living a truly God-centered life is the impact this life has on the lives that come forth from this individual. The person of good fortune will focus more energy on the children's spiritual welfare than on his or her financial fortune, which was addressed in the following verses. The psalmist focused on the next generation and how godly parents could eternally impact their children and their grandchildren in developing their own walk with God. Speaking negatively on the subject of an enduring reputation was Qoheleth.

For the living know that they will die, but the dead know nothing, and they have no more reward, for the memory of them is forgotten. (Ecclesiastes 9:5)

In this section Qoheleth was giving a bleak concept of death and the uncertainty of the afterlife. One of the things that bothered him was that the dead are soon forgotten.

This proverb takes the optimistic approach that living a righteous life will cause the individual to be remembered after his or her life has come to an end. Living a wicked life will also leave a memory, but it will be one that leaves a stench behind. *Are we doing well, or are we doing good?*

> 22:1 – "A good name is to be chosen rather than great riches, and favor is better than silver or gold."

The collection of individual proverbs is full of sayings that speak of riches, both in the positive, and in the negative.

Whoever trusts in his riches will fall, but the righteous will flourish like a green leaf. (Proverbs 11:28)

The reward for humility and fear of the Lord is riches and honor and life. (Proverbs 22:4)

The above proverb is an example of a "better-than" saying. While having riches is great, there is something even greater to possess, namely, having a good reputation. Qoheleth said the same thing.

> A good name is better than precious ointment. (Ecclesiastes 7:1a)

In the ancient world of the author, fine perfume was an expensive luxury item. Its value is demonstrated in the narrative of the woman who anointed Jesus' head before his crucifixion (Matthew 26:6–9). But while fine perfume can make a person smell nice, it cannot cover up the odor of a bad reputation. The same evaluation is true when it comes to monetary things like silver and gold. Money can buy you many things, but it cannot buy a good reputation. Your name is mentioned in public and immediately an opinion of you comes into people's minds. We forge our reputations early in life and it is often the little things we do or do not do that create our reputation.

The Talk of Fools

10:8, 10 – "The wise of heart will receive commandments, but a babbling fool will come to ruin. Whoever winks the eye causes trouble, and a babbling fool will come to ruin."

These two proverbs speak of the self-inflicted ruin brought on by the babbling fool who talks too much. The expression "babbling fool" literally reads "the fool of lips." In the first proverb "the wise of heart" is contrasted with "the fool of lips." A babbling fool is too busy talking to listen to the wise counsel of others, while the wise individual is receptive to biblical instruction. The second proverb compares two other body parts, namely, the winking eye, and once again, "the fool of lips." The babbling fool is just as dangerous as the deceitful individual who sends secret messages with the wink of the eye (6:12–13). Both proverbs warn the fool that his or her babbling will bring about ruin.

10:14 – "The wise lay up knowledge, but the mouth of a fool brings ruin near."

This proverb also contrasts the difference between the wise and the fool. While the wise individual quietly receives knowledge for future use, the noisy fool is busy talking and bringing about his or her own ruin. There is also a contrast in the timing of the two phrases. The wise individual lives for the future, while the fool will speed up his or her own ruin with thoughtless words.

> *14:3 – "By the mouth of a fool comes a rod for his back, but the lips of the wise will preserve them."*

How people talk reveals their level of intelligence, and it determines how others respond to them. While the words of the wise are their greatest protection, what comes out of the mouth of the fool generates a deserved punishment. The wise are careful not to let certain words pass their lips, and they think about their words before they speak. The Hebrew text in the opening phrase reveals the true source of the fool's problem. The text speaks of the "rod of pride" which is the beginning point of all sin.

> *15:2 – "The tongue of the wise commends knowledge, but the mouths of fools pour out folly."*

This proverb teaches the truism that a person's speech reveals their true character. The wise individual promotes knowledge among the listeners with his or her words, while foolish words just spill out of the fool's mouth, much like water running out of the tap when the faucet is turned on.

> *18:2 – "A fool takes no pleasure in understanding, but only in expressing his opinion."*

This proverb says that a fool loves the sound of his or her own voice so much that the fool has no time to listen to the wisdom that others are expressing. The fool finds pleasure in expressing his or her own opinions and is displeased when others try to provide an education.

> *18:6-7 – "A fool's lips walk into a fight, and his mouth invites a beating. A fool's mouth is his ruin, and his lips are a snare to his soul."*

These proverbs try to warn the fool that he or she is his or her own worst enemy. The negative consequences range from verbal fights to actual physical beatings. Like a snare set to capture an unsuspecting animal, the words of a fool set a trap for his or her own ruin. See also Proverbs 14:7; 15:7, 15; 17:7.

Integrity

10:9 – "Whoever walks in integrity walks securely, but he who makes his ways crooked will be found out."

The basic sense of the Hebrew word that is translated "integrity" is that of innocence or blamelessness. The individual who lives a blameless life is open and honest with God and with man. Because of that honesty, the righteous will live securely in the sense that they will not put themselves in harm's way because they have nothing to hide. A similar promise was made by the father to his son in an earlier address.

> For the LORD gives wisdom; from his mouth come knowledge and understanding; he stores up sound wisdom for the upright; he is a shield to those who walk in integrity, guarding the paths of justice and watching over the way of his saints. (Proverbs 2:6–8)

Having a clear conscience is its own reward. On the other hand, the individual who lives a deceptive life, in that he or she pretends to be innocent, will be found out. Since there is no possibility of deceiving God, the finding out will take place in the community. It may take a while for the deceiver's dishonesty to be revealed, but it will eventually take place. The idea of being found out is reminiscent of a warning God issued to the nation of Israel in the Pentateuch.

> But if you will not do so, behold, you have sinned against the LORD, and be sure your sin will find you out. (Numbers 32:23)

11:3 – "The integrity of the upright guides them, but the crookedness of the treacherous destroys them."

The first part of this proverb says much the same thing as the previous proverb, but the second part elaborates on the dangers of being deceptive. The contrast is between two individuals, namely, the upright and the faithless. The reward for living a blameless life is self-preservation, while the consequence of deception is self-destruction. The character Job is a good example of the blameless individual.

> There was a man in the land of Uz whose name was Job, and that man was blameless and upright, one who feared God and turned away from evil. (Job 1:1)

His life is a good example of the guidance provided by integrity for it took some time for him to realize the reward. On the other hand, a life of duplicity will eventually unravel and destroy the deceiver. There is a sense of poetic justice in the wisdom literature for the individual who is trying to harm others through deception will eventually self-destruct.

> *19:1 – "Better is a poor person who walks in his integrity than one who is crooked in speech and is a fool."*

This proverb also addresses the contrast between integrity and dishonesty, but with a "better-than" comparison. Because integrity was so important to the sage, he preferred poverty over prosperity if the prosperity could only be gained through dishonesty. The Old Testament character Joseph, when he first arrived in Egypt due to slavery, is a great example of the first stanza of this proverb. The reference to the "crooked in speech" may indicate how the fool gained a financial advantage.

> *20:7 – "The righteous who walks in his integrity— blessed are his children after him!"*

This proverb promotes the long-term benefits of living a life of integrity. A parent who lives a life of integrity will give his or her children the greatest inheritance of all, which is a godly life to emulate. A righteous life is more valuable than riches, for while riches can fade, righteousness will endure. The Mosaic Law promised blessings on the parents who would live a righteous life before their children (Exodus 20:4–6).

The Fountain of Life

This grouping of four proverbs uses the expression "the fountain of life" to describe something that gives life to its recipient. The image is that of a spring of water that was found in a desert region, whose presence sustained the lives of the inhabitants who lived in this challenging environment. A good illustration of the importance of water, as it pertains to the sustenance of life, comes from the narrative of the life of the patriarch Isaac. As God began to prosper Isaac's life financially as he lived among the Philistines, these coastal plain dwellers retaliated by destroying the wells of his father Abraham.

> Now the Philistines had stopped and filled with earth all the wells that his father's servants had dug in the days of Abraham his father. (Genesis 26:15)

Isaac had his servants dig the wells out again and they proceeded to find new additional wells which brought about more conflict with the Philistines. The conflict over the wells was a life and death issue for the people who lived in that region.

The psalmist used the expression "the fountain of life" when he wrote of the life-giving nature of God.

> How precious is your steadfast love, O God! The children of mankind take refuge in the shadow of your wings. They feast on the abundance of your house, and you give them drink from the river of your delights. For with you is the fountain of life; in your light do we see light. (Psalm 36:7–9)

This is a psalm of sharp contrasts. In the opening stanza, the psalmist examined the destructive nature of the wicked, and in the middle section he described the delights of the LORD. In sharp contrast to the acts of the wicked are the delights of the LORD, reflected in His attributes. His love and faithfulness to His children know no limits. His righteousness goes high and His justice runs deep. All people, whether rich or poor, are dependent on the LORD's sustaining love.

> *10:11 — "The mouth of the righteous is a fountain of life, but the mouth of the wicked conceals violence."*

The wisdom writer proclaimed the life-giving nature of the words that flow from a righteous person's mouth into the ears of others. While the mouth of the wicked spews forth hatred and violence, a righteous person uses his or her words to promote health in the lives of the listeners.

13:14 – "The teaching of the wise is a fountain of life,
that one may turn away from the snares of death."

The words of the righteous come in the form of teaching that instructs others on how to live a wise life. If the advice is followed, the individual will escape the snares that lead to a premature death. And in the process, he or she will go on to enjoy a meaningful life.

14:27 – "The fear of the LORD is a fountain of life,
that one may turn away from the snares of death."

The righteous individual who has a proper reverence for God will avoid the temptations of life because he or she knows they lead to entrapment and eventual death.

16:22 – "Good sense is a fountain of life to him
who has it, but the instruction of fools is folly."

When an individual has a proper fear of the LORD, he or she possesses the understanding that will help make wise assessments in life. But if God is not feared, then the alternative is to turn to the foolish advice of other fools that will lead to destructive decisions in life.

Love Covers All

10:12 – "Hatred stirs up strife, but
love covers all offenses."

This proverb touches on the key quality that is necessary in order to maintain healthy relationships. In every relationship, eventually someone will be offended because human beings are flawed creatures. And when the offense takes place, the injured party has to decide how to respond. If the response is to get angry, then the relationship will be beset by conflict. But if the injured party chooses love over revenge, then the relationship will be protected from further damage. Earlier in the book of Proverbs the father told his son that sowing discord among brothers is one of the things that God hates (6:19). Because this is true, the injured party can minimize the damage by choosing to show love to the offender. This mature response is one of the characteristics of love advocated by the apostle Paul in 1 Corinthians 13:4–7.

Now, choosing love over hatred does not mean the offender is not confronted. Both testaments advocate that sin be dealt with in a loving and direct way.

> You shall not hate your brother in your heart, but you shall reason frankly with your neighbor, lest you incur sin because of him. You shall not take vengeance or bear a grudge against the sons of your own people, but you shall love your neighbor as yourself: I am the LORD. (Leviticus 19:17–19)

And, the apostle Paul wrote these instructions to the church in Galatia.

> Brothers, if anyone is caught in any transgression, you who are spiritual should restore him in a spirit of gentleness. Keep watch on yourself, lest you too be tempted. Bear one another's burdens, and so fulfill the law of Christ. (Galatians 6:1–2)

> *17:9 – "Whoever covers an offense seeks love, but*
> *he who repeats a matter separates close friends."*

This proverb builds on the previous saying by adding a third party to the conflict. When an offense occurs between friends, the offended party has two options from which to choose. The offended individual can speak directly to the friend who caused the offense and seek reconciliation. Or, the offended individual can share the offense with a third person who knows both parties to gain the support of another person. The tendency to share the offense with a third party is due to either immaturity or a lack of courage to confront out of love. But when the offense is shared with a third party, then the damage has been done, for now another person knows the failure of the first individual. So, while the offended party has gained an ally in the cause, he or she has lost a friend and has damaged the relationship between three people. It is also possible that the repeating of the matter could be understood as the injured party continually bringing up the offense with the offender.

> *19:11 – "Good sense makes one slow to anger,*
> *and it is his glory to overlook an offense."*

This proverb builds further on the first two proverbs that promote reconciliation over retribution. The injured individual who chooses not to retaliate when he or she is offended by another person demonstrates wisdom, which is manifested by patience. So, the opposite of wisdom is foolishness, and the opposite of patience is anger. The human tendency is to foolishly strike back in anger when we feel we have been dishonored. But the wisdom writer knew that true honor comes when the injured individual chooses to overlook the offense because he or she understands that human beings are flawed individuals. The offended individual also knows that he or she is a flawed individual as well who has been the offender in the past. And so, having been the recipient of forgiveness, the wise individual will grant the same forgiveness when it is his or her turn.

Wise and Foolish Talk

10:13 – "On the lips of him who has
understanding, wisdom is found, but a rod
is for the back of him who lacks sense."

There is a commercial on the radio that promotes a product designed to increase one's vocabulary. A line in the ad says, "People judge you by the words you use." There are a series of proverbs in the tenth chapter that address one's words and the character of the individual that is revealed by the choice of those words. There are two contrasts in this particular proverb. The first contrast is between a person of understanding and a person of ignorance. The phrase "him who lacks sense" is the Hebrew word for "heart." And so, while it can speak of a lack of intelligence, it is actually a lack of character. The second contrast is between the lips of the one who has understanding and the back of the fool who reveals his or her ignorance. A discerning individual reveals wisdom by the intelligent choice of words. On the other hand, a fool needs constant correction to restrain the ignorant words.

10:14 – "The wise lay up knowledge, but
the mouth of a fool brings ruin near."

The next proverb addresses the consequences of the words we use. A wise individual accumulates knowledge from others when in the instructional phase of life. And because the wise individual stored away this knowledge when young, he or she is careful in the choice of words, and when to speak them. A wise person knows when to speak and what to say at that time. The fool, on the other hand, is quick to speak and often does so before the mind is engaged. Because the fool does not weigh the words and speaks too quickly, the fool is his or her own worst enemy. There are many examples of individuals who have spoken out of turn and out of ignorance, and ruined their careers and reputations. Consider the counsel of James when it comes to our speech.

> Know this, my beloved brothers: let every person be quick
> to hear, slow to speak, slow to anger; for the anger of man
> does not produce the righteousness of God. (James 1:19–20).

*10:21 – "The lips of the righteous feed
many, but fools die for lack of sense."*

This proverb talks about the impact that our words have on other people. A righteous individual speaks with great wisdom, and as a result, the words nourish the lives of the hearers. The apostle Paul said something similar to the church in Ephesus.

> Let no corrupting talk come out of your mouths, but only
> such as is good for building up, as fits the occasion, that it
> may give grace to those who hear. (Ephesians 4:29)

There are no such things as neutral words; either they build others up or tear them down. We need to weigh our words carefully because someday we will give an account of them to God.

> I tell you, on the day of judgment people will give account
> for every careless word they speak, for by your words you
> will be justified, and by your words you will be condemned.
> (Matthew 12:36–37)

A great biblical example of the phrases of this proverb come from the narrative of Abigail and Nabal (1 Samuel 25). Because Nabal was a fool, he spoke harshly to David, which incurred his wrath. But because Abigail was wise, she spoke the right words to David and kept him from killing her husband.

10:32 – "The lips of the righteous know what is
acceptable, but the mouth of the wicked, what is perverse."

One of the signs of having character is knowing what is appropriate to say. This proverb states that the righteous person understands this propriety. But in sharp contrast, the wicked individual has no such self-regulating mechanism. In fact, the wicked chooses to say what he or she knows is perverse.

Wealth and Poverty

10:15 – "A rich man's wealth is his strong
city; the poverty of the poor is their ruin."

We commonly say that money does not buy happiness, and while that sounds pious and is generally true, it is not completely true based on this proverb. This proverb does not speak of happiness, but it does speak of security. The sage contrasts the advantages of wealth with the disadvantages of poverty, without assigning any moral values to the accumulation of wealth and without discussing the root causes of poverty. You will find some proverbs in the collection that speak of wealth in a negative way (11:18; 13:11; 21:6). But given a choice, wealth is to be preferred over poverty due to the security it offers people from the dangers of life. The wisdom writer illustrated the benefits of wealth by comparing it to a fortified city that provided protection to its inhabitants from marauders or an attacking army. In the ancient world of the Middle East a city with walls and gates and towers offered the residents a measure of safety. On the other hand, the lack of money puts a poor person in harm's way for he or she has no resources to deal with unexpected losses. A poor person who lives hand to mouth is living on the brink of financial disaster with little leeway.

14:20 – "The poor is disliked even by his
neighbor, but the rich has many friends."

The wisdom writer is just making an honest observation about human nature. A rich person will attract friends due to the wealth, even though the quality of those friendships can easily be called into question. We can turn to another wisdom book for further insight into how money attracts friends.

When goods increase, they increase who eat them, and what advantage has their owner but to see them with his eyes? (Ecclesiastes 5:11)

The more money you have, the more people come after it. As an individual's means increase, so do the bills. The consumers include the government, relatives, employees, lawyers, accountants, creditors, and the new entourage. We see this in our culture when an individual wins the lottery and becomes surrounded by new friends and distant relatives. We also see it with young people who become professional athletes and come into money. They are surrounded by an entourage as soon as they sign their first contract. But to be poor means you will be disliked by most people because you have nothing to offer them.

All a poor man's brothers hate him; how much more do his friends go far from him! He pursues them with words, but does not have them. (Proverbs 19:7)

18:23 – "The poor use entreaties, but the rich answer roughly."

This proverb addresses another harsh reality in life that reflects the different social standing of the rich and the poor. A person who is poor will often adopt a deferential tone when asking for special favors, for the poor knows that he or she has no clout due to the poverty. We often see this with people who have to ask for financial help to deal with a problem. On the other hand, a rich person can be rude and demanding because the rich know that people are intimidated by wealth which brings people power.

19:4 – "Wealth brings many new friends, but a poor man is deserted by his friend."

This proverb provides another honest observation about how the accumulation of money impacts the accumulation of friends. There is a problem though because the friends who are attracted to money often want some of that money. But for the poor, the lack of money will often cost them the friends they have because they have nothing to offer. Or, the friend is afraid he will be asked for money.

The Wages of the Wicked

*10:16 – "The wage of the righteous leads to
life, the gain of the wicked to sin."*

This antithetical proverb speaks of morality in the monetary terms of loss and gain. And while it admits that both the righteous and the wicked will experience financial gain, the saying is focused on the long-term value of that gain. The second half of the saying makes one think of Paul's statement on the matters of sin and salvation.

> For the wages of sin is death, but the free gift of God is
> eternal life in Christ Jesus our Lord. (Romans 6:23)

While a right standing with God cannot be earned by works, the individual who lives a righteous life will experience God's blessing. But the individual who chooses to live a wicked life will find that what he has gained is a sin-filled life with eternally negative consequences that will end in death.

*11:18 – "The wicked earns deceptive wages, but
one who sows righteousness gets a sure reward."*

This proverb also addresses the matter of morality in monetary terms of wages and reward. The deceptive wages of the wicked can either speak of an income that comes from dishonesty, or an income that deceives the wicked individual into thinking that he is getting ahead in life. So, either the wage earner is deceptive or the wages earned by the wicked are deceptive. What is clear is the second half of the saying. The righteous person is likened to a farmer. What he sows is certain to be rewarded by God. The prophet Hosea also spoke of sowing righteousness.

> Sow for yourselves righteousness; reap steadfast love; break
> up your fallow ground, for it is the time to seek the LORD,
> that he may come and rain righteousness upon you. (Hosea
> 10:12)

The saying is very similar to Paul's statement on sowing.

Whoever sows sparingly will also reap sparingly, and whoever sows bountifully will also reap bountifully. (2 Corinthians 9:6)

13:21 – "Disaster pursues sinners, but the
righteous are rewarded with good."

This proverb speaks of sinners and the righteous, with the promise that God will reward each accordingly. The righteous do not have to pursue after their reward, for God will bestow it on them. On the other hand, those individuals who choose sin will eventually be pursued and overtaken by calamity.

15:27 – "Whoever is greedy for unjust gain troubles his
own household, but he who hates bribes will live."

This proverb also speaks of gain, and it warns the individual who is motivated by greed that avarice will eventually come home to roost with negative consequences for the family. A person who is greedy is not concerned about morality, only money. Therefore, the greedy is willing to accept a bribe. And so, while greed will initially increase the income and help the household, it will eventually increase the misery of the entire family. The Mosaic Law condemned bribery with an explanation.

You shall not pervert justice. You shall not show partiality, and you shall not accept a bribe, for a bribe blinds the eyes of the wise and subverts the cause of the righteous. (Deuteronomy 16:19)

20:17 – "Bread gained by deceit is sweet to a man,
but afterward his mouth will be full of gravel."

This proverb also warns about the long-term consequences of dishonesty. While this saying admits that initially dishonest gain can be pleasant, eventually the sweetness will turn sour. The image of a mouth full of gravel warns the deceptive individual of even more painful consequences to come.

The Path of Life

*10:17 – "Whoever heeds instruction is on the path to
life, but he who rejects reproof leads others astray."*

This antithetical proverb says it is important to choose the right path when it comes to navigating one's way through life. The path that leads to a satisfying life is found when one is teachable and responsive to discipline. The wise person will learn from the mistakes, and will learn from others before he or she makes certain mistakes. This corrective discipline is found in the instruction manual provided by the Author of life. The instruction comes from reading the life manual and obeying it, and from listening to the advice of others who are also heeding the instruction. But the foolish individual who is not receptive to correction will walk down the wrong path that leads to destruction. And in so doing, he or she will lead others astray. This proverb reminds us that the choices we make in life affect more than just ourselves.

*12:26 – "One who is righteous is a guide to his neighbor,
but the way of the wicked leads them astray."*

This proverb speaks of the way of life and the guidance that is offered for the various paths through life. The one who is righteous is so because he or she is receptive to the guidance that God provides to live a godly life. And, because the righteous is receptive to guidance, he or she can in turn be a guide to help others find the right path through life. On the other hand, the wicked is so because he or she has rejected instruction and discipline in how to live life. But the poor choice does not just affect one life, for the wicked will go through life leading other fools astray. This proverb stresses the importance of finding the right person to follow, and the reality that our life choices always affect other people.

*12:28 – "In the path of righteousness is life,
and in its pathway there is no death."*

This proverb also compares life to a path and life choices to a pathway. The first stanza makes a positive statement ("In the path of righteousness is life"), and then it repeats itself by stating it in the negative ("and in its pathway there is no death"). There is a stark contrast between life and death, which is the harsh reality about life. If the individual chooses the right path, it will lead to a righteous life which will experience God's blessing. And all things being equal, the righteous person will likely be protected from a premature death due to not making foolish choices. That being said, this proverb is not a life insurance policy. What it does promise is a life that pleases God and a life that does not put an individual in harm's way. Some biblical scholars take the promise of no death to mean immortality, but it is difficult to determine the author's understanding of eternal life in the Old Testament.

> 15:24 – *"The path of life leads upward for the prudent,*
> *that he may turn away from Sheol beneath."*

This proverb also speaks of the path of life, but it does so, not in the moral sense of right and wrong, or in the traditional sense of wisdom and folly. Instead, it speaks of the path in a directional sense of going up or down. A New Testament reader would be tempted to think of the proverb in terms of heaven and hell, but we need to think in terms of the Old Testament wisdom writer and his limited concept of the afterlife. The proverb views the life of the wise as an upward progression, and in so doing, it will lead the wise individual away from the downward descent that leads to death. The concept of Sheol refers to the grave, with some intimations of the underworld. We saw Sheol talked about in the longer addresses of the father that begin the book of Proverbs (1:12; 5:5; 7:27; 9:18).

Slanderous Lies

10:18 – "The one who conceals hatred has lying
lips, and whoever utters slander is a fool."

This proverb addresses two sins of the tongue that are frequently addressed in both testaments. The first sin is that of hatred, which often causes an individual to lie in order to hide the hatred from the enemy while the revenge is plotted. A biblical example of this sin is the behavior of Absalom who hid his hatred of his brother Amnon who had raped his sister Tamar. After the crime went unpunished by his father King David, the historian wrote of Absalom's silent revenge.

But Absalom spoke to Amnon neither good nor bad, for Absalom hated Amnon, because he had violated his sister Tamar. (2 Samuel 13:23)

Absalom plotted in silence for two years before he had Amnon killed for violating his sister. Rather than hiding our dislike of someone, the Bible advocates an honest confrontation so that the issues are addressed and resolved.

> Therefore, having put away falsehood, let each one of you speak the truth with his neighbor, for we are members one of another. Be angry and do not sin; do not let the sun go down on your anger, and give no opportunity to the devil. (Ephesians 4:25–27)

The second sin of the tongue is that of slander, which is the verbal character assassination of someone else. The one who engages in this type of sin is characterized as a fool. Getting back to the narrative of Absalom, slander was the approach he took to take the kingdom from his father when he returned from his two-year exile after the killing of Amnon. When a citizen would have an unresolved legal issue, Absalom would criticize his father the king to gain the man's favor.

> See, your claims are good and right, but there is no man designated by the king to hear you. (2 Samuel 15:3)

As a result of this implied slander of his father, Absalom stole the hearts of the people of Israel. So, the first sin is the hypocritical concealing of hatred, and the second sin is the foolish revealing of questionable and damaging information.

11:13 – "Whoever goes about slandering reveals secrets,
but he who is trustworthy in spirit keeps a thing covered."

This proverb also addresses the sin of slander which is a common problem in every culture. Slandering the character of someone is achieved by the secret release of certain negative information in the form of harmful gossip to third parties. Rather than a direct attack, the deceitful person brings down the enemy from the shadows through a campaign of whispers. The Mosaic Law condemned this particular sin for its harm effects on a community.

You shall not go around as a slanderer among your people, and you shall not stand up against the life of your neighbor: I am the LORD. (Leviticus 19:16)

But a righteous person will wisely choose to keep private information private for he or she knows the importance of trust in maintaining healthy relationships. The idea of keeping "a thing covered" had been addressed in earlier proverbs (10:12; 17:9).

20:19 – "Whoever goes about slandering reveals secrets; therefore, do not associate with a simple babbler."

This proverb is a warning to people not to associate with individuals who have a tendency to talk too much. Talkative people are dangerous because they cannot keep secrets and because they like to gossip. The danger in associating with talkative people is that while they may give you some juicy information, you are likely to become their topic of conversation with someone else. Speaking of juicy information, consider this later saying in the collection.

The words of a whisperer are like delicious morsels; they go down into the inner parts of the body. (Proverbs 18:8)

Watch Your Mouth

10:19 – "When words are many, transgression is not lacking, but whoever restrains his lips is prudent."

This proverb states an obvious truth. The more a person talks, the more likely he or she is to say something wrong. That is why, in the context of approaching God to worship, the wisdom writer issued this warning.

Guard your steps when you go to the house of God. To draw near to listen is better than to offer the sacrifice of fools, for they do not know that they are doing evil. Be not rash with your mouth, nor let your heart be hasty to utter a word before God, for God is in heaven and you are on earth. Therefore, let your words be few. (Ecclesiastes 5:1–2)

James gave similar advice against talking too much throughout his letter. In the third chapter, he began with a warning to would-be teachers about the presumption of being qualified to teach others. There is an inherent danger in teaching others, and it relates to the fact that the more you talk, the more likely you are to say something wrong. James addressed the topic of the tongue several times in his letter. In the first chapter, he warned of the terrible combination of the tongue and the temper.

> My dear brothers, take note of this: Everyone should be quick to listen, slow to speak and slow to become angry, for man's anger does not bring about the righteous life that God desires. (James 1:19–20)

And then, toward the end of the first chapter, he made one of his harshest statements.

> If anyone considers himself religious and yet does not keep a tight rein on his tongue, he deceives himself and his religion is worthless. (James 1:26)

13:3 – "Whoever guards his mouth preserves his life; he who opens wide his lips comes to ruin."

This proverb also promotes the sparing use of words as a means of self-preservation. The proverb says that when you open wide your mouth to speak, you are also opening up yourself to potential ruin. The individual who engages the tongue without engaging the mind is asking for trouble. A floatation device is also called a life preserver. A great life preserver is when a person sets a guard on the mouth. *I need to grow in this — speak well of others*

17:27-28 – "Whoever restrains his words has knowledge, and he who has a cool spirit is a man of understanding. Even a fool who keeps silent is considered wise; when he closes his lips, he is deemed intelligent."

These proverbs are said with a sense of humor as they advocate the virtue of silence. In the first proverb a "cool" individual is one who is even-tempered, in that he or she controls the anger and the tongue. When a person loses their temper, they generally lose control of the tongue as well (James 1:19–20). A sign of intelligence is knowing when to speak and when to be silent. A modern version of the second proverb says it is better to remain silent and be thought a fool than to speak and remove all doubt. While this saying has been attributed to the American president Abraham Lincoln and to the American humorist Mark Twain, literary research has found no proof. So, it is best to give Solomon the credit for this humorous insight. If a fool follows just this one piece of advice, he or she is not a complete fool.

> *21:23 – "Whoever keeps his mouth and his*
> *tongue keeps himself out of trouble."*

This proverb says that the greatest form of personal protection is to guard your mouth. Trouble can come in many forms, but most calamity is self-inflicted when an individual does not control the tongue. The brevity of this saying reinforces the brevity of our words that it is promoting.

The Power of the Tongue

> *10:20 – "The tongue of the righteous is choice*
> *silver; the heart of the wicked is of little worth."*

In this antithetical proverb, the "tongue of the righteous" is contrasted with the "heart of the wicked" for the wisdom writer knew that out of the heart the mouth speaks. Jesus taught this connection between the heart and the mouth to his disciples.

> The good person out of the good treasure of his heart produces good, and the evil person out of his evil treasure produces evil, for out of the abundance of the heart his mouth speaks" (Luke 6:45)

A righteous person, who knows what to say and when to speak, will say things that will be of great value to the listeners. The righteous person knows when they need correction and when they need comfort. The righteous person will know when to speak and when to be silent. On the other hand, a wicked individual will have very little to say that will be of value to the listeners.

When words proceed from the heart of an individual who is not righteous, the words will have very little benefit for the intended audience. I see the truth of this proverb played out at funeral visitations when people gather to pay their final respects. Most people feel compelled to say something meaningful to the grieving family, but if the individual does not know the Lord, what often is said is trivial and meaningless.

> *10:31 – "The mouth of the righteous brings forth*
> *wisdom, but the perverse tongue will be cut off."*

The first stanza of this proverb basically repeats the thought of the previous saying by commenting on the sage advice that comes out of the mouth of the righteous. People are constantly seeking out advice and the righteous person can give them the direction they need. And then, using hyperbole to make a point, the writer warns that the tongue of the perverse or twisted individual will be cut off. The idea of being cut off is a covenant concept where Moses warned about certain sinful behaviors that would place an individual outside the covenant community (Numbers 15:20). The proverb almost has a directional sense to it in that wise words come out of the mouth of the righteous, while the tongue itself will come out of the perverse individual.

> *12:18 – "There is one whose rash words are like sword*
> *thrusts, but the tongue of the wise brings healing."*

This proverb speaks of the impact that words have on people. Rash words are spoken either out of anger or without thought (see Proverbs 20:25 concerning rash vows). The sage compares the damage caused by these reckless words to the wounds inflicted by a sword. And sometimes the damage is self-inflicted.

> A man of crooked heart does not discover good, and one
> with a dishonest tongue falls into calamity. (Proverbs 17:20)

On the other hand, instead of inflicting wounds, a wise individual speaks words that bring healing to the listeners. A saying from my childhood stated, "Sticks and stones may break my bones, but words will never harm me." This biblical proverb strongly disagrees with this statement.

18:21 – *"Death and life are in the power of the tongue, and those who love it will eat its fruits."*

This proverb makes a bold statement about the power of the tongue in life-and-death situations. History has demonstrated repeatedly that people have died because of what they said or because of what someone else said. And, people have lived wonderful lives because of what they said or because of what someone else said. For that reason, those who love to talk a lot will have to live with the consequences of what they say. Eating the fruits of the tongue refers to the natural consequences of words.

Wealth Enhancement

10:22 – *"The blessing of the LORD makes rich, and he adds no sorrow with it."*

The relationship between people and money has always been a complicated one. While everyone wants money to make life comfortable, the possession of money is not always the blessing one might think it would be. That is because the possession of money can turn into an obsession where money begins to possess the individual. On the other hand, the lack of money is guaranteed to make life difficult. And what further complicates the relationship between people and money is the relationship with God who is the one who provides this money. This proverb focuses on the positive relationship between God and people and the financial blessing that God can bestow on the righteous individual who puts his or her relationship with God first. When the righteous person gets the relationship with God in the right order, then, if God chooses to bless financially, the individual can enjoy the possessions without them possessing him or her. The early days of Solomon's reign saw God financially bless the king, and as long as he honored God, the wealth was a blessing and not a curse (1 Kings 4:20–34; 10:14–29). It was only later in his reign when Solomon turned away from the LORD that the wealth created sorrow.

11:28 – *"Whoever trusts in his riches will fall, but the righteous will flourish like a green leaf."*

This antithetical proverb focuses on the negative relationship with money in the first line, and it concludes with the positive in the second line. There is a danger to money in that the individual can often mistakenly trust in the riches instead of maintain trust in the LORD who gave the riches in the first place. The idea of mistakenly trusting in one's riches is mentioned in a later saying in the collection.

> A rich man's wealth is his strong city, and like a high wall in his imagination. (Proverbs 18:11)

God warned the nation of Israel of this tendency to transfer its trust from God to things when they entered the land of Canaan and began to enjoy the fruits of the land (Deuteronomy 8:11–18). On the other hand, the righteous individual who makes the LORD the object of trust will prosper both financially and spiritually. The metaphor of the green leaf is reminiscent of the opening words of the Psalter.

> He is like a tree planted by streams of water that yields its fruit in its season, and its leaf does not wither. In all that he does, he prospers. (Psalm 1:3)

American Christians are reminded of this proverb every time they look at their currency and see the motto "In God we trust."

22:2 – "The rich and the poor meet together;
the LORD is the Maker of them all."

This proverb recognizes that there will always be financial disparity in life in that there will be the rich and the poor living side by side. Even Jesus said that we will always have the poor with us (Mark 14:7). But the proverb is intended to caution people not to make value judgments on individuals based on their financial condition. God views every one of His human creatures as equal in importance for each person is created in His image (Genesis 1:27). And then, the psalmist saw that death removed the financial disparity that existed in life (Psalm 49:16–19).

contentment

22:4 – "The reward for humility and fear of
the LORD is riches and honor and life."

While the possession of riches and honor can lead to false feelings of superiority and privilege, this proverb reminds people that the LORD is most pleased with individuals who approach Him with true humility and reverential fear (James 4:6–10; 1 Peter 5:5–6).

The Pursuit of Pleasure

10:23 – "Doing wrong is like a joke to a fool, but wisdom is pleasure to a man of understanding."

It is human nature for people to find pleasure in the things of life. For example, as I was working on this proverb, I listened to a recording of Gustav Mahler's Fourth Symphony. Classical music has given me great pleasure since I became a pastor in 1987, and therefore I spend many hours a day listening to the great composers. This proverb understands the natural desire for people to pursue pleasure in their lives. But the wisdom writer also uses the proverb to demonstrate that what one finds pleasure in reveals his true nature or character. The first half of the proverb addresses the fool who takes very few things in life seriously. The fool goes through life with an evil purpose because it gives him or her pleasure. In fact, engaging in behavior that dishonors God and that is harmful to others puts a smile on the face. What God's Word condemns; the fool finds comical. The term that is translated "joke" can also be translated "pleasure" or "laughter." On the other hand, the righteous individual who has insight into what God wants, finds pleasure in the pursuit of wisdom. Speaking of meaningful pleasure, the psalmist spoke of the righteous man and his delight.

> Blessed is the man who walks not in the counsel of the wicked, nor stands in the way of sinners, nor sits in the seat of scoffers; but his delight is in the law of the LORD, and on his law he meditates day and night. (Psalm 1:1–2)

Another psalm promises the righteous a great reward if his delight is focused on God.

> Delight yourself in the LORD, and he will give you the desires of your heart. (Psalm 37:4)

The righteous who truly delight in God will realize all the desires of their heart. And in return, they will find that God delights in them.

15:21 – "Folly is a joy to him who lacks sense, but a man of understanding walks straight ahead."

Tremper Longman uses the blunt term "stupidity" to describe behavior that is done for mindless pleasure. It is deemed stupid or folly because it lacks purpose and it is not permanent. The term "stupidity" reminds me of moments in my childhood and youth when I found pleasure in mindless activities, much to the consternation of my parents and teachers. I can think of wasteful ways I spent my time or my money on things that do not exist today. I am reminded of that waste when I see a child spend their money on a trinket that will be broken before the day is done. In the pursuit of pleasure, we reveal our true character, or our lack of character. And the activities that bring us joy are a reflection of our moral judgment, or lack thereof. The individual who lacks moral judgment will enjoy foolish behavior even though it has no lasting value and it is harmful to those involved. The fool is simply pursuing pleasure without giving any thought to the long-term consequences. But the individual who possesses good judgment sees the benefit of walking the straight course through life instead of taking shortcuts that seem to be appealing. The understanding individual who walks straight ahead has a clear purpose to life and will not be sidetracked by distractions.

21:17 – "Whoever loves pleasure will be a poor man; he who loves wine and oil will not be rich."

This proverb makes an interesting connection between pleasure and poverty. The saying does not condemn pleasure out of hand, but it focuses on the cost of overindulgence or living above one's means. There is nothing wrong with enjoying some of the finer things of life, but those finer things come with a cost. And the individual who wants to live the good life without considering the cost, will become impoverished, because everything comes with a cost. Wine and oil represented the good life of the Old Testament.

You cause the grass to grow for the livestock and plants for man to cultivate, that he may bring forth food from the earth and wine to gladden the heart of man, oil to make his face shine and bread to strengthen man's heart." (Psalm 104:14–15)

A Firm Foundation

10:25 – "When the tempest passes, the wicked is no more, but the righteous is established forever."

This proverb paints a realistic picture about life in that everyone, the wicked and the righteous, will experience storms. Being righteous before God does not protect an individual from trials. Just read the book of Job to get a dose of reality.

> Terrors are turned upon me; my honor is pursued as by the wind, and my prosperity has passed away like a cloud. (Job 30:15)

Asaph had a similar experience and you can read his frustrations as he vented to God in Psalm 73. But this proverb promises that while the righteous individual will experience trials, he or she will survive the trials and be established in the faith, if faith in God is maintained. On the other hand, the wicked individual will also experience his or her share of trials, some brought on by wickedness. But in the end, the wicked will not stand the test because he or she is not relying on anything that will endure. The New Testament version of this proverb is Jesus' parable of the two builders.

> Everyone then who hears these words of mine and does them will be like a wise man who built his house on the rock. And the rain fell, and the floods came, and the winds blew and beat on that house, but it did not fall, because it had been founded on the rock. And everyone who hears these words of mine and does not do them will be like a foolish man who built his house on the sand. And the rain fell, and the floods came, and the winds blew and beat against that house, and it fell, and great was the fall of it. (Matthew 7:24–27)

*12:3 – "No one is established by wickedness, but
the root of the righteous will never be moved."*

This proverb uses the imagery of a plant or a tree to teach the importance of having a good root system to survive the challenges of life. The first line of the proverb warns that a life of wickedness is guaranteed to fail because there is no soundness in the root. But, the second line promises the righteous individual that his or her behavior will bring stability to life.

*16:3 – "Commit your work to the LORD,
and your plans will be established."*

This proverb instructs the righteous individual in the process whereby God will establish one's life. The individual must first devote his or her life's work to the glory of God, and then bring those plans to God for His approval. And if the individual is truly committed to God, if God has other plans for his or her life, the righteous individual will accept the decision and make the necessary adjustments. But once God has been approached in prayer, the approved plans of God will have His blessing. An earlier proverb made the same promise in a memorable way (3:5–6). Another way to make wise decision is to seek the guidance of trusted advisors.

Plans are established by counsel; by wise guidance wage war.
(Proverbs 20:18)

*16:9 – "The heart of man plans his way,
but the LORD establishes his steps."*

This proverb also understands that it is normal for an individual to make life plans. But the second line of the saying reminds us of the sovereignty of God. We may make our plans, but God will have the final say in what actually happens. Proverbs 16:3 reminds us that only the plans approved by God will succeed. Read James 4:13–17. Joseph's understanding of the sovereignty of God helped him forgive his brothers for selling him into slavery.

But Joseph said to them, "Do not fear, for am I in the place of God? As for you, you meant evil against me, but God meant it for good, to bring it about that many people should be kept alive, as they are today." (Genesis 50:19–20)

The Sluggard

10:26 – "Like vinegar to the teeth and smoke to the
eyes, so is the sluggard to those who send him."

We first met the sluggard in the classic passage earlier in the book.

> Go to the ant, O sluggard; consider her ways, and be wise.
> Without having any chief, officer, or ruler, she prepares
> her bread in summer and gathers her food in harvest.
> How long will you lie there, O sluggard? When will you
> arise from your sleep? A little sleep, a little slumber, a little
> folding of the hands to rest, and poverty will come upon
> you like a robber, and want like an armed man. (Proverbs
> 6:6–11)

A series of short proverbs further describes this irritating individual.
Vinegar was a useful food preservative in the ancient world, provided it was
used in the correct way. During biblical times, vinegar was used to flavor
foods, mixed with water and drunk as an energizing drink, and used as a
medicine. After working hard gleaning barley in the fields, Ruth was invited
by Boaz to eat bread and dip it in vinegar (Ruth 2:14). But to drink pure
vinegar without any other food would leave a bitter taste in the mouth. The
wisdom writer compares that bitterness and the irritation of smoke from a
fire in the eyes to the frustration of sending a lazy person on an important
mission.

13:4 – "The soul of the sluggard craves and gets nothing,
while the soul of the diligent is richly supplied."

This proverb acknowledges that everyone has natural cravings. But
cravings need to be acted upon if they are to be realized. The difference lies
in the response to the cravings. The lazy person will daydream about the
cravings, but do nothing to make them a reality. The hardworking person,
on the other hand, will spring to action and make the dreams a reality. A later
proverb also speaks of the desires of the sluggard.

The desire of the sluggard kills him, for his hands refuse to labor. All day long he craves and craves, but the righteous gives and does not hold back. (Proverbs 21:25–26)

> 15:19 – *"The way of a sluggard is like a hedge of thorns, but the path of the upright is a level highway."*

This proverb focuses on the morality of the lazy person by comparing the sluggard to the righteous individual. The lazy person will find his or her way in life filled with obstacles that hinder progress. The righteous person will actually have the same obstacles, for no life is free of detours. But the righteous person will persist through those obstacles and will find that the path through life moves on straight ahead.

> 19:24 – *"The sluggard buries his hand in the dish and will not even bring it back to his mouth."*

The wisdom writers often made the sluggard the butt of their jokes, both to ridicule the lazy individual, and to warn of unavoidable consequences. This proverb exaggerates the laziness of a sluggard to make a point. The picture is of an individual who is so lazy, that even as the hand is down inside a bowl of food, the sluggard lacks the energy to bring the hand to the mouth in order to eat. A later proverb continues this ridicule of the sluggard by having him make a ridiculous statement to try to explain his lack of effort.

The sluggard says, "There is a lion outside! I shall be killed in the streets!" (Proverbs 22:13)

> 20:4 – *"The sluggard does not plow in the autumn; he will seek at harvest and have nothing."*

Due to the climate of the Middle East, the planting season was in the winter, beginning in October and running to March. If the lazy farmer refused to plow his field after the seed had been scattered over the ground, even though he may seek a harvest in the spring, there would be no crop to be found.

The Fear of the LORD

10:27 – "The fear of the LORD prolongs life,
but the years of the wicked will be short."

We first came across "the fear of the LORD" in Proverbs 1:7 with the theme of the entire book. This proverb makes a connection between the health of one's spiritual life and the length of one's physical life. The individual who lives his or her life with a deep reverence for God will enjoy His hand of blessing throughout life. We see this promise of long life in the Ten Commandments. The first four commandments address the individual's relationship with God. And if the relationship with God is characterized by reverential fear, then the relationship with others will also be right.

> Honor your father and your mother, that your days may
> be long in the land that the LORD your God is giving you.
> (Exodus 20:12)

That being said, this proverb does not guarantee that the righteous will always live a long life and that the wicked will die early. You can read the book of Job and the lament of Psalm 73 for the exception to the rule.

14:27 – "The fear of the LORD is a fountain of life,
that one may turn away from the snares of death."

We first encountered the expression "a fountain of life" back in Proverbs 10:11. The image is that of a spring of water that was found in a desert region, whose presence sustained the lives of the inhabitants who lived in this challenging environment. The individual who has a proper reverence for God will avoid the temptations of life because he or she knows they lead to entrapment and eventual death. Speaking of the avoidance of sin, consider another saying in the collection.

> By steadfast love and faithfulness iniquity is atoned for, and by
> the fear of the LORD one turns away from evil. (Proverbs 16:6)

19:23 – "The fear of the LORD leads to life, and whoever
has it rests satisfied; he will not be visited by harm."

This proverb also makes the connection between the fear of the LORD and a life free from harm. But it adds the element of finding rest and satisfaction in that life. Some proverbs focus on a financially prosperous life or a long life, and both aspects are enjoyable. But a life of contentment in God is so special that one cannot put a price on its value. The apostle Paul wrote about such a life of contentment.

← hard to obtain ~ takes great humility and faith

> But godliness with contentment is great gain, for we brought nothing into the world, and we cannot take anything out of the world. But if we have food and clothing, with these we will be content. (1 Timothy 6:6–8)

Paul also wrote about contentment to the church in Philippi.

> Not that I am speaking of being in need, for I have learned in whatever situation I am to be content. I know how to be brought low, and I know how to abound. In any and every circumstance, I have learned the secret of facing plenty and hunger, abundance and need. I can do all things through him who strengthens me. (Philippians 4:11–13)

> 22:4 – *"The reward for humility and fear of the LORD is riches and honor and life."*

This proverb is a biblical math equation where one plus one equals three. The two related qualities of humility and reverence for God lead to the three rewards of "riches and honor and life." Biblical humility is grounded in the character of God. When a pious individual truly understands the holiness of God, the twofold response will be reverential fear and humility before the Creator. The individual who lowers himself or herself before God will be the one that God chooses to elevate.

> God opposes the proud but gives grace to the humble. (James 4:6)

humility + reverence = riches, honor and life

The Way of the LORD

*10:29 – "The way of the LORD is a stronghold to
the blameless, but destruction to evildoers."*

The expression "the way of the LORD" speaks of the direction of life God has established for His covenant people if they are going to enjoy His blessing and avoid sin and misery. The general directions of life were stated in the Ten Commandments, and the fuller Mosaic Law stated them in greater detail. Simply put, obedience to God's way brings blessing, and disobedience brings judgment. There are two contrasts in this proverb. The first contrast is between "the blameless" and "evildoers." The one who is blameless is carefully following the directions for obedience, while evildoers are purposefully engaged in disobedience. The second contrast is between "a stronghold" and "destruction." In the ancient world of the Middle East, a stronghold was a military fortress or geographic highpoint that provided a place of safety when the enemy attacked. David would flee to the stronghold at Engedi when on the run from Saul and his army (1 Samuel 23:29; see Psalm 27:1). The righteous individual is protected because he or she is on the path, and the wicked is harmed because he or she is not on the path. Obeying the LORD protects an individual from the divine and natural consequences of sin.

> Whoever keeps the commandment keeps his life; he who despises his ways will die. (Proverbs 19:16)

*14:2 – "Whoever walks in uprightness fears the LORD,
but he who is devious in his ways despises him."*

The action of walking speaks of the direction of life that one takes, which is expressed in the previous saying with the phrase "the way of the LORD." There is a similarity between the virtue of "uprightness" (which means "straight") in this proverb and "the blameless" of the previous saying. Interestingly, consider a similar saying.

> The highway of the upright turns aside from evil; whoever guards his way preserves his life. (Proverbs 16:17)

The sinful trait of being "devious" or crooked is one of the behaviors that characterize "evildoers."

> The way of the guilty is crooked, but the conduct of the pure is upright. (Proverbs 21:8)

This proverb makes a sharp contrast between the lifestyle of the individual who fears the LORD, and the conduct of an individual who despises God. One's attitude toward God will be demonstrated by the way one walks.

> *15:9 – "The way of the wicked is an abomination to the LORD, but he loves him who pursues righteousness."*

We had encountered the term "abomination" earlier in Proverbs 6:16–19 which provided a list of sinful traits that a holy God finds particularly offensive. It begins with this expression, "There are six things that the LORD hates, seven that are an abomination to him." This proverb goes to the opposite extreme of "the way of the LORD," to speak of "the way of the wicked." The previous proverb said that the crooked individual who chooses to go in the opposite direction that God has established, does so because he or she despises God. And because this willful behavior is contrary to the nature of God, it brings upon the individual harsh condemnation. There is a sharp contrast between what God loves and what God hates. The individual who despises God with willful disobedience will experience divine displeasure.

> *16:7 – "When a man's ways please the LORD, he makes even his enemies to be at peace with him."*

This proverb makes a connection between one's relationship with God and one's relationship with other people. The individual who has the goal to please the LORD by how he or she lives ("a man's ways"), will find God's blessing in the form of peaceful relationships with even the enemies.

The LORD'S Land

10:30 – "The righteous will never be removed,
but the wicked will not dwell in the land."

This proverb is based on the covenant promises God made to the nation of Israel when it entered the land of Canaan. God had Moses clearly communicate to the people the blessings for obedience and the curses for disobedience, and the security of the land featured prominently in the warning (Deuteronomy 28). If the people would obey His commandments, God promised them prosperity in the land and safety from their enemies.

> And you shall eat your bread to the full and dwell in your land securely. I will give peace in the land, and you shall lie down, and none shall make you afraid. (Leviticus 26:5b–6a)

But, if they rebelled against God and persisted in their wickedness despite divine chastisement, He would drive them from the land.

> And I will scatter you among the nations, and I will unsheathe the sword after you, and your land shall be a desolation, and your cities shall be a waste. (Leviticus 26:33)

The acrostic poem of Psalm 37 develops this connection between obedience to God and security in the land.

> Turn away from evil and do good; so shall you dwell forever. For the LORD loves justice; he will not forsake his saints. They are preserved forever, but the children of the wicked shall be cut off. The righteous shall inherit the land and dwell upon it forever. (Psalm 37:27–29)

11:19 – "Whoever is steadfast in righteousness
will live, but he who pursues evil will die."

This proverb also contrasts the opposite behaviors of righteousness and evil, with an emphasis on the effort that one makes in the pursuit of that choice, and the accompanying consequences. To pursue evil indicates a conscious choice has been made to live contrary to the holy character of God. Like Adam and Eve found out, "you will surely die" (Genesis 3:4). But the one who has chosen to live a life of righteousness will also have to make an effort. The idea of being steadfast in righteousness requires a determination on the part of the individual to persist even when the way is hard, when there is opposition, and when righteousness is not immediately rewarded. The final contrast in the proverb is the unavoidable consequences that accompany the choice, namely, life or death.

> 12:7 – *"The wicked are overthrown and are no more, but the house of the righteous will stand."*

This proverb speaks of the respective fates of the wicked and the righteous, with the understanding that both groups will face trials in life. The sage warns the wicked that their decision to live in opposition to God puts them in a vulnerable situation. And when the time of testing comes, and it will surely come, they will fail the test and be overthrown by it. The verb "overthrow" speaks of a sudden and unexpected reversal of fortune. On the other hand, the righteous will also face testing, but they will survive and endure. The image of the house still standing points to Jesus' later parable of the man who built his house on the rock and it survived the flood waters (Matthew 7:24-27). Speaking of a house, consider another proverb.

> The house of the wicked will be destroyed, but the tent of the upright will flourish. (Proverbs 14:11)

> 13:6 – *"Righteousness guards him whose way is blameless, but sin overthrows the wicked."*

This proverb advocates righteous living for the protection it gives the individual as he or she makes his or her way through life. The individual who strives to live a blameless life will be known as a person of integrity. And the reward for integrity is like having a personal guard who goes before you and makes your way safe as you go through life. The wicked, on the other hand, are promised an ultimate defeat.

An Abomination to the LORD

11:1 – "A false balance is an abomination to
the LORD, but a just weight is his delight."

In an earlier address, we looked at a list of sinful traits that God finds particularly offensive (6:16–19). The term "abomination" is used to describe sinful activities or attitudes that a holy God detests in human beings because they offend His moral order. Some of the sinful attitudes are directed toward God, while other sinful activities are committed against fellow human beings. This proverb states that God demands honesty in one's business dealings. Weights were used for measuring out products, and a merchant could cheat the customers by having dishonest weights. The Mosaic Law condemned dishonest business practices (Leviticus 19:35–36; Deuteronomy 25:13–16). The prophet Micah voiced God's criticism of the dishonesty that was rampant in his day.

> Shall I acquit the man with wicked scales and with a bag of deceitful weights? (Micah 6:11)

Proverbs 20:10 and 20:23 address the same sin.

11:20 – "Those of crooked heart are an abomination to
the LORD, but those of blameless ways are his delight."

Because God deals in righteousness, any behavior or attitude that is twisted or perverse falls under God's condemnation. A person with a crooked heart is an individual who spends his or her time thinking of ways to take advantage of others. One way of taking advantage of others was the dishonest merchant with the false weights that was condemned in the above proverb. But a person of integrity, one who lives an open and honest life before God and others, is an individual in whom God delights. And because God delights in him or her, the honest person will enjoy His favor.

12:22 – "Lying lips are an abomination to the LORD,
but those who act faithfully are his delight."

Another form of honesty is in the words that we use to communicate with one another. And while the communication takes place between people, the wisdom writer knew that God was listening in on the conversation and taking note of its honesty. Truthfulness is the basis of every relationship, so when an individual lies to another person, the trust is broken and the relationship is damaged. Lying can become a dangerous habit that requires more lies to cover the first lie.

> The LORD is near to all who call on him, to all who call on him in truth. (Psalm 145:18)

> *15:8 – "The sacrifice of the wicked is an*
> *abomination to the LORD, but the prayer of the*
> *upright is acceptable to him." (also 21:27)*

Throughout the Old Testament, a sacrifice offered to God from a truly repentant worshiper was described as a pleasing aroma. Concerning the burnt offering, Moses gave the instruction to the nation.

> And the priest shall burn all of it on the altar, as a burnt offering, a food offering with a pleasing aroma to the LORD. (Leviticus 1:9)

So, even though the correct offering was sacrificed, if the individual offered it with a wicked heart, God rejected the sacrifice because He found it offensive. This seems to be the reason why God rejected Cain's sacrifice.

> In the course of time Cain brought to the LORD an offering of the fruit of the ground, and Abel also brought of the firstborn of his flock and of their fat portions. And the LORD had regard for Abel and his offering, but for Cain and his offering he had no regard. So, Cain was very angry, and his face fell. (Genesis 4:3–5)

The New Testament version of this proverb is the parable Jesus told of the Pharisee and the tax collector (Luke 18:9–14).

Pride

*11:2 – "When pride comes, then comes
disgrace, but with the humble is wisdom."*

The Hebrew word that is translated "pride" comes from a verb that means "to seethe or to boil up." This is a good word picture of pride as it depicts the feelings of arrogance bubbling up to the surface in a person's life. But the sage warns that when an individual allows pride to come to the surface, with pride comes another feeling, namely, disgrace. The sin of pride never goes unpunished and the negative consequences are unavoidable. But when an individual lives a life of humility, he or she is also living wisely. Pride prevents the fool from listening to the advice of others, but humility allows a person to hear criticism, which helps produce change and growth.

*16:5 – "Everyone who is arrogant in
heart is an abomination to the LORD; be
assured, he will not go unpunished.*

This proverb expresses God's distain for human arrogance. When a human being forgets his or her place in the world, and promotes his or her self-importance, the LORD, Yahweh, the self-existent and eternal God, finds that behavior detestable. And because arrogance is so offensive to God, He will not let it go unpunished. A biblical example of God's punishment of the sin of arrogance was His discipline of Uzziah, the once-godly king of Judah. The historian had this sad commentary on his life.

> But when he was strong, he grew proud, to his destruction. For he was unfaithful to the LORD his God and entered the temple of the LORD to burn incense on the altar of incense. (2 Chronicles 26:16)

*16:18 – "Pride goes before destruction,
and a haughty spirit before a fall."*

This proverb is a succinct commentary on the aforementioned king. Uzziah received a mixed evaluation from the chronicler, "as long as he sought the LORD, God gave him success" (2 Chronicles 26:1–5). God helped him against his enemies and his reputation grew in the region as he became more powerful. He fortified Jerusalem and the land, and he had a powerful army. But after he became powerful, his pride led to his downfall. Uzziah attempted an act in the Temple that could only be performed by the priests. When the priests courageously confronted the king, Uzziah responded in anger and suffered immediate consequences. The LORD afflicted him with leprosy and he suffered from this condition until his death (26:21). Even in death he could not be buried with the other kings of Judah (26:23).

18:12 – "Before destruction a man's heart is haughty, but humility comes before honor."

This proverb is a backhanded way of saying "Pride goes before destruction, and a haughty spirit before a fall" (Proverbs 16:18). When an individual experiences ruin, it is because he or she was expressing arrogance. While the destruction is sudden and unexpected to its victim, the wisdom writer warned that it should have come as no surprise. On the other hand, when an individual experiences honor in life, it was because he or she is expressing humility in the way he or she lived life before the blessing arrived.

21:4 – "Haughty eyes and a proud heart, the lamp of the wicked, are sin."

This proverb sees the inner sin of pride as being reflected in the eyes of the arrogant individual. So, while pride is an inner feeling, it is always expressed outwardly. Eyes are the window to the soul.

The Rewards of Righteousness

11:4 – "Riches do not profit in the day of wrath, but righteousness delivers from death."

How do you measure it

This proverb warns that the pursuit of riches, instead of the pursuit of godliness, will result in ruin on the day of disaster. While riches can buy a measure of happiness and comfort in this life, no amount of financial resources can protect an individual from the "day of wrath." This expression is used several times in the Old Testament in the context of divine judgment. Job vented about the prosperity of the wicked.

> Have you not asked those who travel the roads, and do you not accept their testimony that the evil man is spared in the day of calamity, that he is rescued in the day of wrath? (Job 21:29–30)

Ezekiel warned the nation of Israel that its gold and silver would prove to be worthless when God visited them with disaster.

> They cast their silver into the streets, and their gold is like an unclean thing. Their silver and gold are not able to deliver them in the day of the wrath of the LORD." (Ezekiel 7:19a)

The sage is probably not speaking of "the day of wrath" in the eschatological sense, but in the individual sense of a life-threatening disaster. The only thing that delivers a person from God's wrath is to pursue His righteousness. And the pursuit of God's righteousness results in wise living, which protects an individual from the harm that is associated with foolish choices.

11:5 – "The righteousness of the blameless keeps his way straight, but the wicked falls by his own wickedness.

This proverb defines the pursuit of righteousness as walking on a straight path. The proverb offers several contrasts to demonstrate the two opposing paths through life and their consequences. The first contrast is between "the blameless," the individual who walks with integrity, and "the wicked" who lives in opposition to God. The second contrast is between righteousness and wickedness. The third contrast focuses on the consequences of the two opposing choices. The individual who walks with integrity will walk on a straight path that avoids the pitfalls of sin. But the wicked individual has chosen the crooked path that will cause him or her to be tripped up by sin.

> The light of the righteous rejoices, but the lamp of the wicked will be put out. (Proverbs 13:9)

*11:6 – "The righteousness of the upright delivers them,
but the treacherous are taken captive by their lust.*

This proverb also contrasts the two paths through life, with an emphasis on the security that comes with the choice that is made. When an individual pursues God's righteousness, that choice will lead to deliverance when security is threatened. But the individual who is unfaithful to God because he desires things other than God, will find himself entrapped by his own lust.

*11:10 – "When it goes well with the righteous,
the city rejoices, and when the wicked
perish there are shouts of gladness.*

This proverb focuses on how the choices one makes affects other people. When an individual chooses to honor God, and God honors the individual in return, the divine blessing on that life will be a blessing to other lives. But when an individual chooses to live in opposition to God, that person will also take advantage of others. And so, when the person is finally judged, those individuals who were negatively impacted by that life, will rejoice when the judgment takes place.

Warnings for the Wicked

*11:7 – "When the wicked dies, his hope will perish,
and the expectation of wealth perishes too."*

This proverb begins with a profound statement that is often overlooked as we continue to read the rest of the saying. The sage begins, "When the wicked dies." That in itself is a stark reality, and it was a depressing thought that gripped the writer of Ecclesiastes (2:14–16). The wicked individual is warned that when he or she dies, along with life coming to an end, so too will the hopes and aspirations. And, the specific hope of this wicked individual was financial gain, most likely achieved by taking advantage of someone else. Both testaments provide ample warnings that the wicked will not enjoy financial gain beyond the grave. The psalmist warned,

Be not afraid when a man becomes rich, when the glory of his house increases. For when he dies he will carry nothing away; his glory will not go down after him. (Psalm 49:16-17)

The psalmist warned the wicked that there was no amount of money that would buy their way out of death. The apostle Paul wrote a similar warning to Timothy in the context of advocating contentment in life.

But godliness with contentment is great gain, for we brought nothing into the world, and we cannot take anything out of the world. But if we have food and clothing, with these we will be content. (1 Timothy 6:6–8)

11:31 – "If the righteous is repaid on earth, how much more the wicked and the sinner!"

This proverb uses a "how much more" argument to warn the wicked that divine judgment is certain in this life. The need to remind the righteous of this fact is seen when one reads the frustrations of Job and the author of Ecclesiastes. So, if God will judge the righteous individual for the sins that he or she commits, how much more will God judge the wicked individual for sins. The apostle Peter quoted the Septuagint version of this proverb as he discussed the trials and persecutions that believers experience.

For it is time for judgment to begin at the household of God; and if it begins with us, what will be the outcome for those who do not obey the gospel of God? And "If the righteous is scarcely saved, what will become of the ungodly and the sinner? (1 Peter 4:17–18)

12:21 – "No ill befalls the righteous, but the wicked are filled with trouble."

This proverb should not be taken too literally because all one has to do is read the narrative of Job to know that misfortune can befall the righteous. Job's so-called friends misunderstood this reality, which led to their mistaken assumption that he was hiding some secret sin that needed confession. This proverb is a relative saying, where compared to the wicked, whose lives are filled with trouble because of their sin, the righteous does not experience self-inflicted misery.

> *13:25 – "The righteous has enough to satisfy his appetite, but the belly of the wicked suffers want."*

This proverb speaks about the contentment that can be found in life. The righteous individual who seeks to please God will find a contentment with the blessings that God bestows. The apostle Paul was a great promoter of contentment as he wrote from prison to the church in Philippi.

> Not that I am speaking of being in need, for I have learned in whatever situation I am to be content. I know how to be brought low, and I know how to abound. In any and every circumstance, I have learned the secret of facing plenty and hunger, abundance and need. I can do all things through him who strengthens me. (Philippians 4:11–13)

The second half of the proverb warns the wicked that they will never find contentment in life, for they will always be wanting more. Paul spoke to that problem in his first letter to Timothy as he warned about false teachers who used their position for financial gain (6:5–10).

The Words of the Wicked

Gossip destroys 11:9 – *"With his mouth the godless man would destroy his neighbor, but by knowledge the righteous are delivered."*

When I was a child, I frequently heard the saying, "Sticks and stones may break my bones, but words will never harm me." This saying is similar to a biblical proverb in that it is generally true, but there are always exceptions. This series of proverbs on the words of the wicked state the exceptions to the childhood saying. Words spoken by a wicked person can have a devastating effect on the intended victim of the rumor campaign. The "godless" man destroys his neighbor with his words through hypocrisy, by feigning friendship to his face, but by talking behind his back. If a righteous person is the intended victim, the deliverance comes in the form of knowledge to identify the hypocrisy and end the slander.

Believers are to speak well — of where they live

11:11 – "By the blessing of the upright a city is exalted, but by the mouth of the wicked it is overthrown."

This proverb speaks of the impact that people have on their society. A righteous person, as he or she experiences God's blessing, will positively impact the community. On the other hand, a wicked individual who is rash and vulgar in words will have a devastating impact on the community.

12:6 – "The words of the wicked lie in wait for blood, but the mouth of the upright delivers them."

This proverb provides an interesting word picture as it envisions a group of harmful words hiding in the shadows, waiting for an unsuspecting victim to come by. A wicked person chooses an intended target, and then chooses words to bring harm upon the victim. Through outright lies and secret gossip, the wicked individual sets a trap to bring down the unsuspecting victim. Again, if the intended victim is a righteous person, the skillful use of words will provide a good defense against this verbal attack.

15:28 – "The heart of the righteous ponders how to answer, but the mouth of the wicked pours out evil things."

This proverb contrasts the rash and angry words that spew out of a wicked person's mouth, with the reasoned and cautious response of a righteous individual. The picture of the wicked individual is that of a steady flow of angry and attacking words that pour from the mouth without any thought. On the other hand, the righteous individual is slow and deliberate as he or she carefully weighs each word before the defense is made against the angry attack. In the context of a Christian being attacked for the faith, the apostle Peter had this advice.

> But in your hearts honor Christ the Lord as holy, always being prepared to make a defense to anyone who asks you for a reason for the hope that is in you; yet do it with gentleness and respect, having a good conscience, so that, when you

are slandered, those who revile your good behavior in Christ may be put to shame. (1 Peter 3:15–16)

19:28 – "A worthless witness mocks at justice,
and the mouth of the wicked devours iniquity."

This proverb speaks to the damaging effects of dishonest words to the justice system. A witness is worthless because he or she is wicked and the testimony is a mockery in a court of law. Even as the dishonest words come out of the mouth, the sage pictured the wicked person taking in sin like a person devouring food.

That Makes No Sense

11:12 – "Whoever belittles his neighbor lacks sense,
but a man of understanding remains silent."

The book of Proverbs was written to help individuals develop skillful living and skillful thinking (1:2–6). This series of proverbs describes several public behaviors that reveal a lack of understanding on the part of the fool. The Mosaic Law frequently addressed how an Israelite was supposed to treat his or her neighbor so that the nation could experience a stable society. In fact, the ninth commandment addressed outright lying.

You shall not bear false witness against your neighbor. (Exodus 20:16)

This proverb warns against publicly expressing your contempt for your neighbor, advising the individual to simply remain silent. The proverb is not advocating deception by advising silence. Instead, it is advising against a public forum where disrespect for the neighbor will do no good. The modern version of this proverb is, "If you can't say anything nice about a person, don't say anything at all."

12:11 – "Whoever works his land will have plenty of
bread, but he who follows worthless pursuits lacks sense."

Another sign that a person lacks understanding is the absence of a work ethic which is a popular theme throughout the book of Proverbs. The best-known saying in the book was the comparison of the sluggard to the ant (6:6–11). The nation of Israel was an agricultural society, and when God gave out the inheritance of the land to the tribes, He told them to work hard.

> Six days you shall labor, and do all your work, but the seventh day is a Sabbath to the LORD your God. (Exodus 20:9–10a)

This proverb promotes a strong work ethic, and at the same time, warns against wasting one's energy with "worthless pursuits." These activities which lack substance would include risky financial speculation, schemes to get rich quick at the expense of others, and pursuits that do not glorify God in their results.

> *17:16 – "Why should a fool have money in his hand to buy wisdom when he has no sense?"*

This proverb asks a rhetorical question with an obvious negative answer. The book of Proverbs defines the "fool" as an individual who lacks the sense to gain wisdom in the first place. The proverb envisions a fool with a large amount of money in hand to buy wisdom from a sage. But even if the fool could buy wisdom, the purchase would be a waste of money for he or she would not know what to do with the wisdom.

> *17:18 – "One who lacks sense gives a pledge and puts up security in the presence of his neighbor."*

Another sign of a lack of understanding is getting involved in the financial decisions of others. Earlier in the book, the father warned his son about the consequences of underwriting the bad investments of other people (6:1–5). With a play on words that will only work in the English, the fool who lacks sense will someday lack cents when he has to pay his pledge (see also 11:15 and 20:16).

> *21:16 – "One who wanders from the way of good sense will rest in the assembly of the dead."*

This proverb is a warning to the individual who possesses wisdom, but for reasons unstated, starts making unwise decisions. There are repeated warnings throughout the book not to abandon the possession of wisdom, for it will lead to painful consequences. The author of this section of Proverbs, Solomon, is an example of a wise individual who made foolish decisions with devastating consequences for himself.

We the People

11:14 – "Where there is no guidance, a people falls,
but in an abundance of counselors there is safety."

While the majority of proverbs were written for individuals, the individuals addressed were members of the nation of Israel. And so, this series of proverbs addressed the life of the nation as God's covenant community. This proverb understands that a nation is made up of a collection of individuals, and just as a person needs guidance for in life (1:5), so too does a nation need direction. The nation of Israel was a theocracy which is the direct rule of God over the people.

> Now therefore, if you will indeed obey my voice and keep
> my covenant, you shall be my treasured possession among
> all peoples, for all the earth is mine; and you shall be to me
> a kingdom of priests and a holy nation. (Exodus 19:5–6)

But even when the nation was ruled by a king, the king was to be governed by God and the Mosaic Law (Deuteronomy 17:14–21). And, a wise king would surround himself with a multitude of counselors that he could consult to make wise decisions for the nation. The abundance of counselors is seen in the life of the nation during the leadership of Moses. When the nation came to Mt. Sinai, Moses' father-in-law Jethro advised him to find seventy elders who could help him with the care of the nation (Exodus 18).

14:28 – "In a multitude of people is the glory of a
king, but without people a prince is ruined."

This proverb recognizes that one of the ways to measure the greatness of a king's empire is by the size of the population that he governs. A king with a large number of happy subjects is deemed a great ruler. But a ruler without people willing to submit to his rule will be ruined. The historian gives this summary of the rule of Solomon.

> Judah and Israel were as many as the sand by the sea. They ate and drank and were happy. Solomon ruled over all the kingdoms from the Euphrates to the land of the Philistines and to the border of Egypt. They brought tribute and served Solomon all the days of his life. (1 Kings 4:20–21)

Later on, the queen of Sheba visited Jerusalem and she complimented Solomon on the happy state of his subjects.

> Happy are your men! Happy are your servants, who continually stand before you and hear your wisdom! (1 Kings 10:8)

On the other hand, when Solomon died and his son Rehoboam ascended the throne, this young ruler foolishly rejected the advice of his father's counselors, and as a result, he lost the ten northern tribes (1 Kings 12).

14:34 – "Righteousness exalts a nation, but sin is a reproach to any people."

The opening statement of the book of Proverbs made a connection between wisdom and righteous living (1:2–3). So, as a nation, Israel's greatness was based on its piety, not its politics. A reading of the book of Deuteronomy makes it clear that God was going to deal with the nation of Israel as a covenant community. The book contains three lengthy speeches that Moses delivered to the nation before the people finally crossed the Jordan River and took the land of Canaan through conquest. In these speeches, Moses implored the people to take seriously the covenant that they had entered into with God. In the first address (1:1–4:43), Moses recounted the mighty acts that God had done on behalf of the nation to bring them to this point. The second address (4:44–26:19) restated the covenant laws originally presented in Exodus 20–23. The main point of this address was to apply the Ten

A nation does not rise and fall on its leaders character if the nation chooses what is right

Commandments to everyday life once they entered the Promised Land. The third address was Moses' final challenge to the nation (27:1–31:30). In this section was the ceremony of the blessings and the curses where Moses clearly told the current generation that righteousness would be rewarded and sin would be punished. This proverb is a concise summary of the blessings and curses of Deuteronomy 28.

Honor

11:16 – "A gracious woman gets honor,
and violent men get riches."

There are two obvious contrasts in this proverb that help the sage make his point. The first contrast is between the one "gracious woman" and a group of "violent men." Within this one contrast, we have two separate comparisons. There is the comparison between the use of grace and the use of violence to get what one wants. And then there is the comparison of the one woman and the group of men. While it would appear that a group of powerful men enjoy the upper hand in this scenario, it is actually the gentle and gracious woman who possesses the true power. The second contrast is between what the two entities get, namely, a life of "honor" or temporary "riches." The repeated verb in the proverb actually means "to take hold of" or "to seize," and it fits the violence of the group of men. In this context, the sage disparages wealth because it was obtained by means of violence. There are times in the book of Proverbs that riches and honor go together.

> The reward for humility and fear of the LORD is riches and honor and life. (Proverbs 22:4)

But, in this circumstance, because the riches were gained through violence, there is nothing praiseworthy or permanent. On the other hand, honor gained through noble character is held in high esteem for it cannot be stolen, only earned.

15:33 – "The fear of the LORD is instruction in
wisdom, and humility comes before honor."

This proverb returns us to the theme that opened the entire book.

> The fear of the LORD is the beginning of knowledge; fools despise wisdom and instruction. (Proverbs 1:7)

The individual who possesses a deep reverence for the holy nature of God will be receptive to the instruction of other teachers of wisdom. When an individual properly fears God, there is no room for arrogance. A sign of true humility is the willingness to receive instruction from others. Because of a humble and teachable spirit, God will bestow honor on this individual's life.

> *20:3 – "It is an honor for a man to keep aloof*
> *from strife, but every fool will be quarreling."*

This proverb advocates the avoidance of needless strife as an honorable thing for a person to do. While it is impossible to go through life and not experience conflict with others, this proverb says that it is the sign of a fool who actively looks for quarrels. There are certain personalities who seem to enjoy conflict, but the wisdom writer does not see this as a healthy thing.

> *21:21 – "Whoever pursues righteousness and*
> *kindness will find life, righteousness, and honor."*

This proverb advocates the pursuit of righteousness and kindness as a way to find a meaningful and rewarding life. The pursuit of righteousness begins with our relationship with God, but it also defines how we treat others. Kindness is the attitude that we express toward others. In essence, the two terms are a good summary of the Mosaic Law.

> And one of them, a lawyer, asked him a question to test him. "Teacher, which is the great commandment in the Law?" And he said to him, "You shall love the Lord your God with all your heart and with all your soul and with all your mind. This is the great and first commandment. And a second is like it: You shall love your neighbor as yourself. On these two commandments depend all the Law and the Prophets." (Matthew 22:35–40)

Jesus began by quoting Deuteronomy 6:4–5. He then attached to this important commandment an inseparable companion one by quoting Leviticus 19:18.

Cruel Intentions

11:17 – "A man who is kind benefits himself,
but a cruel man hurts himself."

This proverb contrasts two individuals on opposite sides of the kindness spectrum. The man who is "kind" is one who shows covenant love (*hesed*) to others. This is the type of affection that God showed to His covenant people. The wisdom writer promotes this self-sacrificing love with a somewhat self-serving motivation. The individual who is kind toward others, will, in turn, experience this affection from others. This proverb is similar to the principle Jesus announced in the Sermon on the Mount, known as the Golden Rule.

So whatever you wish that others would do to you, do also to them, for this is the Law and the Prophets. (Matthew 7:12)

This proverb teaches that how we treat others will come back to us. If we treat others with kindness, then we will experience kindness in return. But if we treat others with cruelty, we will eventually bring harm upon ourselves.

12:10 – "Whoever is righteous has regard for the life
of his beast, but the mercy of the wicked is cruel."

This proverb provides an interesting insight into human nature by bringing the animal world into the conversation. The sage believed that how an individual treated an animal revealed his or her true nature. The person who is right with God will treat animals the right way. Even the Mosaic Law addressed the treatment of animals.

You shall not muzzle an ox when it is treading out the grain. (Deuteronomy 25:4)

Even though an ox was a beast of burden, its labor benefitted the owner. So, the wise owner would make sure the ox was properly fed to maintain its strength. The narrative of Balaam's mistreatment of his donkey and their interesting conversation supports the observation of the wisdom writer (Numbers 22). The second half of the proverb warns that when a wicked person shows mercy to someone, his or her compassion is still tainted with cruelty.

*16:29 – "A man of violence entices his neighbor
and leads him in a way that is not good."*

This proverb is a warning to avoid the influence of an individual who resorts to violence to accomplish his or her goals, for it will lead others down a dangerous path. Violence, while it appears to be an effective way to get what one wants, has tragic results for the offending party. Consider another saying that warns about a person of violence.

From the fruit of his mouth a man eats what is good, but
the desire of the treacherous is for violence. (Proverbs 13:2)

*17:11 – "An evil man seeks only rebellion, and
a cruel messenger will be sent against him."*

This proverb seems to provide two warnings to the evil person who rebels against authority. The first warning is for people to avoid the evil person for he or she is rebellious by nature. The proverb assumes that what the evil person is rebelling against is just and authoritative. But the second half of the proverb is a warning to the rebellious person that he or she will surely face judgment for the rebellion. A biblical example of this proverb is seen in the rebellion of David's son, Absalom who sought to wrest the kingdom from his father. Absalom's rebellion was put down when the king's son encountered the king's violent general Joab (2 Samuel 18). A later saying has a similar warning for the man of violence.

The violence of the wicked will sweep them away, because
they refuse to do what is just. (Proverbs 21:7)

This proverb is also a warning about divine retribution. The wicked who seek to inflict violence on others will be done in by their own devices. Judgment is certain for the wicked willingly refuse to change their behavior.

Be Sure Your Sin Will Find You Out

11:21 – "Be assured, an evil person will
not go unpunished, but the offspring of
the righteous will be delivered."

The title for this group of proverbs comes from Numbers 32 where Moses issued a warning to the tribes of Reuben and Gad. These two tribes were attracted to the land on the eastern side of the Jordan River, known as the land of Gilead. This attraction was due to the large pasture lands for their flocks and herds. The leaders of the two tribes promised the other tribes that they would participate in the conquest of the land. Moses accepted their offer, but he also issued them a warning.

> But if you will not do so, behold, you have sinned against the LORD, and be sure your sin will find you out" (Numbers 32:23)

This proverb is an affirmation that is found throughout the Old Testament that righteousness would be rewarded and that wickedness would be punished. But frequently the righteous needed to be reassured that this would take place, especially when it seemed that the wicked were getting away with evil. Read the wisdom psalm of Psalm 73 as the writer Asaph wrestled with his doubts in the justice of God. The assurance in this proverb, translated "be assured," is a Hebrew expression that literally reads, "hand to hand." It might indicate the shaking of hands to finalize an agreement.

12:13 – "An evil man is ensnared by the transgression
of his lips, but the righteous escapes from trouble."

This proverb also contrasts the evil person and the righteous individual, with the similar promise of the ultimate deliverance of the righteous person. The particular emphasis of this proverb is on the speech of the evil individual, and the implied speech of the righteous person in the second half of the proverb. The evil individual brings about his or her ultimate demise by the sinful words that come out of the mouth. The sins of the tongue are manifold, namely, lying, slander, gossip, boasting, to name a few. While the evil person is done in by his or her own words, the righteous person demonstrates wisdom by avoiding self-incriminating talk.

14:32 – "The wicked is overthrown through his evildoing, but the righteous finds refuge in his death."

This proverb is a word of consolation for the righteous person who was troubled by the deeds of the wicked. The righteous person was assured that the wicked would not ultimately succeed in their evil plans. In fact, the demise of the wicked would be self-inflicted. And when the end comes for the wicked, the righteous will find comfort. This seems to be the promise of Proverbs 14:19 and 21:15. There is another way to understand the second phrase of the proverb. Some scholars understand the death to be that of the righteous person, with the promise that justice might not always take place in this lifetime. But in the afterlife, God's judgment is sure. Because the afterlife was not a frequent topic of the wisdom writers, it seems best to understand the death to be that of the wicked.

21:12 – "The Righteous One observes the house of the wicked; he throws the wicked down to ruin."

There are two ways to understand this proverb, and it is reflected in the different translations. The "righteous one" can either be a reference to God, or a reference to an individual who is righteous. If God is "the Righteous One" in the proverb, the wisdom writer was speaking of the omniscience of God in His observance of human sin, and the second part of the proverb speaks to the sovereignty of God who promises to judge that sin. This seems to be the preferred interpretation.

Beautiful Women

11:22 – "Like a gold ring in a pig's snout is a beautiful woman without discretion."

In this proverb, the sage employs an absurd image to grab the attention of young men who are naturally attracted to beautiful women. The writer also taps into the religious and cultural life of Hebrew young men who had grown up with a distaste for pigs due to the food laws (Leviticus 11:7). A physically attractive woman who lacks discretion, which in Hebrew is literally "taste," is a woman who is lacking in taste, both morally and intellectually. Just as a valuable ring of gold would be a wasted ornament on a repulsive pig, so too is physical beauty wasted on a morally shallow woman. This proverb makes one think of the beautiful women in our culture who are famous for being infamous.

> *12:4 – "An excellent wife is the crown of her husband, but*
> *she who brings shame is like rottenness in his bones."*

The first line of this proverb, compared to the above saying, addresses the woman who does possess noble character. While the line does not speak of her physical appearance, a woman with noble character will greatly enhance her husband's life. This was Boaz's assessment of Ruth the Moabitess (Ruth 3:11). A crown was a symbol of strength and nobility, and that is what a woman with character adds to her husband's life. The second phrase of the proverb warns young men to marry wisely, for a wife who behaves shamefully in public will rob her husband of his greatest joy and strength. The wisdom writer known as the Preacher says something similar.

> And I find something more bitter than death: the woman
> whose heart is snares and nets, and whose hands are fetters.
> He who pleases God escapes her, but the sinner is taken by
> her. (Ecclesiastes 7:26)

> *14:1 – "The wisest of women builds her house,*
> *but folly with her own hands tears it down."*

The opening phrase of this proverb is reminiscent of one of Jesus' parables.

> Everyone then who hears these words of mine and does them
> will be like a wise man who built his house on the rock.
> (Matthew 7:24)

In this proverb, the woman is building her house, which speaks of setting up a household and the creation of a family unit. A woman who is wise will invest great time and effort in creating a healthy home life for her husband and children. But if she is foolish, she will destroy that which could give her the greatest joy.

*19:14 – "House and wealth are inherited from
fathers, but a prudent wife is from the* Lord."

While property and inherited wealth can be handed down from a father
to his son, the man who marries well has received a gift that comes directly
from the Lord. And while property and wealth are monetary assets that can
enhance a man's life, a godly wife is a marital asset on which no price can be
set. An earlier proverb made a similar statement.

> He who finds a wife finds a good thing and obtains favor
> from the Lord. (Proverbs 18:22)

The last chapter of the book of Proverbs will elaborate on the good wife
(31:10–31).

*21:9 – "It is better to live in a corner of the housetop
than in a house shared with a quarrelsome wife."*

This proverb is a warning to young men to choose a wife wisely, because
if they do not, there is not a house big enough to escape her hostility. A later
proverb says much the same thing.

> It is better to live in a desert land than with a quarrelsome
> and fretful woman. (Proverbs 21:19)

See also Proverbs 19:13.

Generosity

*11:24 – "One gives freely, yet grows all the richer; another
withholds what he should give, and only suffers want."*

This proverb promotes the practice of generosity by emphasizing the benefits
that come to the giver. The sage encouraged people to be generous because
the act of giving enriches the life of the giver. On the other hand, if the
individual has the opportunity and the ability to give, but does not do so,
selfishness will bring about poverty. The wisdom of the Bible is paradoxical

because most people believe that holding on to their wealth brings about more wealth. The sage urged people to be eager in their generosity. The apostle Paul advocated the same principle when he wrote to the church in Corinth.

> Whoever sows sparingly will also reap sparingly, and whoever sows bountifully will also reap bountifully. Each one must give as he has decided in his heart, not reluctantly or under compulsion, for God loves a cheerful giver. (2 Corinthians 9:6–7)

And while we often think about generosity in terms of financial investments, this proverb would include the generosity of our time and talents.

> *11:25 – "Whoever brings blessing will be enriched,*
> *and one who waters will himself be watered."*

The very next proverb continues the promotion of generosity with two synonymous lines. The first line speaks of being a blessing in the life of someone else and the enrichment that will come to the giver. The expression "to be enriched" is literally in Hebrew "to be made fat." In the culture of the Old Testament, fatness was a sign of prosperity. This is reflection in Isaac's blessed his son Jacob.

> May God give you of the dew of heaven and of the fatness
> of the earth and plenty of grain and wine. (Genesis 27:28)

The second line repeats the rewards for givers by using a figure of speech that would have great meaning in an arid and desert climate where water was a life-and-death matter. The individual who freely shares his or her valuable resources with those in need, will have his or her own needs met as well.

> *19:17 – "Whoever is generous to the poor lends to*
> *the LORD, and he will repay him for his deed."*

This proverb is more specific about the source of blessing that is promised to the generous. The individual who willingly gives to the poor is, in reality, giving money to God. And, the individual willingly makes this investment because he or she realizes God is the source of the resources in the first place.

Moses reminded the nation of Israel of this reality before they entered the land of Canaan.

> You shall remember the LORD your God, for it is he who gives you power to get wealth, that he may confirm his covenant that he swore to your fathers, as it is this day. (Deuteronomy 8:18)

This concept that God is the manager and we are the stewards was taught by Jesus in the parable of the talents (Matthew 25:14–30).

> *21:13 – "Whoever closes his ear to the cry of the poor will himself call out and not be answered."*

This proverb is a warning to those who tend to be miserly with their possessions. The individual who has the resources to help the poor, but turns a deaf ear to their pleas, will be in need someday, and his or her pleas for help will be ignored. While the proverb does not say so, the one who will ignore the pleas for help is God himself. The parable of the rich man and Lazarus (Luke 16:19–31) illustrates the principle expressed in this proverb.

> Abraham said to the rich man, "Child, remember that you in your lifetime received your good things, and Lazarus in like manner bad things; but now he is comforted here, and you are in anguish." (Luke 16:25)

Consequences

> *11:27 – "Whoever diligently seeks good seeks favor, but evil comes to him who searches for it."*

This proverb states that people will find what they are looking for in life. The focus of the saying is not about looking for items that are missing in one's life, but rather about looking for a direction or a purpose to one's life. If an individual is actively pursuing after that which is good, he or she will find God's favor. Noah was an individual who experienced God's favor on his life, and that was because he walked with God when the majority of mankind was living in active disobedience (Genesis 6:1–8). The second line of the proverb was illustrated by the sinful behavior of Noah's contemporaries.

> The LORD saw that the wickedness of man was great in the earth, and that every intention of the thoughts of his heart was only evil continually. (Genesis 6:5)

Because they were pursuing after evil, they found it, and as a result, experienced God's judgment.

> *12:14 – "From the fruit of his mouth a*
> *man is satisfied with good, and the work*
> *of a man's hand comes back to him."*

This proverb also talks about finding good in life, with the emphasis on two key areas of a person's life. The first line of the saying talks about the words that issue from a person's mouth, which is a common theme among the individual proverbs. The person who carefully weighs the words before speaking will speak with wisdom and will find that good things will come to him or her. The second line of the proverb talks about one's work ethic, which is another reoccurring topic among the individual proverbs. The individual who works diligently will also find that good things will come to him or her because God honors a good work ethic. The apostle Paul gave several concrete examples of how the believer's new life must differ from the old life, and he did so by combining the two topics of speech and work (Ephesians 4:25–29).

> *14:14 – "The backslider in heart will be filled*
> *with the fruit of his ways, and a good man*
> *will be filled with the fruit of his ways."*

The above proverb spoke of "the fruit of his mouth," while this proverb speaks of being "filled with the fruit of his ways." Fruit is the natural byproduct of what grows on a tree or a plant. If one plants an apple tree, apples will be the fruit that is produced. The same principle is true in how people live their lives. A "backslider" is an individual who turns aside in his or her heart from doing what is right. Because of this choice, the individual will experience the negative consequences of that wrong choice. On the other hand, an individual who chooses to do what is good will experience the positive rewards of righteous behavior.

> *14:22 – "Do they not go astray who devise evil? Those who devise good meet steadfast love and faithfulness."*

This proverb has a similar expression that was found in the above saying. In 14:14 "the backslider in heart" was an individual who lost heart, and as a result, turned aside from doing what he or she knew to be right. In this proverb, the sage speaks of people who "go astray," which is choosing to depart from the path of righteousness, and as a result, they wander aimlessly through life. Both phrases of the proverb speak of the planning that goes into life. The wicked who plan to do evil will go astray in their lives. On the other hand, the righteous who plan to do good toward others will experience steadfast love and faithfulness in their lives. This common combination of terms describes God's relationship to His people.

Family Inheritance

> *11:29 – "Whoever troubles his own household will inherit the wind, and the fool will be servant to the wise of heart."*

To understand this proverb, we must first determine how an individual could bring trouble on his own family. The second line may provide some hints. The individual who brings trouble on the family is described as a fool who must serve others as a result of his or her foolish actions. Perhaps the individual made foolish financial decisions which resulted in being sold into slavery (Leviticus 25:39). Because of the foolish choices, the individual is said to "inherit the wind," an expression that describes a meaningless existence. This expression is found numerous times throughout the wisdom book of Ecclesiastes where the Preacher lamented a life that lacked substance (1:14). He used the expression in the next chapter as he differentiated between the righteous who pleases God and the sinner who disobeys God.

> For to the one who pleases him God has given wisdom and knowledge and joy, but to the sinner he has given the business of gathering and collecting, only to give to one who

pleases God. This also is vanity and a striving after wind. (2:26)

A biblical example of a man who brought trouble on his household because he foolishly took some items that did not belong to him was the character Achan whose tragic tale is told in Joshua 7.

> *13:22 – "A good man leaves an inheritance*
> *to his children's children, but the sinner's*
> *wealth is laid up for the righteous."*

This proverb provides a positive contrast to the above saying. Instead of making foolish financial decisions that leave one's family with nothing, a good man will live his life with wisdom, and as a result, leave his children and their children a great inheritance. When Israel took possession of the land of Canaan and the territories were allotted to the various tribes, the land was a significant part of one's inheritance.

> The inheritance of the people of Israel shall not be transferred from one tribe to another, for every one of the people of Israel shall hold on to the inheritance of the tribe of his fathers. (Numbers 36:7)

The psalmist also talked about his inheritance as a sign of God's blessing on his life.

> The LORD is my chosen portion and my cup; you hold my lot. The lines have fallen for me in pleasant places; indeed, I have a beautiful inheritance. (Psalm 16:5–6)

The three terms "chosen portion," "my lot," and "a beautiful inheritance" are terms that describe the allocation of land. But the second line of the proverb warns the sinner that his or her wealth will be taken from the children and given to the righteous. The psalmist warned about this as well.

> For he sees that even the wise die; the fool and the stupid alike must perish and leave their wealth to others. (Psalm 49:10)

*14:26 – "In the fear of the LORD one has strong
confidence, and his children will have a refuge."*

While the above proverb emphasized the financial inheritance of land and possessions that a parent can leave for the children, this saying focuses on the spiritual heritage that a godly parent can pass on to the children. The parents who fear the LORD will live with great confidence before their children as they see their parents obey God. And because of this godly example, the children will view God as a spiritual fortress they can flee to when life becomes difficult. In the giving of the Ten Commandments, God told the older generation that their spiritual choices would directly impact the next generation.

> You shall not bow down to them or serve them, for I the LORD your God am a jealous God, visiting the iniquity of the fathers on the children to the third and the fourth generation of those who hate me, but showing steadfast love to thousands of those who love me and keep my commandments. (Exodus 20:5–6)

A Fruitful Life

*11:30 – "The fruit of the righteous is a tree of
life, and whoever captures souls is wise."*

This proverb has two expressions that can be misunderstood if we read our modern context back into this ancient saying. The first mistake is to read of the "tree of life" in the first phrase and think only of the Tree of Life that was in the garden of Eden (Genesis 2:22–24). The second mistake is to think that the sage is speaking of evangelism in the second phrase when he speaks of capturing souls. I remember hearing an evangelist preach a sermon on soul winning when I was in Bible college back in the late 1970s using the King James Version which states, "he that wins souls is wise." This proverb speaks of the rewards that come from living a righteous life. We had noted earlier in the notes that in the arid Middle East, a tree was a picture of life and vitality (Proverbs 3:18). The two images of fruit and a tree are signs of a productive life. And one of the signs of a productive life is having the right kind of influence over the lives of others. Because wickedness abounds in a fallen world, a righteous person can influence people to follow his or her godly example. In a negative example of this influence, Absalom, the rebellious son of David, "stole the hearts of the men of Israel" (2 Samuel 15:6).

12:12 – "Whoever is wicked covets the spoil of evildoers, but the root of the righteous bears fruit."

This proverb notes that while a wicked person can enjoy some financial reward in the form of spoil taken from others, true and lasting reward comes from living a righteous life. The first line of the proverb is difficult to understand because the Hebrew wording is not clear. Based on this English translation, wicked people are motivated by covetousness, and they live their lives taking what rightfully belongs to others. In contrast to a life that benefits by taking advantage of others, the sage says that the real rewards come as a natural byproduct of living a righteous life that enjoys God's blessing.

13:12 – "Hope deferred makes the heart sick, but a desire fulfilled is a tree of life."

This proverb is interesting in that it does not offer any specific advice. It just makes an observation about life. The first line of this proverb understands the deep disappointment a person experiences when dreams are not realized. We see it on the faces of athletes when they lose in the championship game. We feel the discouragement when a loved one gets a bad diagnosis from the doctor. So, with all of the discouragement in life, the second line offers some good news. Every once in a while, we realize our dreams and life is good.

16:31 – "Gray hair is a crown of glory; it is gained in a righteous life."

We often associate gray hair negatively with the dreaded sign of aging. To cover up this fact, we head to the store to buy some hair dye when the first gray hair appears. This proverb celebrates gray hair as a sign of a life lived well. For the sage, gray hair on someone's head is "a crown of glory," something that is very attractive. For the wisdom writer, gray hair is not earned through worry and frustration, but through righteousness and wisdom. An older person with gray hair is enjoying longevity because he or she made wise decisions. It is the making of foolish decisions that ends a life prematurely. The poster boy for gray hair is the good spy of the Promised Land. After forty years of wandering with the children of Israel, Caleb could make this statement to his old friend Moses.

> I am still as strong today as I was in the day that Moses sent me; my strength now is as my strength was then, for war and for going and coming. (Joshua 14:11)

Discipline

> *12:1 – "Whoever loves discipline loves knowledge,*
> *but he who hates reproof is stupid."*

The book of Proverbs begins with the theme of discipline. The Hebrew noun *musar* appears four times in the opening eight verses and is often translated "instruction." While Proverbs promotes the motto, "Learn, and then live," the sage also wanted people to "live and learn." A wise person will want to learn from the mistakes so as not to repeat them. On the other hand, the person who refuses to learn from the mistakes is considered a fool. While a fool resists this correction in life, the wise person will learn to love discipline and corrective instruction.

> The ear that listens to life-giving reproof will dwell among the wise. Whoever ignores instruction despises himself, but he who listens to reproof gains intelligence. (Proverbs 15:31–32; see also 13:18)

The person who rejects correction is behaving like a brutish animal. The Hebrew word translated "stupid" (*ba'ar*) describes a stubborn fool who acts like an animal. The psalmist used this term to describe himself as he struggled to understand what God was doing in his life.

> I was brutish and ignorant; I was like a beast toward you. (Psalm 73:22)

> *13:24 – "Whoever spares the rod hates his son, but*
> *he who loves him is diligent to discipline him."*

This proverb addresses the primary place where discipline needs to begin in a person's life. Discipline must begin in the home and it is promoted by the sage as a sign of genuine love. Once again there is the contrast between love and hate. The parent who is undisciplined in the discipline of his child is actually said to hate the child. While the image of using a rod on a child conjures up the modern problem of child abuse, to keep the issue in perspective, the failure to discipline a child was considered another form of child abuse by the sage.

> Folly is bound up in the heart of a child, but the rod of discipline drives it far from him. (Proverbs 22:15)

This proverb supports the biblical doctrine of human depravity, also known as original sin. The apostle Paul weighed in on the issue and offered some sound parental advice.

> Fathers, do not provoke your children to anger, but bring them up in the discipline and instruction of the Lord. (Ephesians 6:4)

15:10 – "There is severe discipline for him who forsakes the way; whoever hates reproof will die."

This proverb addresses a key reason for why discipline needs to begin in the home, and why it must be practiced consistently and firmly by loving parents. And in the context of the world of the Hebrew wisdom writer, "the way" refers to the way of righteousness that God commanded the Israelite parents to teach to their children (Deuteronomy 6:4–9). If the individual grows into an adult and still hates reproof, he or she will experience a severe form of discipline that will be administered directly by God, or by God using the world to punish bad behavior.

19:18 – "Discipline your son, for there is hope; do not set your heart on putting him to death."

This proverb is a word of encouragement to parents who have grown weary in the task of rearing their child with godly discipline. Consistently addressing the sin nature of a child is exhausting at times, so some parents put off the task until it is too late. Or they started the practice, but the stubborn child has worn down their resolve. The wisdom writer hopes to motivate these exhausted parents by reminding them of what is at stake. If they fail to finish the task of discipline, they are potentially contributing to their child's premature death. A stubborn child who grows into a rebellious adult can die prematurely through foolish decisions and the consequences of those decisions.

Divine Favor

12:2 – "A good man obtains favor from the LORD,
but a man of evil devices he condemns."

This proverb agrees with the basic provisions of the Mosaic Law where God promised to reward righteousness and punish sin. A virtuous person will experience God's blessing because the behavior pleases God, but a devious individual does not deceive God and will receive the due punishment.

15:3 – "The eyes of the LORD are in every place,
keeping watch on the evil and the good."

This proverb speaks of the divine attribute of omniscience, which teaches that God is all-knowing. And one of the things that God knows personally and thoroughly are human beings. In the opening lines of Psalm 139 the psalmist realized there was nothing about him that God did not know, from his thoughts and actions, to the very words that he speaks, even before he uttered them.

> Just as there are no bounds to His presence with me, so there are no limits to His knowledge of me. Just as I am never left alone, so I never go unnoticed. I can hide my heart, and my past, and my future plans, from men, but I cannot hide anything from God. (J.I. Packer)

The sage's purpose was not to make a theological statement about God, but to motivate proper behavior because an all-knowing God was watching. The writer of Hebrews issued the same warning.

And no creature is hidden from his sight, but all are naked and exposed to the eyes of him to whom we must give account. (Hebrews 4:13)

A later saying also speaks of God's omniscience.

The eyes of the LORD keep watch over knowledge, but he overthrows the words of the traitor. (Proverbs 22:12)

15:25 – "The LORD tears down the house of the proud but maintains the widow's boundaries."

This proverb teaches that God's favor is not based on human categories of privilege and status. Instead, God's treatment of people is based on their character and behavior. Widows were particularly vulnerable in the ancient world, and God often addressed how the nation was to care for these women.

You shall not pervert the justice due to the sojourner or to the fatherless, or take a widow's garment in pledge. (Deuteronomy 24:17)

In that section of the Pentateuch God gave examples of how to care for those in need in the following verses. The narrative of Ruth is a classic example of how God cared for widows. On the other hand, because God finds human arrogance so detestable, He promises to punish it.

15:29 – "The LORD is far from the wicked, but he hears the prayer of the righteous."

Even though the attribute of omniscience teaches that God is intimately acquainted with all people, this proverb warns that there is a distance between God and some people. Because the wicked are distant from God, He will be distant from them in their time of need (Saul; 1 Kings 28:6). On the other hand, those who are living righteous lives can approach God in prayer and He will respond to their need.

18:10 – "The name of the LORD is a strong tower; the righteous man runs into it and is safe."

The expression "The name of the LORD" reminds the Bible student of Moses's encounter with God after the golden calf incident.

> The LORD descended in the cloud and stood with him there, and proclaimed the name of the LORD. The LORD passed before him and proclaimed, "The LORD, the LORD, a God merciful and gracious, slow to anger, and abounding in steadfast love and faithfulness. (Exodus 34:5–6)

In words that are reminiscent of the Psalms (61:3), the sage used a military metaphor to describe God's care of the righteous as a place to flee for refuge from the attacks of the world (see 1 Samuel 23:14).

What Were You Thinking?

12:5 – "The thoughts of the righteous are just;
the counsels of the wicked are deceitful."

This proverb is a straightforward assessment of the sharp differences that exist between the righteous and the wicked when it comes to their respective thought processes. And how an individual thinks will affect the value of the advice that they give to others. A righteous person aligns the thoughts with those of God, and as a result, the advice given reflects the justice God demands of His people. In a similar vein, the psalmist concluded his song by considering his words and thoughts, and God's evaluation of them.

> Let the words of my mouth and the meditation of my heart be acceptable in your sight, O LORD, my rock and my redeemer. (Psalm 19:14)

The wicked, on the other hand, are deceitful in their counsel because they have their own interests in mind, not what is best for the one seeking advice.

15:26 – "The thoughts of the wicked are an abomination
to the LORD, but gracious words are pure."

We examined the concept of abomination back in Proverbs 6:16–19 when we studied God's Black List. In that section, the sage offered a list of sinful traits that God finds particularly offensive. We returned to the topic of abomination in a series of individual proverbs (11:1, 20; 12:22; 15:8). This proverb states that God is offended by the thoughts of the wicked because He knows the evil plans they have to harm others. Even if these plans are not made public, God knows the thoughts of everyone (Psalm 139:1–2). What does please God is when the words of advice are gracious because they come from an individual who has a pure heart. Getting back to Psalm 139, the psalmist concluded his thoughts with this prayer.

> Search me, O God, and know my heart! Try me and know my thoughts! And—see if there be any grievous way in me, and lead me in the way everlasting! (Psalm 139:23-24)

> *21:10 – "The soul of the wicked desires evil;*
> *his neighbor finds no mercy in his eyes."*

This proverb could be a commentary on the narrative of King Ahab and his desire to possess the vineyard of his neighbor Naboth (1 Kings 21). The historian described the evil character of Ahab when he came to power in Israel.

> And Ahab the son of Omri did evil in the sight of the LORD, more than all who were before him. And as if it had been a light thing for him to walk in the sins of Jeroboam the son of Nebat, he took for his wife Jezebel the daughter of Ethbaal king of the Sidonians, and went and served Baal and worshiped him. He erected an altar for Baal in the house of Baal, which he built in Samaria. And Ahab made an Asherah. Ahab did more to provoke the LORD, the God of Israel, to anger than all the kings of Israel who were before him. (1 Kings 16:30–33)

Because of his evil nature, when Ahab coveted the vineyard of Naboth which was next to his palace, his neighbor found no mercy as Jezebel implemented her dastardly plan to have Naboth killed so her husband could stop his pouting.

21:30 – "No wisdom, no understanding, no counsel can avail against the LORD."

This proverb celebrates the sovereignty of God that will overcome the thoughts and plans of people that are contrary to the eternal plans of God. No matter the power or the intelligence of the individual, if their plans conflict with those of God, those plans will fail. Even though Eliphaz was wrong about Job, he was correct when he said this about God,

> He frustrates the devices of the crafty, so that their hands achieve no success. He catches the wise in their own craftiness, and the schemes of the wily are brought to a quick end. (Job 5:12–13)

Insight for Living

12:8 – "A man is commended according to his good sense, but one of twisted mind is despised."

The book of Proverbs celebrates the demonstration of intelligence. The Hebrew word that is translated "good sense" speaks of intelligence that is demonstrated by clear thinking. It is the ability to evaluate a difficult situation and have the insight to make a wise decision that addresses the problem. The term was used to describe the discerning nature of Abigail in the narrative that detailed her intervention in the conflict between David and her foolish husband, Nabal (1 Samuel 25:3). In contrast to Nabal's brutish behavior, the historian praised Abigail for her insight to intervene and counsel David out of doing something rash. While the first line of the proverb celebrates the demonstration of intelligence, the second line condemns the dishonest person who fails to exercise insight. A "twisted mind" literally speaks of a disturbed heart. This flawed personality is revealed by the individual who looks at a situation and twists the facts to fit his or her concept of reality. The person who does not exercise this insight will be held in contempt by the community.

13:15 – "Good sense wins favor, but the way of the treacherous is their ruin."

The individual who demonstrates his or her intelligence by clear thinking enjoys the respect of the community. Another motivation for character development is self-interest.

Whoever gets sense loves his own soul; he who keeps understanding will discover good. (Proverbs 19:8)

The ability to analyze a situation and offer intelligent advice is a respected quality. The opposite of respect is ruin, and the individual who gives deceitful counsel will bring about his or her own downfall. The second line of the proverb provides a great commentary on the biblical character Absalom. When Absalom became angry with his father David for the king's failure to punish Amnon for his rape of Tamar, he hid his bitterness for two years until he could get his revenge. When the estranged son returned to Israel, and his father refused to restore their relationship, Absalom began to sow the seeds of discontentment which resulted in a coup against his father. But as the narrative demonstrated, Absalom's deception led to his own ruin (2 Samuel 13–18).

13:20 – "Whoever walks with the wise becomes wise,
but the companion of fools will suffer harm."

This proverb also contrasts the virtue of wisdom and the vice of folly, and the consequences of both pursuits. But it does so by talking about the company that the wise and the foolish keep. An individual who desires to become wise will keep the company of wise individuals because he or she welcomes their influence. Fools, on the hand, choose the company of likeminded individuals, and this combined ignorance will become a self-inflicted wound. I witnessed this behavior as a junior high camp dean for seven years. We had children come to our camp from a dozen churches, and within a few hours, likeminded children found one another. They fulfilled the expression, "birds of a feather flock together." It did not take long for the troublemakers to find one another and begin their plotting.

14:6 – "A scoffer seeks wisdom in vain, but
knowledge is easy for a man of understanding."

The above proverb stated that the search for wisdom is successful when the seeker surrounds himself or herself with wise teachers. The first line of this proverb says that the scoffer also seeks wisdom, but the search will be in vain. The scoffer is an individual who mocks others because he or she thinks they are smarter. An arrogant individual who rejects the advice and insight of others will remain a fool.

Better Than

12:9 – "Better to be lowly and have a servant
than to play the great man and lack bread."

A common expression throughout the book of Proverbs is the "better than" formula that is employed to make comparisons. The comparisons have to do with lifestyle choices. In this proverb, the sage says it is better to live a humble life and be a relative unknown to the majority of people, but where you enjoy a comfortable lifestyle that allows you to employ a servant. This unnoticed lifestyle is preferred over the life that receives attention precisely because the person is trying to be noticed. Some people pretend to live a prosperous lifestyle precisely because it generates attention. This proverb is timely given the phenomenon today in our culture where people become celebrities because they appear to live a rich and fascinating life. But many times, public perception is much different than the private reality. Many of the celebrities who appear to live rich lives are impoverished morally and spiritually.

15:16 – "Better is a little with the fear of the Lord
than great treasure and trouble with it."

While most people would prefer a life of wealth and riches, the sage argues that a godly life is to be preferred even more. The theme of "the fear of the Lord" began the book of Proverbs (1:7), and it is found throughout the entire collection. This proverb promotes a modest lifestyle over a life of wealth, especially if the individual has to sacrifice a meaningful relationship with God to gain the wealth. If God is not properly reverenced, while the person may gain financial wealth, he or she will likely gain all the misery that often accompanies the money. This thought is repeated in another saying.

Better is a little with righteousness than great revenues with injustice. (Proverbs 16:8)

The New Testament version of this proverb is found in Paul's advice to Timothy.

But godliness with contentment is great gain, for we brought nothing into the world, and we cannot take anything out of the world. (1 Timothy 6:6–7)

15:17 – "Better is a dinner of herbs where love
is than a fattened ox and hatred with it."

The very next proverb promotes a similar modest lifestyle. In the ancient world, a diet of meat was a sign of luxury, while a diet of vegetables was a sign of poverty. We see this in the narrative of Daniel, where he and his three Jewish friends, Hananiah, Mishael, and Azariah, better known as Shadrach, Meshach, and Abednego, chose a diet of vegetables to avoid the non-kosher meat of Babylon (Daniel 1). It is better to live in a home that is poor financially, but where the family is rich in love. This is to be preferred to a home that can afford the best food, but where family strife exists. So, love is to be chosen over luxury. A later proverb says much the same thing.

Better is a dry morsel with quiet than a house full of feasting with strife. (Proverbs 17:1)

16:19 – "It is better to be of a lowly spirit with the
poor than to divide the spoil with the proud."

This proverb reminds the reader of the first lengthy address of the father where he warns his son about avoiding certain companions who offer adventure and acceptance.

My son, if sinners entice you, do not consent. If they say, "Come with us, let us lie in wait for blood; let us ambush the innocent without reason; like Sheol let us swallow them alive, and whole, like those who go down to the pit; we shall find all precious goods, we shall fill our houses with plunder; throw in your lot among us; we will all have one purse. (Proverbs 1:10–14)

Borrowing from this thought, the sage says it is better to be humble and associate with the poor, than to be prosperous, but to share ill-gotten gains with the arrogant.

In the Eye of the Beholder

12:15 – "The way of a fool is right in his own eyes, but a wise man listens to advice."

This proverb presents a sharp contrast between the fool and the wise man by emphasizing two different senses. The fool, using the sense of sight, reveals his folly by how he looks at himself. Rather than comparing his actions with the behavior of others, he only looks to himself and assumes the direction of his life is correct. The fool does not seek out the advice of others and is not open to criticism. Another proverb offers a dire warning about the dangers of self-deception.

There is a way that seems right to a man, but its end is the way to death. (Proverbs 14:12; see also 16:25)

The fool rejects the advice of the father to his son from an earlier address in the book.

Be not wise in your own eyes; fear the LORD, and turn away from evil. (Proverbs 3:7)

The first line of this proverb shares the same theme of the book of Judges.

In those days there was no king in Israel. Everyone did what was right in his own eyes. (Judges 17:6)

The wise person, using the sense of hearing, demonstrates intelligence by a willingness to seek out the advice of others. He or she is smart enough to realize the evaluations are not always correct, and so the counsel of other wise people is welcomed.

*16:2 – "All the ways of a man are pure in his
own eyes, but the LORD weighs the spirit."*

This proverb reveals the depth of the sin nature and the extent of God's omniscience. Human beings like to justify their actions and engage in flawed self-evaluation. While we are not good at being honest with ourselves, God, who made mankind, knows His creatures intimately and is a great searcher of the human heart. The prophet Jeremiah had great insight on man's self-deception and God's perfect perception of man.

> The heart is deceitful above all things, and desperately sick; who can understand it? I the LORD search the heart and test the mind, to give every man according to his ways, according to the fruit of his deeds. (Jeremiah 17:9–10)

The psalmist understood God's knowledge of the human heart as well.

> O LORD, you have searched me and known me! You know when I sit down and when I rise up; you discern my thoughts from afar. You search out my path and my lying down and are acquainted with all my ways. (Psalm 139:1–2)

This psalm informs the reader that if an individual is going to have a meaningful relationship with God, that person needs to know that the LORD already has an intimate knowledge of him or her. A later proverb says much the same thing.

> Every way of a man is right in his own eyes, but the LORD weighs the heart. (Proverbs 21:2)

*17:24 – "The discerning sets his face toward wisdom,
but the eyes of a fool are on the ends of the earth."*

This proverb talks about the focus of a person's life and how the ability to concentrate on the right thing will determine the outcome of that life. A person of discernment reveals the determination to get wisdom by a fixation on that pursuit. The fool, on the other hand, is unable to concentrate on the right thing, but spends his or her life looking at many things, without ever finding what he or she should be looking for.

> 20:12 – "The hearing ear and the seeing
> eye, the LORD has made them both."

Proverbs promote the pursuit of wisdom, and the two primary ways to acquire wisdom are through the senses of hearing and seeing. A wise person will be eager to listen to the advice of others and will be careful about what he or she looks at. This proverb reminds the learner that God is the one who made the ears and eyes and that he or she is to honor the Creator by using these senses for their intended purposes.

The Fool and the Prudent

> 12:16 – "The vexation of a fool is known at
> once, but the prudent ignores an insult."

This group of proverbs demonstrates the vast differences that exist between the fool and the one who is prudent. The Hebrew term that is translated "prudent" speaks of an individual who is shrewd, but in a good sense. A fool has a short temper and shows irritation quickly. Life is full of irritating people and frustrating situations, and the fool is easily irritated by these. The prudent person, on the other hand, controls the emotions and does not rashly respond to the offenses of others, thus not making the situation worse. The prudent has the ability, as Jesus put it, to turn the other cheek (Matthew 5:38–39). The apostle Paul offered similar advice to the believers in Ephesus.

> Be angry and do not sin; do not let the sun go down on your anger, and give no opportunity to the devil. (Ephesians 4:26–27)

> 12:23 – "A prudent man conceals knowledge,
> but the heart of fools proclaims folly."

A prudent individual is not only knowledgeable, but also knows when to reveal knowledge and when to conceal it. As a pastor, I frequently have people share some private information about themselves or about someone else. But depending on the situation, it is not always wise to reveal what I know because it would betray a confidence. I had a friend who was a long-time bachelor tell me he was getting engaged, but I could not share this news with his family who attended my church. I withheld this information for months until he announced his engagement to his family at Christmas. A fool, on the other hands, speaks his or her mind and reveals ignorance. The fool blurts out what he or she knows, which is not much.

13:16 – *"Every prudent man acts with knowledge, but a fool flaunts his folly."*

A prudent individual makes sure to have all the facts before taking action, thus ensuring success. A fool, on the other hand, reveals his or her ignorance to everyone who is watching. The prudent person reveals what he or she does know, and the fool reveals what he or she does not know.

14:8 – *"The wisdom of the prudent is to discern his way, but the folly of fools is deceiving."*

A prudent individual is careful to examine his or her motives and the motives of others. The prudent carefully thinks through matters before taking action and thus enjoys success. The prudent wants to be honest with self and with those with whom he or she interacts. And, the prudent wants to know when others are not being honest. A fool, on the other hand, is not only self-deceived, but he or she deceives others who are not wise to their ways.

15:5 – *"A fool despises his father's instruction, but whoever heeds reproof is prudent."*

A fool reveals ignorance early in life when the wise advice of the parents is ignored. Instead of trusting the advice of close acquaintances, the fool assumes greater wisdom than the elders. But the prudent child heeds the correction of the parents because he or she knows they have been placed there by God for their ultimate good. A biblical example of this proverb was King Rehoboam who rejected the wise advice of his father's advisors when he heeded the counsel of his peers.

And the king answered the people harshly, and forsaking the counsel that the old men had given him, he spoke to them according to the counsel of the young men. (1 Kings 12:13–14)

Honesty is the Best Policy

12:17 – "Whoever speaks the truth gives honest evidence, but a false witness utters deceit."

The Old Testament prophets declared that Israel's God was the true God, in contrast to the false gods of the surrounding nations.

But the LORD is the true God; he is the living God and the everlasting King. At his wrath the earth quakes, and the nations cannot endure his indignation. (Jeremiah 10:10)

And, the Old Testament poets portrayed God's Word as the word of truth.

This God—his way is perfect; the word of the LORD proves true; he is a shield for all those who take refuge in him. (Psalm 18:30)

Because of God's veracity, He demanded honesty from His covenant people, and in this context, when it came to a court of law. The Mosaic Law required honesty on the part of witnesses so that the judicial system would not be corrupted.

You shall not spread a false report. You shall not join hands with a wicked man to be a malicious witness. You shall not fall in with the many to do evil, nor shall you bear witness in a lawsuit, siding with the many, so as to pervert justice. (Exodus 23:1–2)

A modern version of this proverb is the oath, "Do you solemnly swear to tell the truth, the whole truth, and nothing but the truth, so help you God?"

12:19 – "Truthful lips endure forever, but
a lying tongue is but for a moment."

This proverb urges honesty by emphasizing the difference between the lifespan of the truth and that of a lie. In comparison to the truth, which will last forever, a lie, compared to eternity, will only last for a moment. The American humorist, Mark Twain, once said, "If you tell the truth, you don't have to remember anything." What he was saying was that if you tell the truth, you don't have to remember what you said. But telling a lie leads to a complicated life because you have to remember the first lie so the second lie does not contradict it. A biblical example of this proverb is the lie the sons of Jacob told their father about the death of their brother Joseph. Even though the lie began when Joseph was seventeen (Genesis 37:2) and it continued to exist when he was elevated in Egypt at the age of thirty (Genesis 41:46), after seven years of plenty, the lie was eventually exposed. A later proverb also emphasizes the lifespan of the truth.

A false witness will perish, but the word of a man who hears will endure. (Proverbs 21:28)

14:5 – "A faithful witness does not lie, but
a false witness breathes out lies."

When I was a student in school many of the exams that I took were true and false statements where I had to discern the truth from error. Some of the questions were phrased in a deceptive way to make me think carefully before I answered. This ability to discern right from wrong was at the heart of the judicial system for the nation of Israel. This proverb simply states that a witness who is faithful to God and to the truth will not lie, while a witness who is false to God will also be false in his or her testimony. A later proverb in this chapter explains how the truth impacts the lives of others.

A truthful witness saves lives, but one who breathes out lies is deceitful. (Proverbs 14:25)

19:5 – "A false witness will not go unpunished,
and he who breathes out lies will not escape."

While the above proverbs talk about the impact of the truth on the innocent person who is on trial, this proverb addressed the negative impact that dishonesty has on the false witness who tells a lie in court. Proverbs 19:9 says the same thing. Another modern saying declares, "If you tell the truth, it becomes a part of your past. But if you tell a lie, it becomes a part of your future."

The Plot Thickens

12:20 – "Deceit is in the heart of those who devise evil, but those who plan peace have joy."

The opening line of this proverb makes the reader think of the observation on human depravity made by the prophet Jeremiah.

> The heart is deceitful above all things, and desperately sick; who can understand it? (Jeremiah 17:9)

Jesus made the same observation about the depraved heart in the Gospels.

> For from within, out of the heart of man, come evil thoughts, sexual immorality, theft, murder, adultery, coveting, wickedness, deceit, sensuality, envy, slander, pride, foolishness. (Mark 7:21–22)

Both Jeremiah and Jesus made the point that deception takes place in the human heart. The sage observed that the human mind is constantly at work making plans for good and for evil. There is a sharp contrast between the person who is devising evil, and the one who is planning peace. Both individuals are using their minds, but one is withholding true intentions because he or she is plotting evil against someone else, while the other can be honest because of honorable intentions. There is also a sharp contrast in the end result of the plans that are made. The one who is planning evil is happy, but the actions will bring sorrow and misery to others. But the person who is planning peace will ultimately bring joy to his or her own life and joy to the lives of others.

14:17 – "A man of quick temper acts foolishly,
and a man of evil devices is hated."

This proverb identifies two flawed character traits, and the second half of the saying is connected in theme to the above proverb. The quick-tempered individual has been the topic of numerous proverbs in the collection (10:19; 12:16; 17:27–28). A short temper gets a person in trouble because he or she reacts to provocation and irritation in a rash manner. Equally flawed is the individual who has evil intentions, and unlike the short-tempered person, this sin against others comes after careful consideration. Because this person goes through life taking advantage of others, he or she is detested by their victims.

16:27 – "A worthless man plots evil, and
his speech is like a scorching fire."

This proverb continues the theme of the person who plots evil against others, and he or she is characterized by the wisdom writer as one who is worthless, in that the depravity goes unchecked. The adjective "worthless" is literally, "the man of Belial." The depravity is demonstrated by the character assassination of his or her victims. The goal is to destroy the reputation of the opponents through the use of slander.

16:30 – "Whoever winks his eyes plans dishonest
things; he who purses his lips brings evil to pass."

Transportation agents who are in charge of providing security for international airports are trained to look for certain deceptive behaviors to identify potential threats. A lists of stress factors include a number of physical behaviors that might reveal the person's true intentions. Those stress factors include the avoidance of eye contact with security personnel, or the exaggerated yawning as the individual approaches the screening process. Agents also look for excessive fidgeting, clock watching, head-turning, shuffling feet, excessive perspiration, facial flushing while undergoing screening, a faster eye blink rate when the individual is requested to submit to screening procedures. Other deceptive behaviors include an increased breathing rate, repetitive touching of the face, sweaty palms, trembling, and whistling as the individual approaches the screening process. The wisdom writer identified two physical mannerisms that betray the evil plotter, namely, the winking of the eye, and the pursing of the lips.

High Anxiety

12:25 – "Anxiety in a man's heart weighs him down, but a good word makes him glad."

This proverb recognizes that life can be difficult, and as a result, the problems of life begin to weigh a person down with overwhelming cares. People become anxious when their mind begins to fixate on their problems and fear takes over their minds. And, continued anxiety leads to depression. The image of an individual who is weighed down by anxiety can be seen in the physical posture of the person who is depressed. The psalmist spoke of this physical state in his description of grieving.

> I went about as though I grieved for my friend or my brother; as one who laments his mother, I bowed down in mourning" (Psalm 35:14)

The sage recognized that a great cure for anxiety is the timely, and well-chosen word of a friend who can provide an objective perspective to give the depressed individual a different outlook on the problem. Getting back to the posture of the depressed, the timely words of a friend can cause a person who is weighed down by cares to cheer up.

14:30 – "A tranquil heart gives life to the flesh, but envy makes the bones rot."

This proverb recognizes that some of our anxieties are self-inflicted. In this case, being discontent with life because we sinfully want what someone else has, will bring unrest into a person's heart. Envy is defined as a feeling of discontentment or covetousness with regard to another person's advantages, success, or possessions. Constantly wanting more will actually leave a person with less. The answer to a happy life is learning to be content with what one has.

15:13 – "A glad heart makes a cheerful face, but by sorrow of heart the spirit is crushed."

This proverb continues the theme of happiness by noting that happiness is found in the heart and expressed on the face. When a person has joy in the soul, there is a smile on the face. But the opposite is true as well. When there is sorrow in the soul, the heartache is hard to hide. Nehemiah, the king's cupbearer, was unable to hide his heartache from Artaxerxes.

> In the month of Nisan, in the twentieth year of King Artaxerxes, when wine was before him, I took up the wine and gave it to the king. Now I had not been sad in his presence. And the king said to me, "Why is your face sad, seeing you are not sick? This is nothing but sadness of the heart." Then I was very much afraid. (Nehemiah 2:1–2)

15:15 – "All the days of the afflicted are evil, but the cheerful of heart has a continual feast."

This proverb recognizes that our emotions are greatly affected by our circumstances. But the saying also acknowledges that our disposition contributes to our frame of mind as well.

> A joyful heart is good medicine, but a crushed spirit dries up the bones. (Proverbs 17:22)

The condition of the mind has a great impact on the physical wellbeing of the individual. I observed this with my father as he went through chemotherapy for lymphoma. Even though the drugs took a toll on his body, he had to daily address his attitude. His faith in the sovereignty of God buoyed his spirit and he found comfort in God's Word. One of the passages that changed his perspective was from the long acrostic poem in the Psalter.

> It is good for me that I was afflicted, that I might learn your statutes. (Psalm 119:71)

15:30 – "The light of the eyes rejoices the heart, and good news refreshes the bones."

When a person is weighed down with care there is nothing better than the arrival of good news to lift the spirits. The "light in the eyes" is on the face of the bearer of the good news. The messenger knows that the good news being delivered is going to bring joy to the friend and change the outlook on life.

Shame on You

*13:5 – "The righteous hates falsehood, but
the wicked brings shame and disgrace."*

In broad generalities, while the West is a guilt-based culture, the Middle East is shame-based. This distinction is the basis of this set of proverbs. The sage notes a key difference between the righteous and the wicked as it relates to honesty. Falsehood can refer to far more things than simply telling a lie. Falsehood speaks of dishonesty in word and action, such as being deceptive. The righteous choose to be honest, not only for conscience sake, but also because they detest dishonesty in themselves and in others. On the other hand, the wicked have no such qualms, and they choose to be dishonest when it suits their purposes. But because they have no such moral conscience, when their dishonesty is revealed, they will bring shameful disgrace on themselves and on their family. The word that is translated "shame" is connected to the idea of a bad odor and we can see this in the narrative of the Exodus. After the first conversation with Pharaoh did not go well, the tribal leaders of Israel complained to Moses.

> The LORD look on you and judge, because you have made us stink in the sight of Pharaoh and his servants, and have put a sword in their hand to kill us. (Exodus 5:21)

*14:35 – "A servant who deals wisely has the king's
favor, but his wrath falls on one who acts shamefully."*

This proverb illustrates the difference between skillful conduct and shameful behavior by going into the palace of a Middle Eastern king. The king is well served by a skillful counselor who provides his sovereign with wise advice and who serves with dignity. But the incompetent counselor whose behavior and advice are disgraceful, will experience the wrath of the king. A biblical example of this proverb is found in the narrative of Absalom's attempted coup against his father David. David had two counselors, Ahithophel and Hushai who stayed in Jerusalem when David had to flee. Ahithophel behaved in a disgraceful way by forsaking David and going over to Absalom. Hushai was instructed by David to stay behind to thwart the advice of Ahithophel. When Ahithophel saw that his counsel was not taking by Absalom, he suffered public shame and he went home and committed suicide by hanging himself (2 Samuel 17:23).

17:2 – "A servant who deals wisely will rule
over a son who acts shamefully and will share
the inheritance as one of the brothers."

This proverb promotes skillful living by using the inheritance laws of antiquity. Very rarely would a servant be promoted from his lowly station to become an heir within a family (Genesis 15:3). But a servant who serves his master with dignity is more valuable than a son who disgraces his father.

18:3 – "When wickedness comes, contempt comes
also, and with dishonor comes disgrace."

This proverb teaches that sinful behavior comes with unavoidable consequences. In a righteous community, sinful behavior is despised by its members and it leads to a loss of respect and public rebuke.

18:13 – "If one gives an answer before he
hears, it is his folly and shame."

When a person speaks before thinking, the advice will be foolish and reveal the speaker to be a fool. Arrogance also leads to public disgrace for it shows the individual did not take the time to listen to the other person before speaking. Disregarding the other person will result in the individual being disregarded by the community.

Wealth Management

13:7 – "One pretends to be rich, yet has nothing;
another pretends to be poor, yet has great wealth."

This proverb teaches that when it comes to money, appearances can be deceptive. The challenge with this proverb is determining the motives of the individuals when it comes to their relationship with money. The first half of the saying suggests a deceptive motive behind the individual who is pretending to be rich. Perhaps the individual wants people to think he or she has money, either to save face, or to be treated with greater respect within the community. The second half of the saying features an individual who wants to give the opposite impression. Why this person wants people to think that he or she is poor is open to conjecture. If the motives are wrong, then the person wants to avoid some responsibility that comes with having money. Perhaps the individual wants to minimize the financial risk to avoid getting robbed or having to give alms to the poor.

> *13:8 – "The ransom of a man's life is his*
> *wealth, but a poor man hears no threat."*

If given a chance, most people would choose wealth over poverty. But this proverb looks at the relative advantages of being poor. If you are poor, you are less likely to be harmed for the sake of money. But if you are rich, and people know you are rich, you are more likely to attract the attention of evil people who will harm you to gain a financial advantage through kidnapping or extortion.

> *13:11 – "Wealth gained hastily will dwindle, but*
> *whoever gathers little by little will increase it."*

This proverb could serve as a commentary on the dangers of playing the lottery. Most people who suddenly come into money do not survive the experience well. I found the following headlines on the internet. "Lotteries can be dangerous to your health." According to the experts, people who experience "sudden financial windfalls" can ultimately expect to feel anxiety, depression, anger, distrust, lack of identity and a sense of loss. Forbes Magazine had an article entitled, "The Pitfalls of Winning the Lottery." The author warned that winning the lottery can bring many challenges to a person's life, most of which cannot be fixed with money. While it sounds exciting to suddenly come into money, the sage knew that it was far better to have a good work ethic and combine that with the patience of saving money over a long period of time. The longer it takes to save the money, the wiser you will spend it.

> *22:7 – "The rich rules over the poor, and the*
> *borrower is the slave of the lender."*

This proverb can first be taken as an observation that the wealthy generally make the rules. It can also be used as a warning against the dangers of debt. Getting into debt can be easy, but getting out of debt can be nearly impossible. While we could take the proverb figuratively, the author probably also had in mind the practice where a poor person could sell himself into slavery to pay off a debt (Exodus 21:2–7).

> *22:16 – "Whoever oppresses the poor to increase his own*
> *wealth, or gives to the rich, will only come to poverty."*

This proverb serves as a warning to people who would use money in an unethical way to gain an advantage over others. If an individual takes advantage of the poor in an attempt to increase wealth, the offender will end up joining the ranks of the poor. And, if one gives money to those who are rich, in an attempt to gain their favor, the investor will simply find that he or she has less money than at the start.

Strife

> *13:10 – "By insolence comes nothing but strife,*
> *but with those who take advice is wisdom."*

In a chapter entitled "The Great Sin," the British theologian who authored the book "Mere Christianity," addressed the sin of pride, which is the theme of this proverb.

> There is one vice of which no man in the world is free;
> which everyone loathes when he sees it in someone else; and
> of which hardly any people, except Christians, ever imagine
> that they are guilty themselves. (C.S. Lewis)

Based on the second half of the saying, the sign of pride in this instance is the rejection of the advice from others. The fool, who rudely will not listen to others, will experience strife from those who were offended when their advice was not followed. On the other hand, those who are wise will listen to the advice of others. And earlier proverb said it well.

The way of a fool is right in his own eyes, but a wise man listens to advice. (Proverbs 12:15)

15:18 – "A hot-tempered man stirs up strife, but he who is slow to anger quiets contention."

Another source of strife is the person who cannot or chooses not to control the temper. When attacked verbally with an accusation, there are two ways to respond. When attacked, a hot-tempered individual attacks back and makes the situation even worse. The other option is to respond calmly and diffuse the situation. Some people like to constantly stir up trouble and a short temper is normally the cause of the problem. The disciplined person who controls his or her temper will calm the contentious situation.

16:28 – "A dishonest man spreads strife, and a whisperer separates close friends."

This proverb identifies two more sources of strife among people, and they both involve the misuse of the tongue, which is a dominant theme of the proverbs. A dishonest person, in this instance, is an individual who spreads lies about other people, and as a result of the falsehoods, spreads strife among those involved. The second sin of the tongue is gossip where an individual whispers secrets and rumors about other people, and as a result of this idle talk, wreaks havoc on close friendships.

17:14 – "The beginning of strife is like letting out water, so quit before the quarrel breaks out."

The sage paints a vivid word picture with this proverb to illustrate how a conflict can begin on a small scale, but then it erupts into a huge problem that quickly gets out of control. He likens the beginning of strife to a small water leak, perhaps in a dam. But once the water begins to leak out, it becomes a raging torrent that cannot be stop before it damages everything in its wake. So, the sage's advice is to quit the conflict before you even begin. Many deep-seated conflicts between people and nations began with a simple misunderstanding or a foolish word.

17:19 – "Whoever loves transgression loves strife;
he who makes his door high seeks destruction."

The emphasis of this proverb will be determined by the understanding of the author's use of the high door reference. Some scholars understand the high door to refer to an individual who builds an unnecessarily pretentious house, and because of arrogance, brings trouble to his or her door. Other scholars take the gate or door to be a figurative reference to the mouth, and understand the sin to be an individual who talks big, and as a result, brings trouble into his or her life. Either way, the first part of the saying is very clear. Some people love a good fight, and because of their antagonistic attitude, will experience strife.

A Word of Advice

13:13 – "Whoever despises the word brings
destruction on himself, but he who reveres
the commandment will be rewarded."

This proverb could be understood simply as a warning not to reject the advice of others, but to seek the counsel of wise people for a rewarding life. But given the context of this book within the life of the covenant people of God, the "word" could be understood as the Word of God and the "commandment" as a reference to the commandments of God as presented in the Mosaic Law. And when that is understood, the word of advice that is given will be based on a knowledge of the Word of God. As we have already seen, the book of Proverbs presupposes the context of biblical revelation from God as the foundation for instruction. For example, take the address that begins the second chapter.

> My son, if you receive my words and treasure up my commandments with you. Then you will understand the fear of the LORD and find the knowledge of God. For the LORD gives wisdom; from his mouth come knowledge and understanding. (Proverbs 2:1, 5–6)

This proverb promises a reward for the individual who will revere the revelation that comes from God. The undefined reward can simply be the good consequences of following biblical advice and the avoidance of mistakes.

15:22 – "Without counsel plans fail, but
with many advisers they succeed."

This proverb continues the theme of seeking the advice of others for a successful outcome. This is true for an individual, and it is also true for a nation. When an individual does not consult others, failure is more likely because there is only one perspective on the issue. But if the person seeks the advice of others, and they are deemed wise, then the individual benefits from multiple perspectives on the matter. But the emphasis is on the quality of the advisors, not just the quantity.

19:20 – "Listen to advice and accept instruction,
that you may gain wisdom in the future."

This proverb repeats the familiar admonition to listen to the wise advice of others and to have a teachable spirit. The book of Proverbs opens with this counsel and the advice is found throughout the book. What is of particular emphasis in this proverb is the future benefit of having a teachable spirit when the student is young. This reminds me of a familiar complaint that is voiced by young people who are in school. High school students often complain to their teachers, "Why do I have to learn this subject? I'm never going to use it in life." This lack of experience and not having a long-term perspective hinders young people from seeing the future value of instruction. Because the book of Proverbs comes from an eternal God, the advice given always looks to the future.

19:27 – "Cease to hear instruction, my son, and
you will stray from the words of knowledge."

The first half of this proverb is intended to shock, for the father tells his son to stop listening to his advice. But then the thought is complete when the father warns about the harmful consequences of doing so. The terminology of "straying from the word of knowledge" conjures up the imagery of a farmer trying to plow a straight furrow through his field from one end to the other. As long as he keeps his eyes fixed on the end of the field, his row will be straight. But if he takes his eyes off the goal, his furrow will become crooked. The same result will happen if the son shuts his ears to the instruction of his father. Instead of staying on the straight and narrow path, he will wander off the path and experience harm.

Healthy Words

13:17 – "A wicked messenger falls into trouble,
but a faithful envoy brings healing."

This proverb is included in this series of sayings that promotes healing words because, in the ancient world, a messenger's task was to deliver messages on behalf of the employer. If the messenger was careless, he would cause trouble for himself and for his master through his foolish conduct and his ungracious words. But if the messenger was reliable, he would enhance the life of his master by accurately conveying his master's wishes.

15:1 – "A soft answer turns away wrath,
but a harsh word stirs up anger."

This proverb promotes the use of conciliatory words to diffuse an argument. When an accuser attacks out of anger, an equally angry response to the accusation will only make the situation worse. But a wise person will control the temper and the gentle answer will calm the tense situation. The sage said much the same thing three verses later.

> A gentle tongue is a tree of life, but perverseness in it breaks the spirit. (Proverbs 15:4)

We have seen this expression, "a tree of life," several times already in the book and it refers to a source of refreshment (11:30; 13:12). A gentle response will bring healing, while dishonest and deceptive words will cause more damage. Words either build people up or tear them down. The apostle Paul said the same thing to the believers in Ephesus.

> Let no corrupting talk come out of your mouths, but only such as is good for building up, as fits the occasion, that it may give grace to those who hear. (Ephesians 4:29)

This policy has served me well over the years as a pastor. When an angry individual comes to my office, I calmly listen to their complaint, and tell them that I will get back to them in several days after I have had the time to prayerfully consider their criticism.

15:23 – "To make an apt answer is a joy to a
man, and a word in season, how good it is!"

This proverb expresses the joy that both the speaker and the listener experience when the advice that is given is both timely and well-thought out. It is a wonderful feeling to give just the right advice at the right time in another person's life. It is equally pleasing to be on the receiving end of timely advice from a wise counselor when the direction of your life is in doubt.

16:21 – "The wise of heart is called discerning, and
sweetness of speech increases persuasiveness."

This proverb continues the theme of timely advice by focusing on the wise counselor. The counselor who is wise has the ability to discern both people and situations before the advice is given. Because of that discerning spirit, the words will be gracious and their impact will be great.

16:24 – "Gracious words are like a honeycomb,
sweetness to the soul and health to the body."

This proverb brings a smile to my face when I read about the honeycomb. I first went to the country of Ukraine in 2002 to teach at a Bible college in the city of Kremenchuk. On that first trip, I was introduced to the Ukrainian custom of hot black tea at meals and at teatimes. My first taste of tea was unpleasant and it remained unpleasant for four years. But one evening during a small group Bible study, I saw a bowl of honey on the table, and when I stirred it into my tea, I found the perfect combination to make tea delicious. The sage found the presence of gracious words to be equally sweet and healing.

The Life of a Fool

13:19 – "A desire fulfilled is sweet to the soul, but to
turn away from evil is an abomination to fools."

This series of proverbs gives the reader a glimpse into the life of a fool, the chief antagonist in this book that promotes wisdom and righteous living. The book of Proverbs encourages wise planning and patient waiting to accomplish anything meaningful in life. An earlier proverb encouraged such patience.

> Hope deferred makes the heart sick, but a desire fulfilled is a tree of life. (Proverbs 13:12)

And when the goal is reached after much time and effort, the feeling of achievement is sweet to the soul. The fool will never feel this sense of satisfaction, for he or she lacks the moral discipline to avoid the evil things in life that will derail every good desire.

14:9 – "Fools mock at the guilt offering,
but the upright enjoy acceptance."

In the Mosaic Law, the guilt offering enabled an offending individual to admit guilt and make reparations for an offense committed against another person (Leviticus 5:14–6:7). The goal of the guilt offering was confession and compensation in order to restore a person to fellowship with God and with his or her fellow man. According to this proverb, fools ridicule any such pangs of conscience. A righteous person will feel compelled to make amends and clear the conscience, but a fool finds such feelings laughable.

14:16 – "One who is wise is cautious and turns away
from evil, but a fool is reckless and careless."

A wise person has a little internal voice that warns of evil actions and harmful consequences. A fool has no such voice. When I was a teenager, my family was visiting our cousins who lived in another state. One day I was walking with my cousin in his neighborhood, and we found a pack of cigarettes. Now, both of us were pastor's kids and we should have known right from wrong. My cousin got excited about this opportunity to try smoking, while I knew that nothing good would come of it. I left him to his experience, and walked away rehearsing the biblical phrase my parents had pounded into my head: "Be sure your sin will find you out."

17:10 – "A rebuke goes deeper into a man of
understanding than a hundred blows into a fool."

A common theme in the book of Proverbs is the need for verbal and corporal punishment to instill discipline into the life of a child. This proverb talks about both means of discipline and the differing impacts they will have on a wise person and on a fool. A person of understanding will take a verbal rebuke to heart, while a fool could be beaten senseless and never learn the lesson. Because of the fool's stubbornness and stupidity, the sage issues a warning two verses later.

> Let a man meet a she-bear robbed of her cubs rather than a
> fool in his folly. (Proverbs 17:12)

Bear experts tell us that most bears prefer to avoid contact with humans, but if a hiker encounters a mother bear with cubs, she will become aggressive. The sage uses hyperbole to warn about the dangers of associating with a fool.

> *21:20 – "Precious treasure and oil are in a wise*
> *man's dwelling, but a foolish man devours it."*

The book of Proverbs advocates saving for the future, and a wise person will do just that. A characteristic of fools is living for the moment and not thinking of the future. The wise person will save for the future, while the fool will squander what he or she has.

Poverty

> *13:23 – "The fallow ground of the poor would yield*
> *much food, but it is swept away through injustice."*

The Mosaic Law frequently addressed the matter of poverty within the nation of Israel and instructed the people on how they should treat the poor within their society. Lenders of money were not to charge interest when the poor had to borrow in order to survive (Leviticus 25:35–38). During harvest time, produce was to be left in the corners of the fields for the poor to reap (Leviticus 23:22). And, when it came to legal matters, the poor were not to be abused in the courts by the wealthy through their money and influence (Leviticus 19:15). In the context of the sabbatical year, Moses made the following statement about the matter of poverty as the nation prepared to enter the land of Canaan.

But there will be no poor among you; for the LORD will bless you in the land that the LORD your God is giving you for an inheritance to possess. (Deuteronomy 15:4)

But, several verses later, Moses expressed the harsh reality that poverty would always exist, even within the covenant people of Israel.

For there will never cease to be poor in the land. Therefore I command you, You shall open wide your hand to your brother, to the needy and to the poor, in your land. (Deuteronomy 15:11)

This proverb expresses both the ideal situation, and the harsh reality of poverty in the land of Israel. If the poor were industrious, their land should provide for their basic physical needs. But injustice will ruin the system that was intended to protect the poor.

14:31 – "Whoever oppresses a poor man insults his Maker, but he who is generous to the needy honors him."

This proverb builds on the above saying, and it makes an interesting connection between one's treatment of the poor and one's relationship with God. Jesus made the same observation in the parable of the persistent widow (Luke 18:1–8).

He said, "In a certain city there was a judge who neither feared God nor respected man." (Luke 18:2)

Both observations were made within a society that claimed to acknowledge the presence of a personal God. Every individual, whether rich or poor, is created in the image of God (Proverbs 22:2), and is therefore deserving of respect.

17:5 – "Whoever mocks the poor insults his Maker; he who is glad at calamity will not go unpunished."

This proverb continues the theme of the above saying with a strong warning of impending judgment on the person who takes pleasure in the misery of others. Making fun of the poor takes place when a person finds a perverse pleasure in their misfortune and blames them for their poverty. While other proverbs connect poverty and laziness (6:6–11; 10:4–5; 12:24, 27; 19:15; 22:13), this proverb does not make that judgment. Being glad at the misfortune of the poor reveals a perverseness that is offensive to God. So, while the offender thinks he or she is merely mocking the poor person, the mocker is actually showing contempt for God, and will suffer the consequences of this judgmental attitude.

> *19:22 – "What is desired in a man is steadfast*
> *love, and a poor man is better than a liar."*

This proverb changes course, even though it continues the theme of poverty. Using the "better than" formula to make comparisons, the wisdom writer lauds the virtue of faithfulness within the covenant community. Because the nation of Israel was built on God's steadfast love for His covenant people (Exodus 34:6–7), this same quality was to be evident in their treatment of one another. So, because the failure to show steadfast love was so offensive, the sage said it was better to be poor than to be a liar.

A Work Ethic

> *14:4 – "Where there are no oxen, the manger is clean,*
> *but abundant crops come by the strength of the ox."*

This proverb makes a fascinating observation about the importance of having a good work ethic and the resulting productivity. The sage makes his point by using a farming illustration that would have been understandable to the ancient first readers, and which is somewhat humorous to the modern reader. In the agricultural world of Palestine, if a farmer wanted to produce crops, he had to own oxen. The energy of the oxen to work the fields would be determined in part by the amount of grain the farmer fed his animals. The Mosaic Law even had a regulation for the treatment of oxen.

> You shall not muzzle an ox when it is treading out the grain.
> (Deuteronomy 25:4)

And once the farmer fed his animals, the oxen produced dung that left the manger messy and in need of cleaning. I have a farmer in my church who used to raise pigs, and pigs produce a lot of manure, which in turn, produces a strong odor. If he wanted to produce an income for his farm, he had to put up with the manure and the odor. When some people in town complained about the smell, he would say, "It smells like money to me." The wisdom writer is making the same observation about a productive life. Life has to be a little messy and it requires a lot of effort for it to be productive.

> 16:26 – *"A worker's appetite works for*
> *him; his mouth urges him on."*

The book of Proverb strongly condemns laziness (6:6–11). And every one of us, due to our sin nature, has a lazy streak that shows up once in a while. This proverb says that one of the cures for laziness is hunger. The appetite for food is a strong motivation to get to work. This hunger is what motivates most of us to get back to work on Monday. The social security system of the Mosaic Law required poor people to work for their food.

> And when you reap the harvest of your land, you shall not reap your field right up to its edge, nor shall you gather the gleanings after your harvest. You shall leave them for the poor and for the sojourner: I am the LORD your God. (Leviticus 23:22)

The apostle Paul picked up on this principle in his second letter to the Thessalonian church when he criticized the idleness that was plaguing the congregation (3:6–12).

> For even when we were with you, we would give you this command: If anyone is not willing to work, let him not eat. (2 Thessalonians 3:10)

> 18:20 – *"From the fruit of a man's mouth his stomach*
> *is satisfied; he is satisfied by the yield of his lips."*

This proverb also speaks of a person's mouth and a harvest, but in a different context from the above saying. The two synonymous lines speak of the productivity of a person's speech. What we say, and how we say things, will either lead to a good harvest or a bad harvest. Just as a farmer plants seeds in the ground, hoping for a good harvest, so too the speaker must carefully choose the words if he or she wants to be satisfied by what they produce.

> *20:21 – "An inheritance gained hastily in the*
> *beginning will not be blessed in the end."*

This proverb has some connection to a work ethic because it warns about the dangers of coming into money without the benefit of hard labor. The book of Proverbs promotes the importance of working hard for a living, with the promise that labor is rewarded (12:11, 14). But if an individual comes into money without the benefit of hard labor, it can have a disastrous effect on the person's life.

Human Emotions

> *14:10 – "The heart knows its own bitterness,*
> *and no stranger shares its joy."*

This proverb identifies the two extremes in emotions that all people experience in life, ranging from the deep bitterness of soul, to the elation of joy. The Hebrew term that is translated "bitterness" (*mara*) was adopted by the Old Testament character Naomi when she returned to the village of Bethlehem after the death of her husband and her two sons in the land of Moab.

> Do not call me Naomi; call me Mara, for the Almighty has
> dealt very bitterly with me. I went away full, and the Lord
> has brought me back empty. (Ruth 1:20–21)

But as you continue to read this narrative that took place in the periods of the judges, Naomi would eventually experience the other emotional extreme. When her daughter-in-law, Ruth, was redeemed by the near kinsman, Boaz, and gave birth to a son, Naomi experienced great joy. This proverb is teaching that while it is good to empathize with people in their joy and in their sorrow, it is impossible to truly understand what another person is going through. For example, I have a deep love of classical music and I have attended the Minnesota

Orchestra where a piece of music moved me. I have tried to explain this feeling of joy to other people, but if they don't love classical music, they really don't understand what I am saying. As a pastor, I talk to people who are dealing with deep emotional and psychological pain in their lives. And while I try to empathize with them, if I have not gone through a similar experience, my ability to understand their feelings of pain is limited. While human beings are limited in their ability to understand another person's heart, God knows the heart.

> Sheol and Abaddon lie open before the Lord; how much more the hearts of the children of man! (Proverbs 15:11)

14:13 – "Even in laughter the heart may ache, and the end of joy may be grief."

The first half of this proverb reminds me of the many visits to the hospital that I have made over the years in my role as a pastor. When individuals in my church deal with serious health concerns, I have spent long hours with the family in the waiting room. To help them pass the time, we will have long conversations. And while we are always mindful of the life-threatening illness that has brought us to the hospital, periodically the group needs to laugh to ease the tension. But while we may be laughing for the moment, the heart is still aching because the threat to their loved one is still present. There is another way to understand this observation by the sage. He may be telling us not to be fooled by appearances. Someone who is laughing may be doing so in an effort to mask their pain. The second half of the proverb seems to be making an observation about the harsh realities of life. There are many experiences in life that bring a feeling of joy to the soul. But many of those joyful experiences can end in grief. For example, getting married can bring the joy of intimacy and companionship. But after many years of marriage, when one of the spouses dies, the feeling of grief is intense. Becoming a parent is an experience of great joy. But that same child can become a source of great sorrow as well if they make poor choices in life.

> A wise son makes a glad father, but a foolish son is a sorrow to his mother. (Proverbs 10:1)

18:14 – "A man's spirit will endure sickness, but a crushed spirit who can bear?"

This proverb teaches that there are both physical and psychological components to life. An individual can have a serious illness that can be life-threatening, but as long as the person has hope and maintains a positive attitude, that attitude can help him or her deal with the challenge. But when a person becomes depressed about the situation, that crushed spirit will find the challenge too overwhelming.

> A joyful heart is good medicine, but a crushed spirit dries up the bones. (Proverbs 17:22)

The Simple

14:15 – "The simple believes everything, but the prudent gives thought to his steps."

We first met the simple person in the opening purpose statement where the sage wrote that proverbs are intended "to give prudence to the simple, knowledge and discretion to the youth" (1:4). The "simple" individual (*peti*) refers to a young person who is naïve and inexperienced when it comes to life. This person is not an idiot, nor an individual who cannot comprehend. Nor is the simple person a fool who despises wisdom. Instead, this individual's exposure to life and wisdom has been limited, and as a result, he or she lacks critical thinking skills. Here is an apt description of this young person.

> For at the window of my house I have looked out through my lattice, and I have seen among the simple, I have perceived among the youths, a young man lacking sense. (Proverb 7:6–7)

Because of this inexperience, this person is gullible and easily influenced, which is the point of this proverb. A young person who is gullible can get into a lot of trouble if he or she is listening to the wrong person. The book of Proverbs identifies several advisors the gullible young person should not listen to in the opening longer addresses. The young person should not listen to peers who offer a life of excitement (1:10–19). Another dangerous advisor is the immoral woman who tells the simple young man what he wants to hear (7:1–27). The opposite of being gullible is a young person who is thoughtful about the direction his or her life is taking. Like the modern proverb, "look before you leap," this biblical proverb advises the taking of careful steps in life. Lady Wisdom invites the simple to "Leave your simple ways, and live, and walk in the way of insight" (Proverbs 9:6).

14:18 – "The simple inherit folly, but the
prudent are crowned with knowledge."

If the translation is accurate, the first half of this proverb would support the biblical doctrine of human depravity that states that children are born with a sin nature. Sin affects every area of a person's life, and in this case, it affects the way the mind functions. We have seen this in a proverb we examined earlier in the book.

> Folly is bound up in the heart of a child, but the rod of discipline drives it far from him. (Proverbs 22:15)

We also see this doctrine in the penitential psalm of David following his adultery with Bathsheba.

> Behold, I was brought forth in iniquity, and in sin did my mother conceive me. (Psalm 51:5)

The New Testament writers also understood how the sin nature affected the mind.

> And you were dead in the trespasses and sins in which you once walked, following the course of this world, following the prince of the power of the air, the spirit that is now at work in the sons of disobedience—among whom we all once lived in the passions of our flesh, carrying out the desires of the body and the mind, and were by nature children of wrath, like the rest of mankind. (Ephesians 2:1–3)

Even though the young are born with folly in their hearts, parental discipline and a pursuit of knowledge can change this behavior. So, while we inherited a sin nature, by responding to biblical discipline, we can have a life that is adorned with knowledge.

22:3 – "The prudent sees danger and hides himself, but the simple go on and suffer for it."

This proverb also has the contrast between the simple individual and the prudent person. If the simple do not learn from their mistakes and refuse to heed the advice of wise counselors, they will go through life repeating their mistakes and paying the price for their stubbornness. This was the case of the simple young man in chapter 7 who walked by the corner of the promiscuous woman. But if the young person develops a discerning eye, he or she will see where the dangers in life lie, and avoid them. A young person can learn from the advice of wise counselors who are older. The young person can also learn from the mistakes of others. So, pain can be minimized in life if we are disciplined to develop critical thinking.

Patience

14:29 – "Whoever is slow to anger has great understanding, but he who has a hasty temper exalts folly."

The book of Proverbs celebrates the wise individual who has understanding, and one of the primary ways that understanding manifests itself in a person's life is with a patient outlook on life. When confronted by irritating people and frustrating circumstances, the wise person chooses to respond carefully and calmly, and thus not aggravate an already difficult situation. The opposite response is to become angry quickly and to intensify an already intense situation. To become angry is to promote folly. One year I was flying home after another teaching trip to Ukraine and our plane had mechanical problems on the tarmac. When the problem could not be fixed, the passengers were told to exit the plane and collect their luggage. All of us passengers had to make new travel arrangements, and I ended up spending the entire day in the terminal as I was able to get the last flight out of the day. There were about ten Americans on the flight and it must have been one passenger's first time to Ukraine. He became so irritated with the delay, that when he finally booked a new flight home, he loudly announced to everyone within his vicinity that he was never coming back to this (expletive) country again.

16:32 – "Whoever is slow to anger is better
than the mighty, and he who rules his
spirit than he who takes a city."

This proverb also celebrates the wise individual who is able to control the temper, and it does so by making a comparison. While every culture celebrates the powerful person, the ability to control one's temper is one of the greatest demonstrations of genuine power. We live in a culture that celebrates the athlete who is a physical specimen. But on a weekly basis, we watch sports highlights where those athletes lose control of their emotions in a competition and they strike out at an opponent or at an official. The sage would see that loss of temper as a sign of weakness. In the ancient world of the wisdom writer, their heroes were military leaders who could capture a fortified city. The historian celebrated King David's mighty men with a rundown of their military exploits (2 Samuel 23:8–39). But in the estimation of the sage, the ability to take a fortified city paled in comparison to the ability to control one's temper.

19:2 – "Desire without knowledge is not good, and
whoever makes haste with his feet misses his way."

The first proverb in this grouping spoke of the individual who had a hasty temper. This proverb talks about the individual who has hasty feet. It is great to have energy and ambition, but that drive needs to be matched with intelligence. I have a bad sense of direction and so the invention of GPS has been a blessing for me. If I was driving somewhere, but got lost, I would joke that I was lost, but was making good time. The ambitious person who does not take the time to plan because he or she is in too much of a hurry, will end up expending all of their energy in a failed enterprise.

19:19 – "A man of great wrath will pay the penalty, for
if you deliver him, you will only have to do it again."

This proverb returns to the theme of the angry individual, with a word of warning to the friends who are tempted to help him or her escape punishment. The person who cannot control the temper will often experience trouble, whether it be legal or financial or otherwise. If you are a friend to an angry person, and you decide to bail that person out of trouble, you had better get used to doing so time and time again.

Wisdom

14:33 – "Wisdom rests in the heart of a man of understanding, but it makes itself known even in the midst of fools."

The first line of this proverb states a theme that is repeated throughout the book. The individual who acquires understanding will possess wisdom deep in the soul. Understanding is the demonstration of discernment toward the complex problems of life. Discernment is gained when an individual responds to the discipline of parents, when he or she listens to the advice of wise counselors, and when the LORD is feared. While the first line of the proverb is clear, the second line has some questions. This translation understands the phrase to say that even though fools reject wisdom, because wisdom is so great, that even among fools, wisdom will reveal itself. The LXX takes the second line as antithetical parallelism so that wisdom does not make itself known to fools.

16:16 – "How much better to get wisdom than gold! To get understanding is to be chosen rather than silver."

This proverb puts a monetary value on wisdom by comparing its worth to the gold and silver standard of the day. While wisdom and wealth are not incompatible, wealth without wisdom will corrupt an individual and turn him or her into a greedy person. If one had to choose between the two items, the sage declares that wisdom is the clear choice, for it is a more permanent possession. Money comes and goes, but wisdom, if it is pursued throughout one's life, will be permanent. Solomon is the poster boy of this proverb. When he came to the throne as a young man, he chose wisdom over wealth (1 Kings 3). But in the later days of his reign, his wealth led him astray and his wisdom turned to foolishness (1 Kings 11). A later proverb makes a similar comparison between wisdom and wealth.

There is gold and abundance of costly stones, but the lips of knowledge are a precious jewel. (Proverbs 20:15)

While people have always been fascinated by shiny objects such as gold and precious stones, a knowledgeable counselor who gives out wise advice is a more valuable commodity. While these two proverbs compare the value of wisdom to wealth, another proverb compares wisdom to power.

A wise man scales the city of the mighty and brings down
the stronghold in which they trust. (Proverbs 21:22)

The tactician who devises the means to scale the walls of a city is more powerful than the armed soldiers who guard the city.

16:23 – "The heart of the wise makes his speech
judicious and adds persuasiveness to his lips."

This proverb also talks about the wise counselor and the impact that his advice has on others. The counselor who is truly wise will not only know what to say, but will know how to say it. By choosing words carefully, the advice will find a receptive audience. This observation is similar to a saying in the same chapter that we studied earlier.

The wise of heart is called discerning, and sweetness of
speech increases persuasiveness. (Proverbs 16:21)

18:15 – "An intelligent heart acquires knowledge,
and the ear of the wise seeks knowledge."

This proverb talks about the effort that must go into the acquisition of wisdom. Because wisdom is such a valuable commodity, great effort must be made to acquire it. It takes an intelligent heart and an open ear to seek earnestly after knowledge in the form of discipline and counsel from other wise people. Through the ear the words come into the heart, and in the heart the counsel is weighed.

The Scoffer

15:12 – "A scoffer does not like to be
reproved; he will not go to the wise."

We first met the scoffer in the book of Proverbs in the second address of the father to his son. The father has Lady Wisdom calling out to three related individuals.

How long, O simple ones, will you love being simple? How long will scoffers delight in their scoffing and fools hate knowledge? (Proverbs 1:22)

The scoffer is the arrogant fool who refuses to accept instruction from the wise. A later proverb emphasizes this ignorance by using three related Hebrew terms to depict the offensive sin of human pride.

"Scoffer" is the name of the arrogant, haughty man who acts with arrogant pride. (Proverbs 21:24)

In Proverb 15:12 the scoffer avoids any relationship with the wise. The second line says either the scoffer will not walk with the wise or he or she will not walk to the wise. The scoffer has progressed to the point where delight is found in ridiculing the advice of the wise. The opening psalm also mentioned the scoffer who is to be avoided if one wants to live the blessed life.

Blessed is the man who walks not in the counsel of the wicked, nor stands in the way of sinners, nor sits in the seat of scoffers. (Psalm 1:1)

19:25 – "Strike a scoffer, and the simple will learn prudence; reprove a man of understanding, and he will gain knowledge."

The emphasis of this proverb is on the impact that discipline has on three different individuals. The scoffer is mentioned first, and the sage admits that discipline is a waste of time for this individual. Whether the discipline is verbal or physical, the scoffer stiffens the resolve and refuses to change. But despite this failure to respond, the scoffer still needs to be punished, because that discipline will produce change in someone else's life. The simple individual is a naive young person whose exposure to life has been limited by time. But by observing the punishment of the scoffer, this young person can learn from that lesson and avoid personal pain. A later proverb makes the same observation about the benefits of discipline.

When a scoffer is punished, the simple becomes wise; when a wise man is instructed, he gains knowledge. (Proverbs 21:11)

While we often hear the motto: "Live and learn," the book of Proverbs promotes the alternative motto: "Learn, and then live." Both proverbs conclude with the impact that discipline has on the wise individual. While the scoffer can be physically beaten and still not respond, the wise individual only needs to hear a word and he or she is responsive.

> 19:29 – *"Condemnation is ready for scoffers,*
> *and beating for the backs of fools."*

This proverb equates the scoffer with the fool, and warns both individuals that punishment is unavoidable. The punishment may come from the family or from society, but ultimately it will come from God because the scoffer and the fool have rejected His wisdom. The punishment can come in the form of legal judgments and monetary penalties, and the beatings can be physical punishment from a parent or a physical beating at the hands of an offended person.

> 22:10 – *"Drive out a scoffer, and strife will go*
> *out, and quarreling and abuse will cease."*

Psalm 1:1 advised not sitting in the seat of scoffers. This proverb depicts a formal meeting where people gather to discuss a serious topic. The presence of a scoffer in the audience will destroy the productivity of the meeting, and so the sage advises that this individual should be removed from the meeting. The scoffer, with the arrogant attitude, is the toxic source of conflict and quarreling.

Divine Omniscience

> 16:1 – *"The plans of the heart belong to man, but*
> *the answer of the tongue is from the* LORD.*"*

This proverb reminds us that while we often act like we are independent from God, that God is sovereignly ruling over the affairs of our lives. A biblical illustration of this proverb is found in the Old Testament narrative where the king of Moab hired the prophet Balaam to pronounce a curse on the nation of Israel (Numbers 22–24). So, Balak, the king of Moab, planned to hire

Balaam to pronounce a curse on his enemies. And Balaam planned to accept the money and perform his task. But God demonstrated His sovereignty by putting words of blessing into the mouth of the prophet instead of the curse that had been paid for. Each time Balaam pronounced a blessing on the nation of Israel, the king of Moab became angry and reminded the prophet that he had paid for a curse. Their exchange is a reflection of this proverb.

> And Balak said to Balaam, "What have you done to me? I took you to curse my enemies, and behold, you have done nothing but bless them." And he answered and said, "Must I not take care to speak what the LORD puts in my mouth? (Numbers 23:11–12)

A later proverb says much the same thing.

> Many are the plans in the mind of a man, but it is the purpose of the LORD that will stand. (Proverbs 19:21)

16:4 – "The LORD has made everything for its purpose, even the wicked for the day of trouble."

This proverb offers some comfort for the righteous person who struggles with the frustration that the wicked seem to be getting away with sin. Read Psalm 73 to hear such frustration. The sage reminds us that God is sovereignly watching over His creatures and that justice will be meted out to the wicked.

16:33 – "The lot is cast into the lap, but its every decision is from the LORD."

This proverb sees divine sovereignty even in the arbitrary ancient human practice of casting lots to make a decision. For example, the sailors cast lots to determine which one of them was responsible for the violent storm at sea (Jonah 1:7). The nation of Israel consulted the Urim and Thummim to determine God's will in a matter (1 Samuel 14:41). While we will not debate the merits of this ancient decision-making process, the sage knew that when God was consulted, that the verdict given revealed the divine will. Precisely because the sage did not know how God made His decisions, it caused him to write the following saying.

A man's steps are from the LORD; how then can man understand his way? (Proverbs 20:24)

> *17:3 – "The crucible is for silver, and the furnace*
> *is for gold, and the LORD tests hearts."*

Just as precious metals need to be put to the test in a hot furnace to remove the dross, and thus, increase their purity, so too God tests the human heart to reveal the sin, and then to purify our motives and thoughts. A later proverb also talks about God searching our conscience.

The spirit of man is the lamp of the LORD, searching all his innermost parts. (Proverbs 20:27)

> *21:31 – "The horse is made ready for the day of*
> *battle, but the victory belongs to the LORD."*

This proverb reflects the reality that when God placed the nation of Israel in the land of Canaan, that He put them in a hostile environment where the surrounding nations wanted to destroy them. The sage reminds his readers that Israel's survival was not based on its military might, but on the nation's dependence on God.

Some trust in chariots and some in horses, but we trust in the name of the LORD our God. (Psalm 20:7)

Royal Proverbs

> *16:10 – "An oracle is on the lips of a king;*
> *his mouth does not sin in judgment."*

As God established the nation of Israel and His direct rule over the nation, known as a theocracy, He anticipated the day when the people would want to have a king like the surrounding nations (Deuteronomy 17:14–20). To protect Israel's king from spiritual and moral corruption, God placed several conditions on the ruler. He was not to collect horses, as a sign of military might. He was not to multiply wives in the form of political marriages. He was not to acquire large amounts of gold and silver. And positively, he was to write out his own copy of the law to remind him that God governed his rule. This series of proverbs allowed the sage to describe the ideal king of Israel which did not happen often in the history of the nation. The Hebrew word that is translated "oracle" described the practice of divination, or the means of determining the will of one's deity in the ancient world. While the pagan practice was condemned (1 Samuel 28:8), in this context it describes the legitimate practice of determining God's will (Isaiah 11:1–5). When Israel's king sought the will of God concerning a matter, he needed to remind himself that he was speaking on behalf of God. If this was the case, the king would choose his words carefully, and when he rendered a judgment, he would not sin with his tongue.

> *16:12 – "It is an abomination to kings to do evil,*
> *for the throne is established by righteousness."*

We have already looked at a list of behaviors that the sage declared to be offensive to God's holy nature in the longer addresses (Proverbs 6:16–19), as well as the individual sayings (11:1, 20, 12:22; 15:8). This proverb states that the king who honors God will find the same behaviors offensive. The king and his administration needed to be characterized by justice, and only then would his reign be established.

> *16:13 – "Righteous lips are the delight of a king,*
> *and he loves him who speaks what is right."*

The first proverb in this grouping spoke of the words of the king, and that when he spoke, he needed to remind himself that he was speaking on God's behalf. This proverb speaks of the words that are spoken by the royal advisors to the king. Rather than surrounding himself with advisors who would simply tell the king what he wanted to hear, a wise ruler would demand that his advisors tell him the truth. A ruler is best served by counselors who are candid and honest.

> *16:14 – "A king's wrath is a messenger of*
> *death, and a wise man will appease it."*

An ancient king possessed the power of life and death over his subjects, so when a king became angry with someone, it could result in loss of life. For example, a word from Solomon brought about the death of his brother Adonijah

(1 Kings 10:25) and the general Joab (1 Kings 10:34). This proverb advises the wise person to learn how to soothe the king's anger when he is displeased.

16:15 – "In the light of a king's face there is life, and his favor is like the clouds that bring the spring rain."

This proverb is the opposite side of the previous saying. While an angry king can result in death for his subject, a happy ruler brings life. The sage likens the favor of the happy king to the coming of the spring rain late in the agricultural cycle to complete the growth of the plants before the harvest.

Honesty

16:11 – "A just balance and scales are the LORD's; all the weights in the bag are his work."

We were first introduced to the topic of a just balance back in an earlier chapter.

> A false balance is an abomination to the LORD, but a just weight is his delight. (Proverbs 11:1)

Weights were used for measuring out products such as grain and spices, and a merchant could cheat his customers by having dishonest weights. The Mosaic Law specifically condemned such dishonest business practices.

> You shall do no wrong in judgment, in measures of length or weight or quantity. You shall have just balances, just weights, a just ephah, and a just hin: I am the LORD your God, who brought you out of the land of Egypt. (Leviticus 19:35–36)

Moses went into more detail about this corrupt practice in the book of Deuteronomy.

> You shall not have in your bag two kinds of weights, a large and a small. You shall not have in your house two kinds of measures, a large and a small. A full and fair weight you shall

have, a full and fair measure you shall have, that your days may be long in the land that the LORD your God is giving you. For all who do such things, all who act dishonestly, are an abomination to the LORD your God. (Deuteronomy 25:13–16)

It is interesting to note the motivation that Moses gave in his condemnation of this practice. The merchants of Israel were to be just in their business dealings because their God was just. This proverb makes the same connection by saying that the balance and scales belong to the LORD.

20:9 – "Who can say, "I have made my
heart pure; I am clean from my sin"?"

This proverb addresses the matter of honesty from the perspective of the individual being honest with himself. Underlining the proverbs is the understanding that human beings have a sin nature, which is reflected in the second line of this proverb. Because of sin, our motives are often questionable and our ability to be honest with ourselves is often compromised. The matter of a pure heart was a frequent topic of discussion between Job and his three friends.

Can mortal man be in the right before God? Can a man be pure before his Maker? (Job 4:17)

While their rhetorical questions were accurate in general, they were wrong about Job hiding secret sins. Getting back to our proverb, even though it is impossible to live a sinless life, it is possible to address the sin in our lives, and this is accomplished by confession and communion. Confession is reflected in the psalmist's prayer.

Have mercy on me, O God, according to your steadfast love; according to your abundant mercy blot out my transgressions. Wash me thoroughly from my iniquity, and cleanse me from my sin! (Psalm 51:1–2)

And communion is found in spending meaningful time in God's Word.

How can a young man keep his way pure? By guarding it according to your word. (Psalm 119:9)

20:14 – "Bad, bad," says the buyer, but
when he goes away, then he boasts."

This proverb returns to the matter of honesty in a business transaction. It depicts a buyer complaining about the quality of an item as he negotiates over the price, but once the deal is struck, he goes home with his purchase and he brags about the deal he got. This proverb brought to my mind my painful initiation into the art of negotiating a price. I was in Israel in 1990 on a three-week study trip with my two brothers and we stopped at a shop one night in Jerusalem as I wanted to buy a souvenir for my wife. The price on the plate was more than I was willing to pay, so I politely returned the plate and tried to walk out of the store. The shopkeeper asked me what I was willing to pay, and he loudly protested when I stated my price. He stood in my way and would not let me leave his store, demanding I negotiate with him. We finally settled on a price that was closer to my original price, but I'm sure he won the competition.

The Wicked

17:4 – "An evildoer listens to wicked lips, and
a liar gives ear to a mischievous tongue."

The book of Proverbs frequently talks about two broad groups of people: the righteous and the wicked. And this series of proverbs addresses the behavior of the wicked and the consequences of that behavior. There are two types of wicked people in this proverb: the one who speaks evil words, and the one who gives the evil speaker an eager audience. As we have seen throughout the collection, evil speech comes in many forms, namely, slander, gossip, lies, character assassination, immoral talk, to name a few. And while the sage condemned those individuals who engage in this evil talk, he also condemned those who find such talk appealing. Take gossip as an example. If people refused to listen to gossip, it would die out. Most people who engage in evil talk will stop talking if they are rebuked.

17:13 – "If anyone returns evil for good,
evil will not depart from his house."

While it is not always wise to quantify wickedness, this proverb states that it is particularly wicked for an individual to do something evil to another person who has shown them a kindness. So, while the apostle Paul wrote, "Repay no one evil for evil" (Romans 12:17), the sage took it a step further when he condemned returning evil for good. A person this evil would bring a curse on his own family. The punishment could be handed out either by God directly, or through other human beings who were repulsed by this dastardly behavior.

> 20:30 – *"Blows that wound cleanse away evil;*
> *strokes make clean the innermost parts."*

In our private moments, every one of us can think of an arrogant individual who would benefit from a good beating. The cleansing cure for wickedness is physical punishment to truly drive the lesson home. While the fool will not learn from a beating, other people will benefit from physical pain. My father believed in loving physical punishment and I quickly learned to change my behavior if I wanted to avoid the pain of a spanking. Some people only require a verbal rebuke to change their ways, but most of us need to feel some physical pain to truly learn the lesson that wicked behavior is offensive to a holy God.

> 21:18 – *"The wicked is a ransom for the*
> *righteous, and the traitor for the upright."*

This proverb may be a word of encouragement to the righteous who is currently suffering at the hands of the wicked and is questioning God's justice. Or, it may be a word of warning to the individual who is contemplating a wicked action. Either way, the sage wants people to know that crime does not pay. Another proverb says much the same thing.

> Thorns and snares are in the way of the crooked; whoever
> guards his soul will keep far from them. (Proverbs 22:5)

> 21:29 – *"A wicked man puts on a bold face,*
> *but the upright gives thought to his ways."*

This proverb contrasts the outward expression of a wicked man, with the inward thoughts of the righteous person. Because appearances can be deceiving, don't be misled by the confidence that a wicked person manifests to others. The confidence may be a means to intimidate others or to conceal his or her own insecurities. In the end, the righteous person who has carefully considered the direction of life will succeed, and the wicked person, though bold, will fail.

The Family

17:6 – "Grandchildren are the crown of the aged,
and the glory of children is their fathers."

This proverb celebrates the importance the family played in the culture of ancient Israel. We see this importance in the many genealogies recorded in the Bible (Genesis 10, 1 Chronicles 1). We also see it in the sadness when a woman was barren (1 Samuel 1). Elderly grandparents would look at their grandchildren with delight because they had lived long enough to see the next generation and they knew the family name would carry on. And children would look at their fathers with respect, knowing he was the leader of the family. While it is natural to impose my fondness for my grandchildren on this Oriental culture, that was not always the case. There are enough accounts in the Old Testament where fathers viewed their children as a necessary function for survival in a hostile environment. For example, daughters were given in marriage without any thought to their feelings or welfare (Genesis 31:14–16).

20:11 – "Even a child makes himself known by his
acts, by whether his conduct is pure and upright."

This proverb takes up a familiar topic of righteous living by looking at the life of a child. The sage believed that one's character was on display very early on in life, and that a child would reveal his or her character, or lack thereof, early on in life. That observation proved true in the lives of my children when they were young as I observed their character traits which are on display now that they are adults.

20:20 – "If one curses his father or his mother,
his lamp will be put out in utter darkness."

The fifth commandment of the Mosaic Law demanded that children show respect to their parents.

> Honor your father and your mother, that your days may be long in the land that the LORD your God is giving you. (Exodus 20:12)

And in cases of extreme disrespect, the law required the death penalty (Exodus 21:17). This proverb reflects the importance of parental respect for a stable society.

> *20:29 – "The glory of young men is their strength,*
> *but the splendor of old men is their gray hair."*

While most cultures celebrate the strength and stamina of youth, the culture of ancient Israel celebrated old age and the outward signs of a long life. This proverb viewed gray hair, not as an embarrassment, but as a sign of wisdom that had been gained throughout a long and meaningful life. While the youth have their energy, the aged have their wisdom and the experience that can only be gained through time.

> *22:6 – "Train up a child in the way he should go;*
> *even when he is old he will not depart from it."*

This proverb may be the best-known, but most misused saying in the collection. Because proverbs are not promises, but general observations and principles, this proverb on child rearing needs to be understood according to the hermeneutical principles of proverbs. The first line places the requirement on the parents to engage in the training of a child through instruction, correction, discipline, and the setting of a godly example. It requires the parents to be consistent in the training and to begin at an early age. The sin nature of the child is assumed in the book of Proverbs. And, according to the book, there are only two courses available to the child, namely, the way of wisdom, and the way of foolishness. If the parents carry out their obligation to train their child, and all things being equal, the child is likely to continue in the way of wisdom as he grows into adulthood.

Bribery

17:8 – "A bribe is like a magic stone in the eyes of the one who gives it; wherever he turns he prospers."

This proverb speaks of the giving of a gift and its guarantee of success, without the sage making a moral judgment on the process. While the Mosaic Law clearly condemned the practice of giving bribes for the purpose of subverting justice (Exodus 23:8), the culture of the Middle East practiced the art of gift-giving to ensure success in various matters. For example, Abraham's servant brought gifts with him when he traveled to Mesopotamia to find a wife for the patriarch's son, Isaac (Genesis 24:10). Another patriarch, Jacob, instructed his sons to bring a gift for the ruler in Egypt on their second journey to buy food during the famine (Genesis 43:11). The sage humorously likened the gift to a magic stone, and the magic was seen in the stone's ability to open doors and make people agreeable to the gift-giver's proposal.

17:23 – "The wicked accepts a bribe in secret to pervert the ways of justice."

While the previous proverb spoke about the matter of gift-giving without judgment, this proverb clearly condemned bribery if it was intended to pervert justice. This saying is in agreement with the Mosaic Law.

> And you shall take no bribe, for a bribe blinds the clear-sighted and subverts the cause of those who are in the right. (Exodus 23:8)

For example, the nation of Israel asked Samuel to give them a king like the surrounding nations, in part, because the prophet's sons accepted bribes, which perverted justice during the period of the Judges (1 Samuel 8:3). The psalmist also included the sin of trying to buy influence with the giving of a bribe in his question and answer about the individual who has the right to come into God's presence.

> Who does not put out his money at interest and does not take a bribe against the innocent. He who does these things shall never be moved. (Psalm 15:5)

We are to be people who handle money with integrity. We are to help others in need without benefitting ourselves, and we are not to change our ethics for financial gain. If we have these qualities in our lives, we will firmly stand.

> *18:16 – "A man's gift makes room for him*
> *and brings him before the great."*

This proverb returns to the practice of gift-giving with a non-judgmental observation about the effectiveness of giving an appropriate gift. The right gift can open doors and give an individual influence with powerful people. A biblical illustration of this practice is seen in the narrative of Saul, the son of Kish, before he became king over Israel. While on a journey to find his father's missing donkeys, Saul and his servant came to the village of Ramah where the prophet Samuel lived. Hoping to receive some direction for his journey, the servant suggested that the young man give the prophet the remaining silver as a present (1 Samuel 9:7–8). A related proverb says much the same thing by looking at the practice of gift-giving from both perspectives.

> Many seek the favor of a generous man, and everyone is a
> friend to a man who gives gifts. (Proverbs 19:6)

While this practice can easily become corrupted, it is an accurate assessment of human nature.

> *21:14 – " A gift in secret averts anger, and*
> *a concealed bribe, strong wrath."*

This proverb looks at the practice of gift-giving, not from the motive of trying to gain favor with a powerful person, but from the purpose of reducing hostility. It might be a husband who is trying to calm his irritated wife. Abigail was commended for giving David a gift to assuage his wrath (1 Samuel 25).

Injustice

17:15 – "He who justifies the wicked and
he who condemns the righteous are both
alike an abomination to the LORD.*"*

Earlier in the book we looked at a list of human behaviors that God finds particularly offensive to His holy nature (6:16–19), and injustice is another sin to add to the list. When God established the Mosaic Covenant, He told the nation to be holy, because He was holy (Leviticus 19:2). God promised to reward righteousness and to punish wickedness. So, when individuals did the opposite, that is, reward wickedness and punish righteousness, that reversal was offensive to God's holy nature. This miscarriage of justice was a common complaint of the prophets during the latter days of the nation before God sent His people into exile.

So the law is paralyzed, and justice never goes forth. For the wicked surround the righteous; so justice goes forth perverted (Habakkuk 1:7)

17:26 – "To impose a fine on a righteous man is not
good, nor to strike the noble for their uprightness."

This proverb identifies two forms of punishment that a corrupt legal system could use to intimidate the righteous. The righteous could be hurt financially and forced to pay a fine, or they could be intimidated physically with corporeal punishment. The apostle Paul experienced a physical beating in Philippi and a financial fine in Thessalonica for preaching the Gospel on the second missionary journey (Acts 16–17).

18:5 – "It is not good to be partial to the wicked
or to deprive the righteous of justice."

Whether the injustice takes place in a private relationship, or whether it takes place in a public court of law, the sage condemns the practice of partiality when the wicked are favored and when the righteous are deprived of justice. The expression "to be partial" literally reads in Hebrew "to lift up the face." The modern symbol of Lady Justice with a blindfold illustrates the form of justice that God wants.

*20:22 – "Do not say, "I will repay evil"; wait
for the LORD, and he will deliver you."*

When injustice takes place, this proverb advocates patience on the part of the offended, and a willingness to trust God to right the wrong. Instead of the eye for an eye, the spiritually wise individual will trust in God's form of justice and in His timing of retribution. The apostle Paul taught that revenge is wrong for the believer.

> Beloved, never avenge yourselves, but leave it to the wrath of God, for it is written, "Vengeance is mine, I will repay, says the Lord." To the contrary, "if your enemy is hungry, feed him; if he is thirsty, give him something to drink; for by so doing you will heap burning coals on his head." (Romans 12:19–20)

*21:3 – "To do righteousness and justice is more
acceptable to the LORD than sacrifice."*

The theme of this proverb is featured in the narrative of King Saul and his failure to obey God's instructions to devote the nation of Amalek to destruction. Having failed his earlier tests as Israel's first king, the LORD now sent the prophet Samuel to deliver to Saul his greatest challenge to see if he would completely obey the LORD. Samuel instructed Saul to take his army and to go down to the southern edge of the country into the Negev to attack a group of people known as the Amalekites. Samuel reminded Saul of the history of hostility that existed between the Israelites and their distant relatives the Amalekites. 500 years earlier, on the Exodus out of Egypt, the Amalekites had attacked this nation of former slaves in an attempt to keep them from entering the Promised Land (Exodus 17). The seriousness of their offense demanded a serious response and now was the time to respond. God had placed this nation under the ban which required complete destruction of the nation, men, women, and children, along with the wholesale slaughter of their animals. When Saul spared the king and the best of the animals, an angry Samuel rebuked the king.

> Has the LORD as great delight in burnt offerings and sacrifices, as in obeying the voice of the LORD? Behold, to obey is better than sacrifice, and to listen than the fat of rams. (1 Samuel 15:22)

This was a common criticism of the prophets (Isaiah 1:11–17; Micah 6:6–8).

> *22:8 – "Whoever sows injustice will reap*
> *calamity, and the rod of his fury will fail."*

This proverb agrees with the biblical principle that an individual reaps what one sows (Galatians 6:7), and puts it in the context of injustice. The person who practices injustice will have his or her power to do so destroyed.

Friendship

> *17:17 – "A friend loves at all times, and*
> *a brother is born for adversity."*

This proverb defines the difference between a genuine friendship and a casual acquaintance. A genuine friendship is demonstrated by affection and loyalty in the good times and in the bad. The bad times are characterized as "adversity" when the depth of the friendship is put to the test. The second line of the saying is synonymous parallelism, so the brother is not necessarily a blood relative. The narrative of David and Jonathan comes to mind with this proverb. After David killed the Philistine champion Goliath, the king's son Jonathan developed a close friendship with him.

> As soon as he had finished speaking to Saul, the soul of Jonathan was knit to the soul of David, and Jonathan loved him as his own soul. (1 Samuel 18:1)

After Saul grew paranoid of David's popularity within the nation, and after he attempted to kill David several times, Jonathan, the king's son and heir to the throne, risked his life to protect his friend. After Saul and Jonathan were killed by the Philistines, David lamented his friend's death.

> I am distressed for you, my brother Jonathan; very pleasant have you been to me; your love to me was extraordinary, surpassing the love of women. (2 Samuel 1:26)

18:1 – "Whoever isolates himself seeks his own
desire; he breaks out against all sound judgment."

This proverb places the blame for the lack of friends on the individual who does not make the effort to have friends. This antisocial individual chooses not to have friends because he or she lives an isolated and selfish life. In order to have friends, one must be friendly and be willing to invest in others. A selfish individual is not willing to make that kind of effort, and even though it is unreasonable, he or she will do so to their own harm.

18:24 – "A man of many companions may come to ruin,
but there is a friend who sticks closer than a brother."

This proverb continues the contrast between the casual acquaintance and the intimate friend. It is better to have one genuine friend than to have many casual companions. But the distinction between the companion and the friend will not be understood until the friendship is put to the test. And when the need for a genuine friend is the greatest, the many companions will not be available. And when the companions fail to be friends, the individual in need will be devastated. Casual friends are always available for the good times, but trying times reveal their unreliability. A genuine friend will remain loyal through thick and thin. This proverb reminds me of a young couple that I had led to Christ and then discipled. They were going to move from their third story apartment over a downtown store to a third story apartment in a large house. When I asked if they needed help moving, they accepted my offer but assured me that a group of friends had promised to help as well. But on the day of the move, it was raining and none of their friends materialized. I was the only friend to show up to help that day and the move was exhausting.

20:6 – "Many a man proclaims his own steadfast
love, but a faithful man who can find?"

This proverb warns that talk is cheap when it comes to genuine friendship. When the friendship is not being tested by adversity, it is easy to proclaim one's loyalty. But when a trial puts the relationship to the test, the faithful friend will prove to be a rare commodity. The Old Testament character Job found that out the painful way when his time of testing came (Job 2:11–13). The apostle Paul talked about being abandoned by his friends when he was put on trial for his faith.

At my first defense no one came to stand by me, but all deserted me. May it not be charged against them. (2 Timothy 4:16)

Deep Waters

18:4 – "The words of a man's mouth are deep waters;
the fountain of wisdom is a bubbling brook."

There are two ways to understand this proverb. If the sage was using synthetic parallelism, the second line of the saying further develops the thought of the first line. If that is the case, the sage was extolling the profound source of wisdom that comes from wise counselors. The "deep waters" would express the large reservoir of wisdom that is available to the individual who wants to learn and become wise. And the wise sayings of the sages are profound, thought-provoking, and life-giving. The water metaphor continues in the second line with the bubbling brook that pictures the steady stream of wisdom that comes to the surface when someone surrounds himself with wise counselors.

The second way to understand the proverb is to see the sage using antithetic parallelism in the second line. If this interpretation is correct, the sage was issuing a warning to carefully listen to what others were actually saying. The "deep waters" then tell us to look beneath the surface of what an individual says to find out the true motives. If this is the case, the sage was contrasting the deceptive words of so-called sages with the honest advice that flows from the mouths of wise counselors. This interpretation reminds me of an encounter I experienced as a young pastor. We had a new family visit our church on a Sunday morning, and after the service they stayed for a long time to visit. The husband was excessive in his praise of the sermon I had delivered that morning. His compliments raised my suspicions (I know I'm not that good!), and I made a call that afternoon to their previous pastor. The pastor warned me that this family had abused the generosity of his church. Armed with this information, I was not surprised when the family returned for the evening service and asked to meet with me and the deacons. When they asked for some financial assistance, I informed them that I had talked to their previous pastor and that he had warned me not to get involved with them.

20:5 – "The purpose in a man's heart is like deep
water, but a man of understanding will draw it out."

This proverb uses the imagery of deep water to describe the challenges of understanding the motives of other people. When you get to know an individual, you can listen to their words and watch the expressions on their face, but it takes a while to discern their true motives. I have been going to the same lake in Ontario, Canada for the past twelve years with a group of men from my church. The lake is large and deep, but thanks to sonar technology, we are able to look beneath the surface to discern the contours on the bottom of the lake to find the fish. While there is no technology to look beneath the surface of a person's heart, wisdom and understanding will draw out their true motives.

22:14 – "The mouth of forbidden women is a deep pit;
he with whom the LORD is angry will fall into it."

This proverb takes us back to the opening addresses of the father to his son and his warnings about the deceptive and immoral woman (2:16–19; 5:1–14; 6:20–35). The father goes into greater detail in the seventh chapter.

> With much seductive speech she persuades him; with her smooth talk she compels him. All at once he follows her, as an ox goes to the slaughter, or as a stag is caught fast till an arrow pierces its liver; as a bird rushes into a snare; he does not know that it will cost him his life. (Proverbs 7:21–23)

This immoral woman knows how to flatter with her words, and her mouth is accurately described as a "deep pit." The individual with whom God is angry is the man who does not care about morality. God will use the immoral woman as His form of divine judgment on the adulterous man.

Disputes

18:17 – "The one who states his case first seems
right, until the other comes and examines him."

This proverb warns against making hasty judgments without asking critical questions. The sage teaches that there are always two sides to a story, and both sides need to be heard to get a fair hearing. The first individual to present his or her case will often sound convincing, and if the individual is not questioned, the judge will rule in his or her favor. But the wise judge will always allow the other party to present his or her version of events and to call into question the accuracy of the first presenter. Only when both parties have presented their case can the judge weigh the evidence, ask the critical questions, and render a fair verdict. There is a biblical illustration of this proverb from the narrative of Solomon's life in 1 Kings 3. Two prostitutes came into his throne room with a conflict over a male baby. The two women lived together and both women had given birth to a baby within three days of one another. Both women claimed to be the mother of the living baby, and both blamed the other woman for smothering the dead baby in her sleep. In this instance, it was the first presenter who was right, but Solomon needed to hear both women present their evidence. Using the great wisdom with which God had endowed him, Solomon was able to correctly determine the genuine mother by using a clever ploy.

18:18 – "The lot puts an end to quarrels and decides between powerful contenders."

This proverb on disputes can only be understood in the context of a previous proverb that describes an ancient way of divining God's will.

> The lot is cast into the lap, but its every decision is from the LORD. (Proverbs 16:33)

When God established the nation of Israel, he gave the high priest two items called the Urim and the Thummim that were to be placed in his breastpiece to be used in divining God's will for the nation.

> And in the breastpiece of judgment you shall put the Urim and the Thummim, and they shall be on Aaron's heart, when he goes in before the LORD. Thus Aaron shall bear the judgment of the people of Israel on his heart before the LORD regularly. (Exodus 28:33)

Scholars believe these two items were stones or sticks that were black and white and allowed people to divine God's will by asking yes and no questions. Joshua 7:14–18 provides a biblical illustration of this process. This proverb states that even when two influential individuals are involved in a conflict, with strong evidence to favor their side, when God is consulted and when He renders a verdict, the dispute is easily solved.

> *18:19 – "A brother offended is more unyielding than a
> strong city, and quarreling is like the bars of a castle."*

This proverb warns that disputes that erupt between good friends and close relatives can degenerate into deep-seated conflicts where grudges are harbored for years. The sage likens an offended brother to a walled city that cannot be scaled. And that quarreling between friends can erect barriers that never come down. I have seen this proverb play out in families and in church congregations. The apostle Paul wrote about this problem in the church at Corinth and offered the following advice because he understood the damage that can ruin a church.

> But brother goes to law against brother, and that before
> unbelievers? To have lawsuits at all with one another is
> already a defeat for you. Why not rather suffer wrong? Why
> not rather be defrauded? (1 Corinthians 6:6–7)

I was once asked to arbitrate a family conflict for a family outside of my church. The dispute involved the repayment of money that was borrowed from elderly parents. When the other siblings confronted the guilty party, the animosity that was expressed back and forth was deep-seated, and the issue was never resolved.

The Fool

> *19:3 – "When a man's folly brings his way to
> ruin, his heart rages against the Lord."*

This proverb is an observation on fallen humanity, also known as human depravity. People like to have someone else to blame for their problems, and the fool is a prime example. The first line of the saying states that the misery is caused by the individual's foolish decisions, and yet the fool refuses to accept personal responsibility. The book of Proverbs teaches that if the fool would accept personal responsibility, he or she could learn from the mistakes and make progress in life. The tendency to blame God for one's mistakes is as old as creation. When

Adam and Eve disobeyed God in the garden of Eden and fell into sin, when God questioned Adam, the first man found someone else to blame.

> "Who told you that you were naked? Have you eaten of the tree of which I commanded you not to eat?" The man said, "The woman whom you gave to be with me, she gave me fruit of the tree, and I ate." (Genesis 3:11–12)

In one reply, Adam first blamed God for giving him Eve, and then he blamed his wife for his mistake. This tendency to blame God for the misery that comes from making foolish choices is found throughout scripture and is still practiced today.

> *19:10 – "It is not fitting for a fool to live in luxury,*
> *much less for a slave to rule over princes."*

In this proverb the sage describes two unbearable situations. It bothered the sage to see a fool live in luxury, where vast wealth allowed a life of extravagance even though foolish choices were made with the money. This condition was one of the things that bothered the psalmist in Psalm 73 as he contemplated the prosperous fool.

> Their eyes swell out through fatness; their hearts overflow with follies" (Psalm 73:7)

I had two employers that fit this description when I went to seminary. I got a job detailing used cars when I went to school in Minneapolis and the business was owned by two young men who enjoyed their fathers' wealth. The two owners were unethical in their business practices in how they dealt with their customers and how they treated their employees. But their fathers' money kept their business afloat. Getting back to the second line of the proverb, the only thing worse than a rich fool was a slave who rose to power, for it would likely lead to abuse. The wisdom writer known as the Preacher commented on the same two unbearable situations.

> There is an evil that I have seen under the sun, as it were an error proceeding from the ruler: folly is set in many high places, and the rich sit in a low place. I have seen slaves

on horses, and princes walking on the ground like slaves. (Ecclesiastes 10:5–7)

> *20:1 – "Wine is a mocker, strong drink a brawler,*
> *and whoever is led astray by it is not wise."*

This proverb teaches that alcoholic beverages and foolish behavior are a dangerous combination. Wine, made from grapes, and strong drink, made from grains, were common beverages in the Old Testament. In the context of talking about making a pilgrimage to Jerusalem, Moses told the nation of Israel about to enter the land of Canaan.

> Spend the money for whatever you desire—oxen or sheep or wine or strong drink, whatever your appetite craves. And you shall eat there before the LORD your God and rejoice, you and your household. (Deuteronomy 28:7)

So, while the beverages were not forbidden, intoxication was condemned in the covenant community. The individual who chooses to become intoxicated is making a foolish decision that will result in embarrassing and aggressive behavior where the senses are no longer in control. I was a senior in high school when I saw my classmates exhibit such foolish behavior on the way home from a basketball game. After a loss at the state tournament, the alcohol began to flow on the school bus and young people lost control of their inhibitions and engaged in shocking behavior.

Royal Proverbs

> *19:12 – "A king's wrath is like the growling of a*
> *lion, but his favor is like dew on the grass."*

A sovereign ruler in the ancient world held the power of life and death over his subjects, and so the sage used this proverb to teach his students to avoid the king's wrath and to curry his favor. He used two vivid similes to demonstrate the opposing emotional states of the king. If the king was angry at one of his subjects, it was likened to the terror that one would feel if they heard the unmistakable sound of a lion's growl. If an individual was walking through the Judean countryside and heard the growling of a lion, he knew he was in grave danger. But the king's favor was likened to the refreshing and life-giving qualities of the dew that fell overnight on the land of Canaan. In this arid climate, dew played an important part in the water supply of Palestine. In areas where the skies are normally clear in the summer and the air cools at night, heavy dews are produced wherever moisture is present in the atmosphere. A later proverb made the same observation by solely focusing on the king's anger.

> The terror of a king is like the growling of a lion; whoever provokes him to anger forfeits his life. (Proverbs 20:2)

The narrative of Daniel's life offers examples of both emotional states of a sovereign. With Nebuchadnezzar, Daniel and the other wisemen of Babylon were in danger of losing their lives when the king's dream could not be interpreted (2:12–13). But when God enabled Daniel to reveal the dream, he was promoted (2:46–49).

20:8 – "A king who sits on the throne of judgment winnows all evil with his eyes."

The king who sat on Israel's throne was expected to carry out God's justice, and this proverb explained how the justice system was supposed to function. The king was supposed to exercise discernment as he heard the cases and evaluated the merits of the defendants. And when he determined the guilty party, he was supposed to hand out a verdict that was intended to punish the wicked and remove it from his realm. The verb "to winnow" comes from the agricultural world where the farmer would separate the chaff from the grain. Another proverb in this chapter makes a similar observation.

> A wise king winnows the wicked and drives the wheel over them. (Proverbs 20:26)

20:28 – "Steadfast love and faithfulness preserve the king, and by steadfast love his throne is upheld."

When God established the covenant with David, He promised He would never remove His steadfast love from the Davidic house and that his kingdom would be firmly established (2 Samuel 7:15–16). The divine attributes of steadfast love and faithfulness, or truth, were to characterize the king who sat on the throne of Israel. If the king manifested these qualities in his administration, his throne would be established and stability would characterize his reign. A related proverb states that if an individual within the kingdom also possesses these qualities, he would become a friend of the king.

> He who loves purity of heart, and whose speech is gracious,
> will have the king as his friend. (Proverbs 22:11)

> *21:1 – "The king's heart is a stream of water in the*
> *hand of the LORD; he turns it wherever he will."*

This proverb also speaks of the king, but in the context of the sovereignty of the LORD. While the ancient king was a sovereign ruler, the sage knew that the sovereignty of the LORD trumped the human sovereign. And, he likened the decisions of the king to a farmer who channeled the water to go where he wanted it to reach his crops. Even pagan rulers such as the Babylonian Nebuchadnezzar (Jeremiah 25:9) and the Persian Cyrus (Isaiah 45:1) made decisions that were determined by the sovereignty of God.

An Introduction to the 30 Sayings (22:17–21)

> ¹⁷ Incline your ear, and hear the words of the wise,
> and apply your heart to my knowledge,
> ¹⁸ for it will be pleasant if you keep them within you,
> if all of them are ready on your lips.
> ¹⁹ That your trust may be in the LORD,
> I have made them known to you today, even to you.
> ²⁰ Have I not written for you thirty sayings
> of counsel and knowledge,
> ²¹ to make you know what is right and true,
> that you may give a true answer to those who sent you?

Another collection of the sayings of the wise includes the material from 22:17–24:22, with another brief section of sayings that runs from 24:23–34. In this introduction to the thirty sayings of the sage, the author lists three incentives for his readers to carefully heed the words of the wise. Before he gets to his incentives, he employs some familiar expressions that are found throughout the book of Proverbs. The expression "incline your ear" (4:20; 5:1) conjures up the image of a person leaning in to the speaker to carefully hear every word that is spoken. Several years ago, my wife and I had the opportunity to take a study trip to the land of Israel with a highly respected guide, Dr. Doug Bookman of Shepherd's Theological Seminary in Cary, North Carolina. In order to take advantage of the educational opportunity to learn about Bible geography, we remained as close as we could to our guide to hear all of the information he was dispensing as we traveled from site to site. While other members from the group explored a site on their own, if our guide was walking and talking, we were on his heels. In addition to hearing "the words of the wise," the serious student will be careful to apply this knowledge to life. And, the changed behavior will be a reflection of the heart condition.

The first incentive for heeding the advice of the sage is a practical or esthetical (this adjective is characterized by an appreciation of beauty or good taste) one in that it will lead to a pleasant life. As the book of Proverbs has demonstrated repeatedly, life can be very unpleasant for the fool who behaves in a stubborn and foolish manner (5:1–14). But when the advice of the wise is carefully heeded, then internalized, and finally followed, mistakes are avoided and the individual responds favorably with proper behavior and words. When the advice has been internalized ("you keep them within you"), then the proper words will flow from the individual's lips ("all of them are ready on your lips").

The second incentive to follow the wise counsel of others is a theological one in that it will deepen an individual's trust "in the LORD." The book of Proverbs is not merely a collection of wise sayings that are practical in nature. These sayings are revelations from God so that a person's relationship with God is deepened. It is important to remember the theme of the book of Proverbs.

> The fear of the LORD is the beginning of knowledge; fools
> despise wisdom and instruction. (Proverbs 1:7)

While many of the sayings emphasize human relationships, the ultimate relationship is between the individual and the Creator. When the advice is followed, and the individual experiences God's blessing, the trust in God will grow deeper.

The third incentive to listen to the right advice is an intellectual one in that it will help the individual to be more discerning when it comes to right and wrong. Choosing between right and wrong can be confusing to the simple, so if the naïve person listens to the right advice, he or she will make the right choices. And when making right choices becomes a habit, the individual can become a wise adviser to others.

Don't Exploit the Poor (22:22–23)

²² Do not rob the poor, because he is poor, or crush the afflicted at the gate,
²³ for the Lord will plead their cause and rob of life those who rob them.

In the Mosaic Law, God frequently addressed the treatment of the poor within the covenant community.

> You shall not oppress a hired worker who is poor and needy, whether he is one of your brothers or one of the sojourners who are in your land within your towns. You shall give him his wages on the same day, before the sun sets (for he is poor and counts on it), lest he cry against you to the Lord, and you be guilty of sin. (Deuteronomy 24:14–15)

In any culture, the poor are often exploited simply because they are poor and lack the resources to defend themselves legally. The reference "at the gate" is where legal disputes were settled in Israeli society (Ruth 4:1–12). Like the incentive given in the Mosaic Law concerning God's omniscience in human affairs, the sage reminds his readers that God is the Protector of the poor whom He has made (Proverbs 17:5) and He notices how the vulnerable are treated.

Don't Associate with the Angry Man (22:24–25)

²⁴ Make no friendship with a man given to
anger, nor go with a wrathful man,
²⁵ lest you learn his ways and entangle yourself in a snare.

In the context of debating believers who were denying the bodily resurrection, the apostle Paul advised, "Do not be deceived: "Bad company ruins good morals" (1 Corinthians 15:33). This was true for the apostle theologically, and it was true for the sage socially. The sage agreed with this sentiment for he knew that the bad behavior of the people we associate with will eventually become our bad behavior. One of the opening addresses of the book warned about choosing bad companions because of the disastrous consequences (1:8–19). If one becomes friends with a hot-tempered person, he or she will eventually get in hot water as well. It is human nature to adopt the behavior of the people with whom we spend time.

Don't Make Rash Vows (22:26–27)

²⁶ Be not one of those who give pledges, who put up security for debts.
    ²⁷ If you have nothing with which to pay, why
        should your bed be taken from under you?

While generosity is encouraged in wisdom literature, the sage warns against making rash vows when it comes to the bad debts of other people (see Proverbs 6:1–5). This warning is heightened when the individual who is making the vow lacks the financial resources to meet the obligation. The fool could lose everything, including his or her bed, which is equivalent to our saying of losing one's shirt.

Don't Steal from Others (22:28)

²⁸ Do not move the ancient landmark that your fathers have set.

When the land of Canaan was handed out to the tribes of Israel, beginning in Joshua 15, boundaries markers that consisted of a pile of rocks were used to designate the property lines among the tribes and within the clans. The inheritances were sacred (1 Kings 21:3) and considered permanent. The sage is warning against the sin of stealing by the simple task of moving a boundary marker.

> You shall not move your neighbor's landmark, which the
> men of old have set, in the inheritance that you will hold in
> the land that the LORD your God is giving you to possess.
> (Deuteronomy 19:14)

Don't Be Lazy (22:29)

²⁹ Do you see a man skillful in his work?
He will stand before kings; he will not stand before obscure men.

The sage tells his readers to look around and note the industrious individual, for he is someone worthy of emulation. By encouraging these observations, he is exhorting people to work hard at developing their skills, with the promise that such diligence generally is rewarded with promotion. The lazy and undisciplined individual will never get ahead in life, but hard work is recognized and rewarded by people in authority. Joseph in Egypt is a biblical example of this proverb. Joseph served diligently in each capacity, and because of his work ethic, he eventually stood before Pharaoh and was promoted to leadership.

Don't Eat Too Much (23:1–3)

¹ When you sit down to eat with a ruler, observe
carefully what is before you,
² and put a knife to your throat if you are given to appetite.
³ Do not desire his delicacies, for they are deceptive food.

This saying reflects the culture of ancient Israel where the king was a sovereign ruler who would surround himself with courtiers to serve him. The sage warns individuals who have been invited to the king's feast to mind their manners when it comes to the meal. The feast and all the royal delicacies are actually a test to see how the individual conducts himself in the court. Like Haman, who became excited because he had been invited to Esther's private feast, little did he know the fatal outcome of that meal (Esther 5). The vivid expression to "put a knife to your throat" tells the dinner guest to demonstrate self-control before the king, for it he does not, with his ravenous appetite he will cut his own throat.

Don't Accumulate Wealth (23:4–5)

4 Do not toil to acquire wealth; be discerning enough to desist.
5 When your eyes light on it, it is gone,
for suddenly it sprouts wings, flying like an eagle toward heaven.

This saying is one of the many memorable warnings in scripture concerning the fleeting nature of riches. While the sage does encourage hard work to get ahead in life (22:29), this saying addresses the motivation when it comes to money. Money is useful when it is properly invested in meeting the physical needs of one's family, or in showing compassion for the poor. But if the goal is merely to accumulate wealth, the sage warns that money can be easily lost. Jesus gave a similar warning at the end of the parable of the rich fool who merely wanted to accumulate money.

> But God said to him, 'Fool! This night your soul is required of you, and the things you have prepared, whose will they be?' So is the one who lays up treasure for himself and is not rich toward God. (Luke 12:20–21)

Paul offered Timothy similar advice about money.

> But godliness with contentment is great gain, for we brought nothing into the world, and we cannot take anything out of the world. But if we have food and clothing, with these we will be content. But those who desire to be rich fall into temptation, into a snare, into many senseless and harmful desires that plunge people into ruin and destruction. For the love of money is a root of all kinds of evils. It is through this craving that some have wandered away from the faith and pierced themselves with many pangs. (1 Timothy 6:6–10)

Don't R.S.V.P. (23:6–8)

⁶ Do not eat the bread of a man who is stingy; do not desire his delicacies,
⁷ for he is like one who is inwardly calculating.
"Eat and drink!" he says to you, but his heart is not with you.
⁸ You will vomit up the morsels that you have
eaten, and waste your pleasant words.

In an earlier proverb the sage warned about eating the delicacies of the king, for it was actually a test to examine one's behavior in the presence of power and wealth (23:1-3). This saying now warns about accepting a dinner invitation from a stingy person, which, literally, is a person with an "evil eye." While the food may appear to taste good, the evening will turn out to be an unpleasant experience once the invited guest realizes the motive behind the invitation. While the food appears to be delicious, because the host is stingy, it will not taste good. And, the attempt at pleasant conversation will prove to be a waste of time when the host reveals his or her true character.

Don't Talk to Fools (23:9)

⁹ Do not speak in the hearing of a fool,
for he will despise the good sense of your words.

While the large collection of proverbs was written with the fool in mind (1:20–33), the sage realizes that giving advice to a confirmed fool is a waste of time. One of the chief characteristics of a fool is that he or she thinks he or she is smarter than everyone else.

A fool takes no pleasure in understanding, but only in expressing his opinion. (Proverbs 18:2)

While the advice is characterized as "good sense," the fool considers the guidance to be nonsense. In the context of the message of the kingdom, Jesus gave a similar word of advice to his disciples.

Do not give dogs what is holy, and do not throw your pearls before pigs, lest they trample them underfoot and turn to attack you. (Matthew 7:6)

Don't Rob the Poor (23:10–11)

¹⁰ Do not move an ancient landmark or enter the fields of the fatherless,
¹¹ for their Redeemer is strong; he will plead their cause against you.

We already examined the warning against stealing when the sage used the expression of moving an ancient landmark in an earlier proverb (22:28). Now, the warning is repeated in the context of social justice, as the sage addresses how an individual treats the most vulnerable neighbors. The land of an orphan, and its produce, are not to be stolen because the orphan has no protector. The fatherless appears to be vulnerable because there is no earthly father to protect the orphan from an aggressor. But this proverb warns the potential thief that the victim has a heavenly Father, a "Redeemer" who will avenge the wrong done.

Be a Good Listener (23:12)

¹² Apply your heart to instruction and your ear to words of knowledge.

This general proverb instructs the individual to make a concerted effort to listen to the instruction of the wise, a saying similar to Proverbs 22:17.

Don't Spoil Your Children (23:13–14)

¹³ Do not withhold discipline from a child; if you
strike him with a rod, he will not die.
¹⁴ If you strike him with the rod, you will save his soul from Sheol.

A common literary technique of wisdom literature was the use of hyperbole to get the reader's attention so that an important point could be made. The sage was not promoting child abuse, though he was writing in a much different time and culture where corporal punishment was widely practiced. We live in a time when the legitimate issue of child abuse has caused our society to overreact, and now, very little corporal discipline of children is practiced. As a result, modern parents fail to give their children the firm discipline that is needed to address the sin nature. The sage seemed to know that he was writing to lenient parents when he said about the protesting child, "he will not die." In effect, he was actually saying that the failure to discipline a child was another form of child abuse. The parents who fail to discipline may have an unbiblical definition of love, or simply may be lazy. Because he knew the terrible consequences of an undisciplined child, the sage's focus on Sheol, or the grave, looked at the fatal and unavoidable consequences that the world has for an undisciplined individual. I once talked to a child psychologist who was troubled by my practice of spanking my children when they disobeyed. She questioned me as to why I had to hurt my children. I told her that I would rather hurt my children in a loving way, instead of waiting for the world to hurt my children in an unloving way.

Make Your Parents Happy (23:15–16)

¹⁵ My son, if your heart is wise, my heart too will be glad.
¹⁶ My inmost being will exult when your lips speak what is right.

This saying is connected to the preceding proverb, in that it served as a motivation for parents to be loving and consistent disciplinarians. When a child grows up, the child will either bring joy to the parents, or the child will be the source of great sorrow. Anyone who has children knows this to be true. The father knew that if his son demonstrated wisdom when he was older, he would be a happy father, and he would be thankful that his discipline produced a wise child. And, when he heard his son speak words of truth, he would rejoice, and he would know that his loving discipline did the job.

Don't Envy the Wicked (23:17–18)

¹⁷ Let not your heart envy sinners, but continue
    in the fear of the LORD all the day.
¹⁸ Surely there is a future, and your hope will not be cut off.

This proverb acknowledges the common frustration that was expressed by the psalmist.

I was envious of the arrogant when I saw the prosperity of the wicked. (Psalm 73:3)

Later in the psalm this faulty perception of the wicked caused the psalmist to draw a conclusion.

All in vain have I kept my heart clean and washed my hands in innocence. (Psalm 73:11)

The sage understood the frustration of the righteous that it didn't seem to pay to live a righteous life when the wicked appear to be prosperous and getting away with sin. To help his readers put this frustration in the proper perspective, he told them to change their focus. Instead of looking at the present, where sinners appear to be prosperous, look to the future. And in the future, only the righteous will ultimately be satisfied. The psalmist saw the bleak future of the wicked.

Truly you set them in slippery places; you make them fall to ruin. (Psalm 73:18)

Live a Disciplined Life (23:19–21)

19 Hear, my son, and be wise, and direct your heart in the way.
20 Be not among drunkards or among gluttonous eaters of meat,
21 for the drunkard and the glutton will come to poverty,
and slumber will clothe them with rags.

The father wanted his son to live a well-ordered life, so he identified two habits that demonstrate self-indulgence. He didn't want his son to associate with individuals who drank too much or who ate too much. While the modern church focuses most of its attention on the abuse of alcohol, lately I have been directed to think of the oft ignored sin of gluttony, which was the focus of the ancient church. I have been watching an online course by Gary Thomas entitled Spiritual Formations, and he had an excellent discussion on the topic of gluttony. The related sins of gluttony and sloth were viewed by the ancient church fathers as gateway sins, in that they caused the gluttonous Christian to become accustomed to disobedience. The thinking is that if an individual is undisciplined in the daily decisions of food, he or she will become undisciplined in the larger decisions of life. Thomas quotes two church fathers who saw the connection between gluttony and other sins.

> In the eating of meat, and the drinking of wine, and the fullness of stomach, is the seed-bed of lust. (Saint Jerome)

> To be gluttonous, yet expect to be chaste, is to wish to extinguish fire with oil. John Climacus)

The father emphasized the consequence of poverty, both physical and moral, that would result from living an undisciplined life.

Listen to Your Parents (23:22–25)

²² Listen to your father who gave you life, and do
not despise your mother when she is old.
²³ Buy truth, and do not sell it; buy wisdom, instruction, and understanding.
²⁴ The father of the righteous will greatly rejoice; he
who fathers a wise son will be glad in him.
²⁵ Let your father and mother be glad; let her who bore you rejoice.

The father pleaded with his son to listen to his advice, and to honor his mother's advanced age. These parents were to be honored because they had spent many years acquiring this valuable knowledge. Speaking in financial terms, the father told his son to invest in wisdom and knowledge, for these acquisitions would prove to be a great investment over time. And, the son would not be the only one who would be delighted in this purchase. It would also bring great joy to his parents who not only gave him his physical life, which is emphasized three times, but also gave him the skills to live life well.

Avoid Immorality (23:26–28)

²⁶ My son, give me your heart, and let your eyes observe my ways.
²⁷ For a prostitute is a deep pit; an adulteress is a narrow well.
²⁸ She lies in wait like a robber and increases the traitors among mankind.

The father was concerned about his son's heart condition. He wanted his son to give his heart to the acquisition of knowledge, which the father was trying to demonstrate. He was urgent for he knew that as his son got older, that there would be women who would also try to capture his heart. There were two types of immoral women to avoid, namely, the unmarried prostitute and the unfaithful wife. Both women were likened to a thief who would rob an unsuspecting youth of his purity.

Don't Abuse Alcohol (23:29-35)

²⁹ Who has woe? Who has sorrow? Who has strife? Who has complaining?
Who has wounds without cause? Who has redness of eyes?
³⁰ Those who tarry long over wine; those who go to try mixed wine.
³¹ Do not look at wine when it is red,
when it sparkles in the cup and goes down smoothly.
³² In the end it bites like a serpent and stings like an adder.
³³ Your eyes will see strange things, and your heart utter perverse things.
³⁴ You will be like one who lies down in the midst of the sea,
like one who lies on the top of a mast.
³⁵ "They struck me," you will say, "but I was not hurt;
they beat me, but I did not feel it.
When shall I awake? I must have another drink."

With the opening series of questions, the sage posed a riddle for his listeners as he prepared them for his address on the dangers of abusing alcohol. Because his description of the intoxicated individual is so vivid, it seems unnecessary to comment on the particulars. Instead, I will describe some personal experiences where I saw these biblical truths firsthand in the lives of individuals who abused alcohol. While I have no personal experience with alcohol, I have counseled individuals who were addicted. And, I witnessed the misery that alcohol brought into their lives and into the lives of their loved ones.

I grew up in the home of a Baptist pastor where alcohol was not allowed and where I only heard about its evils. My first exposure to the effects of alcohol took place when I was living in the small town of White, South Dakota. During my childhood, our country was involved in the Vietnam War and college students began to protest against the government's involvement in the war. One Saturday, on May 17, 1969, hundreds of college students from the Dakotas and Minnesota descended on our small town and took it over. They spent the day drinking, and by the afternoon, most of them were intoxicated. I remember the legs of intoxicated girls hanging out of the trunks of the vehicles that lined the streets of our small town. In the evening the National Guard escorted everyone out of town and the streets were littered with beer bottles.

My next exposure to alcohol occurred when I was a high school senior in New Prague, Minnesota. Our high school basketball team qualified for the state tournament and so I rode the school bus to St. Paul for the playoff game. Even though it was a mild March day, many students were wearing long winter coats. When a bottle of liquor dropped out of a coat and smashed on the ground, I realized why my classmates were dressed so warmly. We lost the game, and as the depressed students rode the school bus home, the alcohol started to flow. I witnessed firsthand the change in behavior as the alcohol took effect. Classmates who were normally loud, became quiet and sullen. One classmate who was naturally quiet and shy, became loud and aggressive with the girls. Having lived an isolated life, I was shocked at the change in behavior brought on by alcohol.

Several years ago, a young man started attending my church and I learned that he had a serious addiction to alcohol where he would drink to excess and need to be hospitalized. One evening he came to my home to talk about his addiction and I shared with him the Gospel that could free him from his addiction. The portrayal of the sage was a perfect description of his misery. Fortunately for this young man, he responded to the Gospel, and with help with others who understood addictions, found freedom.

Don't Envy Evil Men (24:1–2)

¹ Be not envious of evil men, nor desire to be with them,
² for their hearts devise violence, and their lips talk of trouble.

This proverb is similar to a saying we studied in the previous chapter.

Let not your heart envy sinners, but continue in the fear of the Lord all the day. (Proverbs 23:17)

The antidote to envy, when sinners seem to be prospering because of their evil deeds, is to keep one's eyes fixed on the LORD, and to have a greater regard for His eternal nature than for sinful man's temporary success. The opening words of Psalm 37 state a similar refrain.

> Fret not yourself because of evildoers; be not envious of wrongdoers! For they will soon fade like the grass and wither like the green herb. (Psalm 37:1–2)

In the present proverb, the sage had a word of warning for his readers who were tempted to idolize the powerful because of their success. He advised them to focus instead on the violence that is conceived in the minds of these evil men, and to pay attention to the coarseness that characterizes their talk.

The Wise Builder (24:3–4)

³ By wisdom a house is built, and by understanding it is established;
⁴ by knowledge the rooms are filled with all precious and pleasant riches.

In contrast to violence which evil men use to get ahead (24:1–2), this proverb advocates the commodity of wisdom to build something truly worthy and lasting. I am not very handy when it comes to tools and construction. I am more at home in a bookstore than in a home improvement store. My father was a very good carpenter, along with being a pastor, but I must have had my nose in a book when he was trying to teach his sons some construction skills. So, if I ever did build a house, I would have to hire a skillful carpenter to do the work for me. Skill and wisdom are synonymous concepts in wisdom literature. Early in the book of Proverbs, Lady Wisdom built her house.

> Wisdom has built her house; she has hewn her seven pillars.
> (Proverbs 9:1)

In this saying the sage advocates the necessity of wisdom in the construction of one's house, in the figurative sense of the psalmist.

> Unless the LORD builds the house, those who build it labor in vain. (Psalm 127:1)

The sage elaborated on the house metaphor and imagined the rooms beautifully furnished in fine details. Such is the life that is built on wisdom.

Brains Enhance Brawn (24:5-6)

> [5] A wise man is full of strength, and a man of
> knowledge enhances his might,
> [6] for by wise guidance you can wage your war,
> and in abundance of counselors there is victory.

With this saying the sage gives a complete definition of true strength. While physical strength and military might are needed in battle, what is even more effective is when that physical strength is guided by wise strategy from multiple counselors. It is another way of saying that brains are greater than brawn. The Preacher made a similar observation.

> Wisdom gives strength to the wise man more than ten rulers
> who are in a city. (Ecclesiastes 7:19)

Because the context of this proverb is that of battle, two things are needed to wage an effective war. The physical strength of the warriors is a necessity, but brute strength is not enough. The soldiers need to be guided in battle by the strategy of wise counselors who will make the best use of their military might.

The Silent Fool (24:7)

> [7] Wisdom is too high for a fool; in the gate he does not open his mouth.

This proverb utilizes several themes that are frequently used in the collection of wise sayings. There is the fool who is a frequent focus of proverbs. Then, there is the gate which describes the public square of ancient Israel where issues were debated, agreements were made, and where the community leaders gathered for counsel. The sage made the observation that in this public arena the fool was out of his element because he had nothing of intelligence to contribute to the conversation.

The Schemer, the Sinner, and the Scoffer (24:8–9)

⁸ Whoever plans to do evil will be called a schemer.
⁹ The devising of folly is sin, and the scoffer is an abomination to mankind.

This proverb identifies three individuals who are related in an evil purpose. In reality, all three individuals are probably the same person in the mind of the sage. First, there is the "schemer" who spends time and energy thinking up ways to take advantage of others. Second, there is the "fool" who spends time and energy engaged in the pursuit of activities that are bluntly defined as sin. The fool is not unintelligent, but sadly, he or she uses the mental resources for activities that are condemned by God. And then there is the "scoffer" who mocks what the community upholds as moral and good, and as a result, the scoffer is denounced by the community.

High Anxiety (24:10)

¹⁰ If you faint in the day of adversity, your strength is small.

Because we live in a fallen world, times of adversity are inevitable and varied. My adversity came several years ago in the form of a panic attack, though at the time I did not know that. At the conclusion of a vigorous workout one morning, my extremities began to oddly tingle and I could not breathe. As I fought to breathe, I began to suspect I was having a heart attack. I woke up my wife and told her something was wrong. We finally called for an ambulance and I was taken to the hospital for tests. After the stress test, the doctor told me he had good news and bad news. The good news was I was in excellent health with no sign of a heart attack or stroke. The bad news was the doctor did not know what was wrong with me. The first Sunday after the attack, I was not able to preach my sermon because I could not breathe in the pulpit. Because the attack came after a workout, and because I had no history of anxiety, I pursued a medical solution at first. Later in the year, when I was teaching at the seminary in Ukraine, I had another bad attack and descended into a week-long bout of high anxiety. I was terrified to go to sleep at night and had no interest in eating during the day. The long bus ride to the airport in Kiev to fly home was the worst night of my life. When I returned home, I realized I needed to seek some mental help, so I went to see a clinical psychologist. At the first meeting, I wanted to find out what brought on the panic attack, and when it would go away. To my disappointment, he told me I would probably never know, and that the anxious feelings might never go away completely. Even though I did not like the news, it was good for me to hear it so I could come to terms with my problem. I took some medicine for the first year to minimize the symptoms, but when I realized the problem was in my head, I stopped taking the medicine. I made some changes to my lifestyle to limit the panic attacks, and I find that talking about my problem with others actually helps.

Get Involved (24:11–12)

[11] Rescue those who are being taken away to death;
hold back those who are stumbling to the slaughter.
[12] If you say, "Behold, we did not know this,"
does not he who weighs the heart perceive it?
Does not he who keeps watch over your soul know it,
and will he not repay man according to his work?

The precise interpretation of this proverb is made difficult by its vague statements. The sage does not say why human lives are in danger. The threat to human life could be injustice, or it could be ignorance on the part of the endangered person. While the threat to human life is unclear, the application is quite clear. The sage tells his audience that they need to get involved in the lives of those who are endangered. If the threat to human life is due to injustice, then the reader needs to take up the cause of the oppressed. If the threat is due to ignorance, then the reader needs to warn the fool of the deadly consequences of poor decisions. And, the sage warns his readers that they should not try to justify their lack of involvement with the excuse that they did not know. He reminds us that there is an omniscient God who is watching how we care for others. Because God is just, He will treat us the way we treat others.

Pass the Honey (24:13–14)

¹³ My son, eat honey, for it is good,
and the drippings of the honeycomb are sweet to your taste.
¹⁴ Know that wisdom is such to your soul;
if you find it, there will be a future, and your hope will not be cut off.

I think the sage must have been a tea drinker, for he compared the pursuit of wisdom for the soul to the sweetness of honey to the palate. When I started teaching at the seminary in Kremenchuk, Ukraine in 2002, I was introduced to the practice of drinking black tea, which was not a part of my American culture. I would drink tea with my Ukrainian friends to connect with their culture, but I did not enjoy the experience at first. Then, one evening at a group Bible study, there was a jar of honey on the table, and I found the perfect blend of honey and tea. The sage likened that sweetness to the pursuit of wisdom. When the individual has added wisdom to life, he or she will find the future to be much more hopeful.

The Righteous Will Rise (24:15–16)

¹⁵ Lie not in wait as a wicked man against the dwelling of the righteous;
do no violence to his home;
¹⁶ for the righteous falls seven times and rises again,
but the wicked stumble in times of calamity.

The sage issued a warning for anyone who was thinking about attacking a righteous person. He warned that such an attack would be foolish and futile because of the character of the righteous. Because a righteous person is pursuing God, the righteous has the fortitude to get back up when he or she has been knocked down. In fact, the righteous person can be knocked down numerous times, but will get back up because of the strength that comes from walking with God. On the other hand, the wicked lacks the capacity to endure calamity.

Don't Gloat (24:17–18)

¹⁷ Do not rejoice when your enemy falls,
and let not your heart be glad when he stumbles,
¹⁸ lest the LORD see it and be displeased, and turn away his anger from him.

This proverb reminds me of something I was guilty of when I was a freshman in college. There was a girl in my class that I liked, but she already had a boyfriend. One day in a chapel service her boyfriend embarrassed himself in front of the student body, and I found myself enjoying his humiliation. When we enjoy the misfortune of others, whether it is in the form of publicly rejoicing, or it is inner gloating, the sage condemned such behavior. This type of bad behavior is something Job talked about.

> If I have rejoiced at the ruin of him who hated me, or exulted
> when evil overtook him. (Job 31:29)

In a sense, when we take pleasure in the misfortune of people we dislike, we take on the role of their judge, which is solely God's task. And even if no one else sees our gloating, the LORD does, and He may turn His attention from our enemy's behavior, and focus on correcting our bad behavior. This proverb reminds us of the admonition of the apostle Paul.

> Beloved, never avenge yourselves, but leave it to the wrath of
> God, for it is written, Vengeance is mine, I will repay, says
> the Lord. (Romans 12:19)

Don't Worry about Others (24:19–20)

¹⁹ Fret not yourself because of evildoers, and be not envious of the wicked,
²⁰ for the evil man has no future; the lamp of the wicked will be put out.

While the previous proverb talked about our enjoyment of our enemy's misfortune, this proverb warns us not be envious of their success (also Proverbs 23:17–18; 24:1–2). There are two improper reactions on the part of the righteous when the wicked prosper. We can get irritated with their success and struggle with the unfairness. Since God promised to reward righteousness and punish wickedness, why are the wicked prospering and I am not? The classic biblical example of this reaction is found in Psalm 73. Or, we can become envious of their present success and be tempted to emulate their bad behavior. The sage put their present success in perspective when he looked at their bleak future. The sage trusted God to ultimately right the wrongs in life and to deal with the wicked when the time was right.

Don't Rebel (24:21–22)

²¹ My son, fear the LORD and the king, and do
not join with those who do otherwise,
²² for disaster will arise suddenly from them,
and who knows the ruin that will come from them both?

The sage lived in an age when the government over his nation was in the form of a monarchy. The sage warned his students not to rebel against this ruler, or to join with others who wanted to depose their leader. While this proverb does not lay out any exceptions to this rule, in this situation the sage understood that God had placed this individual in authority over them. Dietrich Bonhoeffer came to a different conclusion when living under Hitler's Nazi government. In the situation of the proverb, the rebellion was unfounded and the agitators were, in reality, rebelling against God. The apostle Peter made reference to the first half of verse 21 in his section on submission to human authority (1 Peter 2:13–17). The apostle Paul had similar instructions in Romans 13:1–7.

Don't Play Favorites (24:23–25)

²³ These also are sayings of the wise.
Partiality in judging is not good.
²⁴ Whoever says to the wicked, "You are in the right,"
will be cursed by peoples, abhorred by nations,
²⁵ but those who rebuke the wicked will have delight,
and a good blessing will come upon them.

This additional set of "sayings of the wise" begins with a statement condemning the showing of favoritism in judgment. The saying could be specifically addressed to the judges who handed out legal decisions in the nation of Israel (Exodus 18). The Pentateuch specifically condemned favoritism among the judges of Israel.

> You shall do no injustice in court. You shall not be partial to the poor or defer to the great, but in righteousness shall you judge your neighbor. (Leviticus 19:15)

But its application can be applied to anyone who has to render a decision in a dispute between individuals. The sage condemned a decision that was not based on the facts of the case, but was influenced by the individuals involved in the dispute. Jesus spoke of such a judge in his parable on the unjust judge (Luke 18:1–6). The sage assumed that the wicked individual involved in the dispute was in the wrong, simply because of his bad reputation. But, if his reputation influenced the judge in his favor, perhaps through a bribe, then the dishonest judge would be roundly condemned by the community as it heard the verdict. But, if the judge was guided by the facts and brought a verdict of guilt against the wicked individual, he would receive the praise of the people for upholding justice.

Tell the Truth (24:26)

²⁶ Whoever gives an honest answer kisses the lips.

This proverb states that honesty is the best policy. The image of a kiss on the lips signifies a close relationship between individuals who enjoy intimacy.

> Let him kiss me with the kisses of his mouth! For your love is better than wine. (Song of Solomon 1:2)

The individual who tells the truth to a friend demonstrates true friendship by this honesty. The individual who is less than honest, for whatever reason, is not a genuine friend. This proverb also requires the recipient of the truth to be accepting of the truth, even if it is painful.

Do Your Homework (24:27)

²⁷ Prepare your work outside;
get everything ready for yourself in the field,
and after that build your house.

This saying promotes preparation and hard work so that a venture will be successful. The wording of the proverb reflects the agricultural life of the ancient Israelite. The young man is admonished to prepare his fields and to plant his crops, so that he will have food to feed his family once his household is established. The building of a house could be the actual structure, or it could refer to the creation of a home through marriage and the birth of children. Either way, the sage urged the individual to be thorough in his preparation so that when he started his family, he would enjoy success.

Don't Lie (24:28)

²⁸ Be not a witness against your neighbor without cause,
and do not deceive with your lips.

The integrity of the judicial system in ancient Israel was based on people telling the truth. To protect from false accusations, the Mosaic Law required multiple witnesses in capital punishment cases.

> On the evidence of two witnesses or of three witnesses the one who is to die shall be put to death; a person shall not be put to death on the evidence of one witness. (Deuteronomy 17:6)

The Mosaic Law repeatedly condemned the bringing of a false accusation in court.

> You shall not spread a false report. You shall not join hands with a wicked man to be a malicious witness. You shall not fall in with the many to do evil, nor shall you bear witness in a lawsuit, siding with the many, so as to pervert justice, nor shall you be partial to a poor man in his lawsuit. (Exodus 23:1–3)

The Mosaic Law connected the giving of a false report to the showing of partiality, which was the focus of a previous saying (Proverbs 24:23–25). When we take this proverb outside the courtroom, the sage was condemning dishonesty and deception in our dealings with our neighbors, who are the people we encounter in life.

Don't Retaliate (24:29)

²⁹ Do not say, "I will do to him as he has done to me;
  I will pay the man back for what he has done."

While the Mosaic Law followed the principle known as *lex talionis* which is expressed as "eye for eye, tooth for tooth" (Leviticus 24:17–23), the sage was addressing the matter of one's personal conduct. Instead of contemplating retaliation for an offense, the sage advocated forgiveness, mercy, and a gracious spirit. Jesus advocated the same reaction in the Sermon on the Mount (Matthew 5:43–45). The apostle Paul wrote similar words to the believers in Rome (Romans 12:17–21). My father used to say, "The more you try to get even, the more you get at odds.

Don't Be Lazy (24:30–34)

³⁰ I passed by the field of a sluggard,
  by the vineyard of a man lacking sense,
³¹ and behold, it was all overgrown with thorns;
the ground was covered with nettles, and its stone wall was broken down.
³² Then I saw and considered it; I looked and received instruction.
³³ A little sleep, a little slumber, a little folding of the hands to rest,
  ³⁴ and poverty will come upon you like a robber,
    and want like an armed man.

This passage is similar to the classic description of the sluggard in Proverbs 6:6–11. The sage lived in an agricultural society and he noted that an individual's laziness was publicly displayed by the appearance of one's vineyard. I have helped harvest grapes for friends who own a local vineyard and I know the hard work the owners exerted to have a productive vineyard.

The presence of thorns and thistles, and a broken-down wall told the passerby the work habits of the owner. The overgrown vineyard served as an object lesson for the passerby not to be lazy like the owner. In this case, the poverty was self-inflicted.

The Proverbs of Solomon (25:1–29:27)

> **25:1** These also are proverbs of Solomon
> which the men of Hezekiah king of Judah copied.

The historian gave this assessment of the wisdom of King Solomon.

> And God gave Solomon wisdom and understanding beyond measure, and breadth of mind like the sand on the seashore, so that Solomon's wisdom surpassed the wisdom of all the people of the east and all the wisdom of Egypt. For he was wiser than all other men, wiser than Ethan the Ezrahite, and Heman, Calcol, and Darda, the sons of Mahol, and his fame was in all the surrounding nations. He also spoke 3,000 proverbs, and his songs were 1,005. (1 Kings 4:29–32)

Solomon reigned over Israel for forty years from 971–931 B.C. and was the last king of the united monarchy. Over two centuries later, during the reign of King Hezekiah (715–687 B.C.), his scribes copied out the following proverbs that were attributed to Solomon. The events of the reign of Hezekiah are recorded in 2 Kings 18–20 and 2 Chronicles 29–32. While Hezekiah had some lapses of judgment later in his reign concerning the kingdom of Babylon (Isaiah 38-39), overall, he was a godly king who sought to bring spiritual reform to the southern kingdom of Judah during the rise of the Assyrian Empire (2 Kings 18:3–6). That Hezekiah would value and want to preserve these proverbs that address the life of the king fits what we know of his godly nature.

> **2** It is the glory of God to conceal things,
> but the glory of kings is to search things out.
> **3** As the heavens for height, and the earth for depth,
> so the heart of kings is unsearchable.

These two proverbs can be linked together for they both speak of the need for investigation and the reality of incomprehensibility. The first saying reminds us that anything we can learn about God is solely due to the fact that He chooses to make Himself known through natural and special revelation. The apostle Paul spoke of God's use of natural revelation to disclose His presence to mankind in Romans 1:18–20. And while this is true, because God is infinite, He is beyond man's ability to completely fathom even with special revelation.

> It is not true to say that God is unable to be understood, but it is true to say that he cannot be understood fully or exhaustively. (Wayne Grudem)

Consider the following biblical statements on the topic. Job made a fascinating statement concerning the incomprehensibility of God after he listed some of the acts of God in human history that displayed His power.

> Behold, these are but the outskirts of his ways, and how small a whisper do we hear of him! But the thunder of his power who can understand? (Job 26:14)

Moses spoke about the incomprehensibility of God and also His self-revelation to the nation of Israel prior to the Conquest.

> The secret things belong to the LORD our God, but the things that are revealed belong to us and to our children forever, that we may do all the words of this law. (Deuteronomy 29:29)

The psalmist marveled at the greatness of the God he served.

> Great is the LORD, and greatly to be praised, and his greatness is unsearchable. (Psalm 145:3)

After a lengthy section on God's great plan of redemption for lost mankind, the apostle Paul broke out into praise.

> Oh, the depth of the riches and wisdom and knowledge of God! How unsearchable are his judgments and how inscrutable his ways! (Romans 11:33)

So, even though God can never be fully known, it is still the task of the king to inquire after God and to make the divine will known to the people. On a secondary level, the next proverb reminded the people that they could never fully understand the mind of their king either. The king would always have more information on a situation, some of which he could not share with the people due to confidentiality. This advice was probably directed to those who would serve the king.

⁴Take away the dross from the silver, and the smith has material for a vessel;
    ⁵take away the wicked from the presence of the king,
        and his throne will be established in righteousness.

This proverb uses an illustration from metallurgy to make a point about purity in the palace of the king. In the ancient world, a silversmith had to heat the precious metal with fire to remove the dross. As the impurities rose to the surface, the craftsman would skim them off. This process of refinement had to be repeated several times until the silversmith could see his reflection in the metal. Just as a silversmith had to remove the dross from the silver before he could make a vessel, so too, the king had to remove wicked counselors from his throne room if he wanted to rule his nation properly. The presence of impurities in the form of wicked counselors would always be a poor reflection on the king's ability to rule in righteousness. There is an excellent example of this principle in scripture.

> And Jehoash did what was right in the eyes of the LORD all his days, because Jehoiada the priest instructed him. (2 Kings 12:2)

The psalmist made a similar vow to remove impure people from his life.

> No one who practices deceit shall dwell in my house; no one who utters lies shall continue before my eyes. (Psalm 101:7)

⁶Do not put yourself forward in the king's presence
        or stand in the place of the great,
    ⁷for it is better to be told, "Come up here,"
        than to be put lower in the presence of a noble.

This proverb uses the scenario of a king's throne room to teach a lesson in humility. If an individual is invited to the palace, an attitude of humility should be demonstrated in the presence of the king. This proverb could be connected to an earlier saying that advocated self-control when invited to dine at the king's table (23:1–2). The invitation to dine was probably a test to evaluate a potential courtier's behavior when in the presence of power. It is likely that Jesus was thinking of this proverb when he told the parable of the wedding feast (Luke 14:7–11). Jesus concluded the parable with this moral: "For everyone who exalts himself will be humbled, and he who humbles himself will be exalted."

What your eyes have seen [8] do not hastily bring into court,
for what will you do in the end, when your neighbor puts you to shame?

The proverb seems to be intentionally vague so it is difficult to be precise in the application. What is clear is that the sage was describing a private matter, which a witness might be tempted to make a public matter by bringing it to the courts. The sage warned his students that they needed to have their facts straight before they started making accusations. He might also have been addressing the importance of keeping confidences.

[9] Argue your case with your neighbor himself,
and do not reveal another's secret,
[10] lest he who hears you bring shame upon you,
and your ill repute have no end.

This proverb is similar to the previous saying in that it addresses how to handle a conflict with a neighbor. It is important to settle our disputes privately. We should not bring a third party unnecessarily into the conflict, similarly to Jesus' instructions concerning church conflicts (Matthew 18:15–17).

[11] A word fitly spoken is like apples of gold in a setting of silver.

While the ancient image of "apples of gold in a setting of silver" is not certain to the modern reader, what is clear is the great value the sage placed on the wise use of words. There is nothing more satisfying than saying the right thing at the right time. The right words spoken at the appropriate time is a thing of beauty and is quite rare. The scriptures praise the ability to deliver a well-turned phrase.

> Let your speech always be gracious, seasoned with salt, so that you may know how you ought to answer each person. (Colossians 4:6)

> ¹² Like a gold ring or an ornament of gold is
> a wise reprover to a listening ear.

This proverb conjures up the image of a beautiful gold earring adorning a woman's ear. Sometimes the "word fitly spoken" comes in the form of a word of rebuke delivered by an esteemed teacher to a receptive student. Once again, the sage used the image of an ornament made of gold to express the value that he placed on the right words spoken at the right time. The right rebuke at the right time is most valuable when it is received by the person in need of correction. Even the apostle Peter was in need of a strong rebuke (Galatians 2:11–14). So, how receptive are you to correction from others?

> ¹³ Like the cold of snow in the time of harvest
> is a faithful messenger to those who send him;
> he refreshes the soul of his masters.

As I worked on this proverb in the month of March, there was snow on the ground since I live in Minnesota. Because of those factors the simile of snow being refreshing initially escaped me. There were three times of harvest in the Middle East, with the barley harvest taking place in April near the Feast of Passover (Ruth 1:22), the wheat harvest taking place seven weeks later at the Feast of Pentecost (Exodus 34:22), and the fruit harvest taking place in October during the Feast of Tabernacles (Leviticus 23:24). Harvest time could be hot and exhausting work (2 Kings 4:18–20), and so, the cold of snow, perhaps in the form of cooler weather or a cold drink, would be refreshing to the workers. Important communication in the ancient world was accomplished by means of using messengers, and so, the arrival of a faithful envoy with good news would refresh the spirits of those who waited on him. The focus of this proverb is on the one who serves as the messenger and the need for one to be faithful. The apostle Paul commended such a group of faithful people as he concluded his first letter to the church in Corinth (1 Corinthians 16:15–18).

^{14} Like clouds and wind without rain
is a man who boasts of a gift he does not give.

While the previous proverb praised faithfulness, this saying bemoans the individual who makes great promises, but sadly, does not produce. In the ancient Middle East, before the science of meteorology, the appearance of clouds or the presence of strong winds made the people hopeful that needed rain was soon to fall. When the rain did not materialize, the disappointment was great. Individuals who talk a good game, but who fail to live up to the expectations they have created, will be a great disappointment to the people who count on them. Peter used similar imagery to describe false teachers.

> These are waterless springs and mists driven by a storm. For them the gloom of utter darkness has been reserved. For, speaking loud boasts of folly, they entice by sensual passions of the flesh those who are barely escaping from those who live in error. (2 Peter 2:17–18)

^{15} With patience a ruler may be persuaded, and
a soft tongue will break a bone.

An effective tool to influence powerful people is the combination of patience and persuasion. The sage was giving this advice to individuals who would serve in the court of the king. If they wanted to have influence in the court over the decision-makers, they needed to have a keen sense of timing and tact. Abigail's influence over an angry David is an illustration of this saying (1 Samuel 25).

^{16} If you have found honey, eat only enough for you,
lest you have your fill of it and vomit it.

This proverb puts a smile on my face because honey plays an important role in my life since I started going to Ukraine. Prior to my first trip in 2002 to teach at the seminary in Kremenchuk, I had never tasted tea. But at the first meal I was served a cup of black tea and I found the taste unpleasant. Since I wanted to identify with this culture, I became a social drinker even though I did not like the taste. But one evening at a small group Bible study, I spied a jar of honey on the table and added a spoonful to my tea. The combination of tea and honey was the perfect match for my palate. Since then, with the help of honey, I start every day with a pot of tea. This proverb warns that too much of a good thing can quickly become a bad thing. This proverb, like other passages of scripture, advocates moderation in all things.

> ¹⁷ Let your foot be seldom in your neighbor's house,
> lest he have his fill of you and hate you.

This proverb reminds me of my father and his sense of humor. One evening after the Sunday evening service, a young man in our church came over to the house to visit and have refreshments with our family. Because we were having such a good time together, he stayed late into the night. As he was leaving for home, my father told him, with a smile on his face, to read Proverbs 25:17 when he got home. Since we were raised on the King James Version, when he got home, the young man read these words.

> Withdraw your foot from your neighbor's house; lest he be
> weary of you, and so hate you. (Proverbs 25:17)

While my father meant it as a joke, the sage was serious about his advice which is timeless. Do not wear out your welcome.

> ¹⁸ A man who bears false witness against his neighbor
> is like a war club, or a sword, or a sharp arrow.

With the ninth commandment God told Israel, "You shall not bear false witness against your neighbor" (Exodus 20:16). The primary setting for this prohibition was the courtroom, but its application will extend to social discourse. The sage agreed with this prohibition and likened the weapon of dishonest words to three dangerous weapons of war. The narrative of Jezebel's slander against the character of Naboth to acquire his vineyard for her husband is a biblical illustration of this saying (1 Samuel 21). Positively stated, there needs to be a commitment to the truth.

> ¹⁹ Trusting in a treacherous man in time of trouble
> is like a bad tooth or a foot that slips.

Because no one is self-sufficient, we all have to rely on others from time to time, and especially in difficult times. The sage warned that relying on an undependable person will prove to be troublesome, like biting down on food and finding out you have a painful cavity.

> ²⁰ Whoever sings songs to a heavy heart
> is like one who takes off a garment on a cold day,
> and like vinegar on soda.

If it were not for the two negative similes in the latter part of the saying, the first line could be understood in a positive sense. Like David playing his stringed instrument for the troubled king, music generally has a soothing quality (1 Samuel 16:14–23). However, in this proverb the sage was talking about the unkind use of music when an individual was still in mourning. Read Psalm 137 for a biblical illustration of using music, not to comfort, but to afflict more pain. The first illustration of musical misery is likened to taking a person's means of warmth when they are cold. The second illustration is the explosive chemical reaction that takes place when vinegar and soda are combined. The wise individual knows when to commiserate with those who are in mourning (Romans 12:15), and when it is time to lift their spirits.

> ²¹ If your enemy is hungry, give him bread to eat,
> and if he is thirsty, give him water to drink,
> ²² for you will heap burning coals on his head,
> and the LORD will reward you.

When I went to seminary, I worked with a man who followed this motto: Do unto others before they do unto you. The sage's advice was not only the exact opposite, but it went even further. We are to treat our enemies with kindness, and if we do so, there are two positive results. First, our unexpected kindness will serve as a rebuke to our enemy for his or her mistreatment of us. Second, God will reward our generosity with His own generosity in some fashion. The apostle Paul quoted this proverb in his discussion of the marks of a true Christian as he wrote to the church in Rome (Romans 12:20). He concluded the section with the admonition, "Do not be overcome by evil, but overcome evil with good" (12:21). The reference to "burning coals" has numerous interpretations, from burning shame to a change of mind. In the Old Testament the metaphor was usually a negative one when divine judgment was involved (2 Samuel 22:9; Job 41:20–21; Psalm 140:10; Proverbs 6:27–29). This emphasis on divine judgment fits the previous verse where

Paul says, concerning vengeance, to "leave it to the wrath of God." Jesus had an extended discussion on this topic in his Sermon on the Mount (Matthew 5:38–48).

> [23] The north wind brings forth rain,
> and a backbiting tongue, angry looks.

The sage once again used a meteorological metaphor to illustrate the damaging impact of gossip (25:14). The sage was speaking figuratively for the west wind, not the north wind, brings the rain in the land of Canaan (1 Kings 8:41–46). When gossip is finally exposed, it only produces dirty looks.

> [24] It is better to live in a corner of the housetop
> than in a house shared with a quarrelsome wife.

This saying is identical to Proverbs 21:9. This proverb is a warning to young men to choose a wife wisely, because if they do not, there is not a house big enough to escape her hostility. A later proverb says much the same thing.

> It is better to live in a desert land than with a quarrelsome
> and fretful woman. (Proverbs 21:19)

To be fair to women, the book of Proverbs was written from a male perspective. If the sage had been writing to his daughter, he would have warned her not to marry an abusive man.

> [25] Like cold water to a thirsty soul,
> so is good news from a far country.

This proverb reminds me of something I experienced when I was in college. I spent the summer of 1979 in the country of Peru on a Missionary Apprenticeship Program living with missionaries who served in this South American country. This was in the days before Facebook, cell phones, and emails. And while I thoroughly enjoyed my first time of being away from home, I had not heard from my family the entire time. After a month of living in the city of Lima, we moved to the countryside and made it all the way up into the Andes Mountains. While staying with missionaries in the town of Nazca, I received seven letters from home and I read those letters from family and friends numerous times. The sage captured this feeling as he compared the hearing of good news to a refreshing cold drink of water on a hot day.

> ²⁶ Like a muddied spring or a polluted fountain
> is a righteous man who gives way before the wicked.

While the above proverb celebrates the refreshment that cold water brings, this saying laments the contamination of good water. The book of Proverbs consistently promotes the righteous life (see 10:30; 12:3), and so this proverb laments when the righteous individual does not endure in the face of the wicked. The sage lived in the arid climate of the Middle East where water made the difference between life and death. As an example, read the narrative of the patriarch Isaac as he lived among the Philistines and had conflict with them over a series of wells (Genesis 26:12–33). The sage picked an apt metaphor of a polluted source of water to describe the disappointment that is felt when a righteous individual experiences defeat at the hands of the wicked. The proverb does not reveal the nature of the loss, whether it was due to the moral failure of the righteous, or it was due to the plotting of the wicked.

> ²⁷ It is not good to eat much honey,
> nor is it glorious to seek one's own glory.

The sage returned to the topic of eating too much honey (25:16) to illustrate how too much of a good thing can be unhealthy. In this instance, self-promotion is distasteful for it is a sign of a shallow individual. Absalom, the embittered son of King David promoted himself to his own demise (2 Samuel 15–18).

> ²⁸ A man without self-control
> is like a city broken into and left without walls.

While self-promotion was condemned by the sage in the previous saying, equally troubling is the absence of self-discipline. He likened an individual without restraint to the sad state of a city that had been attacked and left without its walls for protection. This image brings to mind the state of the city of Jerusalem at the beginning of the book of Nehemiah and the report of the returning exiles.

The remnant there in the province who had survived the exile is in great trouble and shame. The wall of Jerusalem is broken down, and its gates are destroyed by fire. As soon as I heard these words I sat down and wept and mourned for days, and I continued fasting and praying before the God of heaven. (Nehemiah 1:3–4)

An individual who does not control his or her emotions will always be vulnerable to attack from within and from without.

> 26:1 Like snow in summer or rain in harvest,
> so honor is not fitting for a fool.

From the very beginning of the book of Proverbs, the fool has been consistently condemned for arrogance and obstinance. Because of this boorish behavior and a resistance to correction, the fool will experience negative natural consequences and some manmade punishment. Just as it would be wrong for it to snow in the Middle East during the heat of summer, and for rain to fall in harvesttime (see 1 Samuel 12:17–25 for the exception), it would be wrong for a fool to have standing in the community. The modern phenomenon of achieving fame for doing something infamous comes to mind with this proverb.

> 2 Like a sparrow in its flitting, like a swallow in its flying,
> a curse that is causeless does not alight.

As a child I would visit my grandparents on their dairy farm in western Wisconsin during the summertime, and one of my chores was to mow the lawn. As I cut the grass near the barn, sparrows would divebomb me as I neared their nests. While I felt threatened as a young boy, the sparrows never actually harmed me. The same thing is true of a superstitious curse that is uttered. As Balaam learned, the power of a curse is not in the speaker, but in the Creator (Numbers 22).

> 3 A whip for the horse, a bridle for the donkey,
> and a rod for the back of fools.

Just as a horse or donkey does not respond to reason, but needs brute force to make it useful, so too a fool needs to feel some physical pain to get him or her to change the direction of life. This proverb makes me think of my father who was very proper in his language and who punished any form of swearing. But when his boys were acting foolish, if he called me a jackass, I knew I was in trouble.

⁴Answer not a fool according to his folly, lest you be like him yourself.
⁵Answer a fool according to his folly, lest he be wise in his own eyes.

These two proverbs serve as a good object lesson to remind us of the general nature of proverbs. Proverbs are not legal guarantees but are general statements of truth. If the advice is heeded, success is likely to follow. The two proverbs at hand actually contradict one another, and yet both sayings are correct because they contain an element of truth. The first proverb warns of the danger of getting involved in the life of a fool. If you stoop to the fool's level with correction, you are in danger of becoming just like him or her. Dealing with a fool can be an irritating experience, and you may find yourself becoming angry and wasting your time with an argument you cannot win. But the second proverb encourages the individual to correct the fool so he or she realizes the mistake. Discernment is needed on the part of the individual to determine whether or not to get involved in a fool's life.

⁶Whoever sends a message by the hand of a fool
cuts off his own feet and drinks violence.

This proverb warns us not to entrust important matters to a fool for it will come back to haunt us. In the ancient world couriers were utilized to carry important messages between individuals. Because the courier served as the sender's feet, if the courier was unreliable, it was like cutting off one's own feet. And, based on the sensitivity of the matter, sending an unreliable messenger was like a self-inflicted wound.

⁷Like a lame man's legs, which hang useless,
is a proverb in the mouth of fools.

This proverb continues the threefold theme of the previous saying that spoke of the fool, the message, and a pair of legs. A fool may try to appear to be wise by quoting a proverb, but it is obvious to the audience that he or she clearly does not understand what was just said. Wisdom in the mouth of a fool is just as useless as a pair of legs on a paralyzed person.

⁸ Like one who binds the stone in the sling is one who gives honor to a fool.

This proverb is similar to Proverbs 26:1 in that it bemoans the impropriety of seeing a fool receive honor. The sage changed the simile to that of a stone in a sling. An ancient sling had a leather pouch attached on two sides by a long strand of rope. Slingers would put a rock or a lead ball into the pouch, swing it around in increasingly wider and faster circles, and then release one end of the rope, hurling the rock forward. Slinging took an extraordinary amount of skill and practice. But in experienced hands, the sling was a devastating weapon. Back to the proverb, because the stone was secured in the sling, it would not release the stone. Giving honor to a fool is likewise a waste of time.

⁹ Like a thorn that goes up into the hand of a drunkard
is a proverb in the mouth of fools.

This proverb is similar to Proverbs 26:7 in that it describes the painful experience of hearing a fool quote a proverb. A fool may be able to recite a wise saying, but the audience knows his or her life contradicts what was said. The sage likened the fool's quotation of a proverb to the damage a drunk individual could cause as he wielded a thornbush in an inebriated state.

¹⁰ Like an archer who wounds everyone
is one who hires a passing fool or drunkard.

This proverb is similar to Proverbs 26:6 in that it warns against hiring a fool to perform an important task. Entrusting a passing fool with an important task was likened to the randomness of an archer shooting arrows from his bow. Eventually, someone is going to get injured. The death of King Ahab provides a biblical illustration of the sage's warning.

> But a certain man drew his bow at random and struck the
> king of Israel between the scale armor and the breastplate.
> (1 Kings 22:34)

¹¹ Like a dog that returns to his vomit is a fool who repeats his folly.

As a dog owner, I have seen this proverb acted out in person and it is disgusting to behold. I walk my dog early in the morning while it is still dark and he occasionally finds a scrap of food and eats it before I can pull back on the leash. The sage created this visual word picture to elicit an emotional reaction from his students. A fool rarely learns his or her lesson, but tends to repeat the mistakes again and again, even if the consequences are unpleasant. The apostle Peter quoted the first line of this proverb as he warned about the captivating nature of sin (2 Peter 2:22). I once counseled a recently divorced woman not to marry her new boyfriend, but she ignored my advice. Several years later she invited me to her home to talk about her marital problems with her current husband. I asked her why she was seeking my counsel again, since she did not listen to me the first time.

> ¹² Do you see a man who is wise in his own eyes?
> There is more hope for a fool than for him.

While the fool is the chief object of the sage's withering criticism, there is one person who is even more hopeless than the fool. The person who thinks he or she is the smartest individual in the room is even more pitiful than the fool. We first saw the expression "wise in his own eyes" back in Proverbs 3:7 when the father advised his son, "Be not wise in your own eyes; fear the LORD, and turn away from evil." The prophet Isaiah condemned this arrogance in his day as the nation of Judah substituted their own wisdom in place of divine wisdom.

> Woe to those who are wise in their own eyes, and shrewd in
> their own sight! (Isaiah 5:21)

The opposite of humility is hubris, which is defined as excessive pride or arrogance. Back in 1998 the British historian Ian Kershaw wrote a two-volume biography on the German dictator Adolph Hitler, and the first volume which detailed his rise to power was appropriately entitled "Hubris." Fortunately for the world, this man's arrogance ultimately led to his downfall.

> ¹³ The sluggard says, "There is a lion in the road!
> There is a lion in the streets!"
> ¹⁴ As a door turns on its hinges,
> so does a sluggard on his bed.

¹⁵ The sluggard buries his hand in the dish;
it wears him out to bring it back to his mouth.
¹⁶ The sluggard is wiser in his own eyes
than seven men who can answer sensibly.

This extended parody on the sluggard reminds us of the classic statement in Proverbs 6:6–11 where the sage cited the work ethic of the ant to warn his readers against the dangers of laziness. In this section, the sage mocks the ridiculous excuses the sluggard offers up to explain his or her inactivity. We first heard the excuse of the lion in the street back in Proverbs 22:13. Instead of leaving the house to find work, the sluggard's only exercise is to turn from side to side on the bed as the day is wasted sleeping. The epitome of the sluggard's laziness is the unwillingness to exert any effort even to eat (see 19:24). And then, citing the above proverb, the sluggard thinks he or she is smarter than the seven sages who are warning of the dire consequences of laziness. We recently had a story in the news where an older couple from New York had to take their thirty-year old son to court to have him evicted from their home. The excuses this grown man offered to the news reporters to explain his inactivity was as laughable as the excuses the sage used to describe the sluggard in his day.

¹⁷ Whoever meddles in a quarrel not his own
is like one who takes a passing dog by the ears.

This proverb reminds me of the iconic picture of the American president Lyndon Baines Johnson holding his beagle by the ears. The president had two beagles named Him and Her and the picture was published by Life magazine in 1964. Hundreds of phone calls, telegrams, and letters came in from angry dog lovers criticizing the president. The sage was not thinking of a beloved household pet, but he probably had in mind a stray dog that wandered through the village looking for food (Psalm 59:14–15). Getting involved in a quarrel that is none of your business is likely to become a source of personal pain for the busybody. The sage is not encouraging a life of indifference in the lives of others. But the wise individual needs to show discernment to determine whether or not he or she needs to intervene in a matter.

¹⁸ Like a madman who throws firebrands, arrows, and death
¹⁹ is the man who deceives his neighbor and says, "I am only joking!"

The sage understood the destructive nature of deception within relationships, and he compared the deceiver to a madman whose insanity endangered the lives of those around him. While a madman may not realize he is harming others, the deceiver clearly knows the harm he or she is doing to a neighbor. In this particular proverb it is difficult to determine whether the deceiver engages in deception as a joke, or whether the deceiver merely said he or she was joking when the deception was discovered. Either way, an individual who is given to deception will cause significant harm to the lives of others. This saying reminds me of a video I saw online where a woman on a public beach was caught in the act of taking items that belonged to someone else. And yet, when she was confronted by the owner, she claimed innocence as she walked away from the camera.

> [20] For lack of wood the fire goes out,
> and where there is no whisperer, quarreling ceases.

The sage provided a great word picture to illustrate the individual who stirs up trouble with gossip. When a campfire is burning down, one merely needs to stir the dying coals by blowing on them and then put on more wood to get the fire raging again. So, too, the gossiper, with slander and innuendo, can increase the intensity of the conflict by his or her continued talking. The most effective way to limit the damage of gossip is to refuse to lend a listening ear, and then to rebuke the whisperer. Most people who engage in gossip are cowards, which is why they engage in this secretive talk. But if the gossiper is confronted, he or she will lose the audience and the damage will be minimized.

> [21] As charcoal to hot embers and wood to fire,
> so is a quarrelsome man for kindling strife.

The sage continued with his campfire metaphor to describe another troublemaker. In the previous saying the campfire was about to go out, but in this one proverb the fire is still hot with the embers glowing red. And while both the whisperer and the quarrelsome man are troublemakers, the man in this saying is not trying to hide his intentions. Instead of using private gossip, this man is quite public. The argumentative individual is continually stirring up conflict among acquaintances with this seeming love of controversy. Whether it is in person or with social media, certain individuals seem to love to stir up strife. By describing this quarrelsome man, the sage was warning his readers to avoid this type of company.

> ²² The words of a whisperer are like delicious morsels;
> they go down into the inner parts of the body.

This saying is a repetition of Proverbs 18:8. The sage returned to the whisperer and he compared juicy gossip to tasty delicacies that we find tempting. It's like the junk food that we love, but we know it is bad for our health and it lacks any nutritional value. All of us have experienced the regret of giving in to our appetites. Gossip never does anyone any good, but it is often too tempting to avoid. Gossip harms the individual who is the subject of the gossip, but it equally harms the gossiper and the listener. The mature individual knows that gossip is unhealthy for everyone involved and he or she passes on the tempting opportunity and rebukes the gossiper.

> ²³ Like the glaze covering an earthen vessel
> are fervent lips with an evil heart.
> ²⁴ Whoever hates disguises himself with his lips
> and harbors deceit in his heart;
> ²⁵ when he speaks graciously, believe him not,
> for there are seven abominations in his heart;
> ²⁶ though his hatred be covered with deception,
> his wickedness will be exposed in the assembly.

This set of proverbs is connected by the themes of duplicity and persuasive speech. The sage warned his students of the evil person who hid hatred and evil intentions behind gracious and persuasive words. He likened the deception to a potter in ancient Israel who baked an earthenware vessel, who then concealed the flaws of the clay by painting the vessel with a decorative glaze. The sage warned that a gifted individual can conceal evil intentions with persuasive speech. The sage found this deception to be one of the most loathsome practices ("seven abominations") that can be committed for it violated the honesty God demanded of His people. Throughout history, charismatic characters have been able to sway the masses to follow their leadership and join them in executing their evil plans. A highly persuasive individual can hide his or her true intentions for a while, but eventually this hatred will finally be revealed. But the damage may have been done. The sage enjoins us to exercise great discernment when it comes to the people to whom we listen.

> ²⁷ Whoever digs a pit will fall into it,
> and a stone will come back on him who starts it rolling.

The sage believed in poetic justice because he also believed that a sovereign God governed the affairs of mankind (Proverbs 1:17–19). Because of his theological perspective, he taught his students that God would eventually right the wrongs and bring back on the heads of the wicked their own evil devices. The unstated advice behind this proverb is not to take matters into your own hands in the form of vengeance, but to wait on the Lord for justice (Romans 12:19). The digging of a pit was for the purpose of laying a trap for an unsuspecting victim (Psalm 57:6). The rolling of a stone might be for the purpose of entrapping someone in a cave (Joshua 10:16–18), though this biblical example had God's approval. A biblical example of poetic justice would be the hanging of Haman on his own gallows (Esther 7:10).

> ²⁸ A lying tongue hates its victims,
> and a flattering mouth works ruin.

With this saying the sage returned to the topic of the destructive nature of false speech. He identified two forms of false speech, namely outright lying, and the subtler false flattery which is harder to detect. Lying about an individual is a form of hatred because it is character assassination, like what Jezebel did to Naboth to take possession of his vineyard (1 Kings 21). False flattery is employed to appeal to a person's ego for the purpose of manipulation to make the unsuspecting victim act on the behalf of the flatterer.

> ²⁷:¹ Do not boast about tomorrow,
> for you do not know what a day may bring.

The sage warned his students not to presume about the future because life is uncertain. He would not discourage them from making plans, for that is a wise thing to do (Proverbs 15:22). But to foolishly assume success in future endeavors ignores the realities of life. James developed this thought in his letter.

Come now, you who say, "Today or tomorrow we will go into such and such a town and spend a year there and trade and make a profit"— yet you do not know what tomorrow will bring. What is your life? For you are a mist that appears for a little time and then vanishes. Instead you ought to say, "If the Lord wills, we will live and do this or that." As it is, you boast in your arrogance. All such boasting is evil. (James 5:13–16)

These Christian businessmen to whom James wrote ignored three realities of life. They ignored the uncertainty of life, the brevity of life, and the futility of man. Boasting is the confident speech of a person who does not take God into account but acts as if he or she alone is in control of life and the future. In such talk the failure to acknowledge God's sovereignty over your life is the evil that James condemns.

> ² Let another praise you, and not your own mouth;
> a stranger, and not your own lips.

Self-promotion makes a person look shallow and needy. Self-promotion is actually a sign of pride which God finds particularly offensive for it ignores His presence in our lives and His provision. If praise does come from someone else, acknowledge it, appreciate it, but do not let it go to your head. The greatest protection for pride is to redirect the praise to God. Consider the words of the prophet Jeremiah.

> Thus says the Lord: "Let not the wise man boast in his wisdom, let not the mighty man boast in his might, let not the rich man boast in his riches, but let him who boasts boast in this, that he understands and knows me, that I am the Lord who practices steadfast love, justice, and righteousness in the earth. For in these things I delight, declares the Lord. (Jeremiah 9:23–24)

> ³ A stone is heavy, and sand is weighty,
> but a fool's provocation is heavier than both.

The sage cited two physical objects that are literally heavy to bear and compared them to something that is emotionally unbearable. When I was young, our family would help our grandfather clear his field of stones and Polk County in western Wisconsin produced some heavy stones. While moving heavy objects is exhausting work, dealing with a fool is emotionally draining. When we removed heavy stones from the field, at least we saw some progress. When you deal with a fool, you make the effort but there is no satisfaction for nothing has been accomplished.

> [4] Wrath is cruel, anger is overwhelming,
>   but who can stand before jealousy?

The sage identified three closely related character flaws and made a comparison as to which was the worst vice to deal with. Wrath can cause a person to become cruel and being the object of someone's anger can be emotionally overwhelming. But they pale in comparison to dealing with a person who is driven by feelings of jealousy. Especially in cases of domestic violence, a jealous spouse can commit some heinous acts in a failed attempt not to lose someone.

> [5] Better is open rebuke
>   than hidden love.

This is one of the "better than" proverbs that shows a comparison. There are two contrasts in the saying. There is the contrast in the nouns where "rebuke" is normally thought of as negative and "love" is considered positive. There is the second contrast between the adjectives "open" and "hidden." When it comes to the discipline of a child or the rebuke of an adult, "hidden love" is the failure to say anything negative for fear that the rebuke will be rejected and the relationship will be strained. The sage is saying that "hidden love" may not, in fact, be love. Genuine love is expressed in the willingness to speak up and rebuke a person who is not acting correctly. The Bible says that rebuke is actually a form of genuine love (Proverbs 3:11–12; 13:24).

> [6] Faithful are the wounds of a friend;
>   profuse are the kisses of an enemy.

This saying picks up on the previous proverb as it focuses on the relationship between two friends. A genuine friend will rebuke his or her companion when the behavior is wrong even though the words are painful to speak and hear. The person who is giving the rebuke must be willing to risk the friendship in order to strengthen it. The individual who is the recipient of the rebuke needs to recognize the sign of a genuine friend. A kiss, which is normally an expression of affection, may hide a false friend (Matthew 26:48–50). This proverb demands two questions. As a friend, are you willing to speak truth into the life of another person? And, are you receptive to the correction of others?

> 7 One who is full loathes honey,
> but to one who is hungry everything bitter is sweet.

The sage used the human appetite for food to serve as a commentary on the human appetite for finances, possessions, and achievements in life. Beginning with the food items, I love honey because I use it to sweeten my Earl Grey tea with which I begin every day. But I also know that too much honey can become sickening (Proverbs 25:16). And, when it comes to hunger, I can remember feeling starved as a young man and going through my parents' cupboards looking for anything to satisfy my hunger. Food that I would have normally rejected in lieu of better options, suddenly appeared appetizing because I was hungry. The individual who grows up poor is generally more appreciative than the person who grows up with wealth. As a general rule, the more things we have, the less we appreciate them. And, the harder it was to accomplish something, the more we value the achievement.

> 8 Like a bird that strays from its nest
> is a man who strays from his home.

Infidelity has been a problem as long as marriage has been a God-ordained institution. The sage likened the unfaithful husband to a bird that strays from its nest. In the nest the bird enjoys safety, but outside the nest it is susceptible to predators. God designed marriage to provide the same type of protection. Consider the warning of the apostle Paul.

> But because of the temptation to sexual immorality, each man should have his own wife and each woman her own husband. Do not deprive one another, except perhaps by agreement for a limited time, that you may devote yourselves to prayer; but then come together again, so that Satan

may not tempt you because of your lack of self-control. (1
Corinthians 7:2, 5)

> ⁹ Oil and perfume make the heart glad,
> and the sweetness of a friend comes from his earnest counsel.

Every culture has certain luxuries that make life a little more pleasant
when it becomes difficult. The sage was thinking of the arid climate of the
Middle East when he identified olive oil and perfume as two resources that
bring relief to an individual on a hot day. The psalmist spoke of God as
anointing his head with oil to cool the traveler's head (Psalm 23:5). One can
read the opening lines of the Song of Solomon as the woman speaks of the
fragrant anointing oils (1:1–3). The sage then likened these two resources to
the refreshing advice of a trusted friend when life becomes complicated and
confusing. The book of Proverbs promotes the wisdom of seeking counsel
from trusted advisors.

> ¹⁰ Do not forsake your friend and your father's friend,
> and do not go to your brother's house in the day of your calamity.
> Better is a neighbor who is near
> than a brother who is far away.

While the institution of the family was highly prized in the tribal life of the
nation of Israel, long-term friendships were also important. The sage spoke of a
friend who had been intimate with the family for several generations, in that he
was a friend of the individual's father. Because of that long-term commitment
to the family, in this situation, friendship trumped family. A negative biblical
illustration was the folly of Rehoboam when he failed to heed the advice of the
counselors who had served his father Solomon (1 Kings 12:6–8). If you have a
relative who physically lives far away, it is better to have a trusted friend who can
be an active part of your life on a daily basis. This proverb would reinforce the
saying that while you cannot choose your relatives, you can choose your friends.

> ¹¹ Be wise, my son, and make my heart glad,
> that I may answer him who reproaches me.

This simple saying speaks to several profound truths. It stresses the
importance of consistent parental discipline in the life of a child with a

concentration on the future behavior of that child as a mature adult. It also speaks to the impact the proper behavior of a child will have on the happiness and the reputation of the parent. The saying understands that a child who grows to maturity is the greatest compliment a parent can receive in life. The emphasis of the saying on reproach tells us that a child who grows to maturity is the best defense to one's critics. The saying is also true when the son is a student who responds to the instruction of his teacher. A well-taught student validates the effectiveness of the teacher.

> 12 The prudent sees danger and hides himself,
>   but the simple go on and suffer for it.

One of the signs of a well-taught child or student is the ability to detect hazardous situations and dangerous people, and then to avoid them. The young person who lacks experience will ignore the warning signs and suffer the harmful consequences. The book of Proverbs advocates the motto of "learn, and then live," instead of the world's motto "live and learn." This saying is identical to Proverbs 22:3.

> 13 Take a man's garment when he has put up security for a stranger,
>   and hold it in pledge when he puts up security for an adulteress.

This saying speaks to the painful consequences that need to occur when an individual makes a foolish financial decision that is connected to the making of bad moral decisions. The saying is similar to Proverbs 20:16. The first line addresses the custom of taking an individual's garment as security for a financial loan. In one of the early addresses of the book, the father warned his son to do whatever it took to get out of a bad financial decision (6:1–5). The second line of the proverb connects that foolish financial decision to a bad moral decision. A biblical illustration would be the patriarch Judah who gave a pledge to a woman he thought to be a prostitute, who turned out to be his daughter-in-law Tamar (Genesis 38). With this proverb the sage realized the only way a fool will learn his or her lesson for making foolish financial decisions is by experiencing the pain that comes with it.

> 14 Whoever blesses his neighbor with a loud voice,
>   rising early in the morning, will be counted as cursing.

The proverb is connected to the well-known adage that says "timing is everything." It also shows the vast difference between morning people and those who are not early risers. Pronouncing a blessing on one's neighbor, either as a greeting or a compliment, is generally greatly appreciated by the recipient. But when the blessing is said with a loud voice, and the loud voice is heard too early in the morning, instead of being appreciated, it becomes a source of irritation. This saying is similar to Proverbs 15:23 that also touches on the timing of words.

¹⁵ A continual dripping on a rainy day and a quarrelsome wife are alike;
¹⁶ to restrain her is to restrain the wind or to grasp oil in one's right hand.

It is important to remember that the book of Proverbs was written from a male perspective, as a father offered advice to his son on a wide variety of topics to help the young man live a wise and productive life. With these two proverbs, the father addressed the personality traits of a prospective wife, focusing on a critical spirit. But if the father had been talking to his daughter, he would have warned her against marrying a man who demonstrated the same negativity. Back in chapter 5:15–19, the father praised the joy of finding marital bliss. And, the collection will end with the acrostic poem that lauds the positive impact the ideal woman will have on her husband (31:10–31). The sage warned that marital life is guaranteed to turn miserable when an individual is married to a mate who is a complainer. He likened the nagging to the annoying dripping sound of rain that never quits on a rainy day. The home is supposed to provide shelter from the storms of life, but when a spouse is given to bitterness, it is like living with a roof that leaks. Then, with very picturesque language, the sage warned that trying to restrain a critical spirit was like trying to stop the wind. His final warning was if the son foolishly thought he could change this woman; he would have better success trying to hold oil in his hand. It is interesting to me that I wrote my comments on this set of proverbs the same week my youngest son married a wonderful sweet Christian young lady.

¹⁷ Iron sharpens iron,
and one man sharpens another.

While there are numerous biblical warnings about the consequences of unhealthy friendships (Proverbs 27:6; 1 Corinthians 15:33), this proverb advocates having authentic friends who will sharpen our character with their constructive criticism. Just as a whet stone is needed to sharpen a knife, we need to surround ourselves with wise individuals who will challenge our thinking and our character.

> [18] Whoever tends a fig tree will eat its fruit,
> and he who guards his master will be honored.

The sage used an agricultural illustration to motivate his students to fulfill their social obligations. In poetic terms this is known as emblematic parallelism. Serving others is one of the key purposes of life, and the sage encouraged his students to take pride in their service. The motivation to serve others well is the promise that the one who serves well will be honored for the dedication. To illustrate his point, the sage spoke of the gardener who labored to care for a fig tree. The gardener who lavished care on the fig tree would be rewarded with a productive tree with succulent fruit. So too, is the promise of reward for faithful and diligent labor. A New Testament version of this proverb is Paul's promise.

> Therefore, my beloved brothers, be steadfast, immovable, always abounding in the work of the Lord, knowing that in the Lord your labor is not in vain. (1 Corinthians 15:58)

The Christian serves God by serving others.

> [19] As in water face reflects face,
> so the heart of man reflects the man.

The sage used a common experience to make a profound observation. We have all looked at our reflection while near a body of water. I like to fish and I have leaned over the side of the boat and looked at my reflection in the calm water. While the surface of the water reflects what I look like physically, a closer examination of my heart will reflect the type of person that I truly am. In the Hebrew language, the heart is used to connote the feelings, thoughts, and aspirations of an individual. So, if you want to know the true character of an individual, try to get inside his or her heart.

> [20] Sheol and Abaddon are never satisfied,
> and never satisfied are the eyes of man.

I thought of this proverb as I walked from my house to church and passed the funeral home in my town. Every week there are new names posted in the window and this morning there were three names listed for upcoming funerals. The sage used two Hebrew terms for the underworld to describe the insatiable appetite of death. Sheol referred to the grave and Abaddon spoke of destruction (Proverbs 15:11). The Preacher made this blunt assessment of life and death.

> It is better to go to the house of mourning than to go to the house of feasting, for this is the end of all mankind, and the living will lay it to heart. (Ecclesiastes 7:2)

Having gained his readers' attention with his talk of death, the sage turned his attention to the living and made this observation. Just as the grave is never satisfied, but always wants more, so too tend to be the hearts of mankind as they live their lives. The person who needs something more to be satisfied will never be satisfied. The apostle Paul warned Timothy of the dangers of covetousness as he argued for a spirit of contentment (1 Timothy 6:6–10). Return to the experience of the Preacher who realized his pursuit of things did not bring him satisfaction (Ecclesiastes 2:1–11).

> [21] The crucible is for silver, and the furnace is for gold,
>   and a man is tested by his praise.

While no one likes trials, the sage understood their necessity in the removal of character flaws. Just as the heat of the furnace is necessary for the removal of dross, so too each individual must experience the heat of trials to develop character. While the first line of the proverb is clear, the second line is not. Either the individual reveals character by how he or she responds to praise, or by what he or she chooses to praise.

> [22] Crush a fool in a mortar with a pestle along with crushed grain,
>   yet his folly will not depart from him.

One of the reoccurring themes of the book of Proverbs is the incorrigibility of the fool (17:10). The fool is incapable of being corrected or reformed because he or she rarely learns from the mistakes. And, physical punishment, implied by the metaphor, is not a good deterrent either. A pestle is a hard tool with a rounded end that is used for pounding or crushing substances, such as medicines, in a deep bowl, called a mortar. In the sage's world, grains were crushed in a pestle to be made into flour. The sage did not believe that stupidity could be beaten out of a fool. The takeaway from this proverb is the need for consistent and loving parental discipline of a child before the child becomes deep-seated in the folly.

> [23] Know well the condition of your flocks,
> and give attention to your herds,
> [24] for riches do not last forever;
> and does a crown endure to all generations?
> [25] When the grass is gone and the new growth appears
> and the vegetation of the mountains is gathered,
> [26] the lambs will provide your clothing,
> and the goats the price of a field.
> [27] There will be enough goats' milk for your food,
> for the food of your household
> and maintenance for your girls.

This extended proverbial section addresses a number of the key topics that are highlighted throughout the book of Proverbs, namely, riches and possessions and diligence and hard work. Speaking to an agricultural audience, the sage advocated a commitment to hard work and attention to detail when it came to the care of one's flocks. The shepherd who cared for his flocks of sheep and goats would see these animals provide for his household. If the shepherd would work hard to feed his sheep and goats, reflected in the gathering of the grass from the hillsides, then these animals would feed and clothe the people who lived in his home. The sage urged his readers to engage in hard labor because he knew that riches do not last forever. This was a reality, not just for the common people, but also for the wealthy, which is hinted at with the reference to the "crown." The subject of this section was wealthy enough to own female servants ("your girls"). Speaking to a modern audience, this section instructs us to work hard at our occupations and to take care of our possessions and property. Prosperity is not a bad thing, but we need to be reminded of the transitory nature of money and possessions. The New Testament reinforces these truths with a negative example with the parable of the rich fool in Luke 12:13–21.

^{28:1} The wicked flee when no one pursues,
but the righteous are bold as a lion.

One of the negative side effects of being wicked is having a guilty conscience. The wicked individual knows that what he or she is doing is wrong, which is why the unethical business is normally conducted in secret (Proverbs 17:23). We see this flight in Adam and Eve's behavior when they hid from the presence of God after they had disobeyed and eaten from the tree of the knowledge of good and evil (Genesis 3:8). One of the positive benefits of living a righteous life is having confidence and living a life of purpose. We see this confidence in David as he approached the Philistine champion in battle (1 Samuel 17). With this proverb the sage advocates godliness over wickedness with the reward of a clear conscience.

² When a land transgresses, it has many rulers,
but with a man of understanding and knowledge,
its stability will long continue.

This proverb could serve as political commentary on the history of the nation of Israel. The first line describes the constant turnover of kings who sat on the throne of the northern kingdom of Israel after the kingdom divided (1 Kings 12–2 Kings 17). The second line summarizes the long and relatively stable reigns of David and his son Solomon. The saying describes how wise leadership will lead to stability and longevity, while corrupt leadership will result in instability and brief reigns. The principle of wise and stable leadership applies to governments, institutions, and ministries.

³ A poor man who oppresses the poor
is a beating rain that leaves no food.

Numerous proverbs condemn the rich for oppressing the poor (14:31; 22:7; 22:16). And while the oppression of the poor by those in power is despicable, even worse in the sage's estimation is when one poor person oppresses another poor individual. He likens the damage to a pounding rain that destroys a crop instead of providing necessary moisture. Some translations change the first line to "a ruler who oppresses the poor" because they do not see the poor as having the power to oppress anyone. But, the Hebrew reads "a poor man who oppresses the poor" and so this is the preferred translation.

⁴ Those who forsake the law praise the wicked,
but those who keep the law strive against them.

The scope of this proverb will be determined by how one understands the word translated "law" in the opening phrase. If the term *torah* is limited to general instruction, then it refers to the instruction of the sages. But if *torah* is extended to God's law as defined by the Mosaic Law, then its perspective is broadened. I prefer the broader view because of the emphasis on the wicked (see 28:9). The basic lesson of the Mosaic Law is that God rewards righteousness and punishes wickedness. Read the blessings and curses of Deuteronomy 28. With this proverb the sage challenged his readers to align their lives with God's Word. If they abandon the Law, they will find themselves approving the sinful behavior that God condemns. But if they treasure God's Word, they will actively resist the evil conduct of the wicked. This proverb teaches that one cannot be neutral when it comes to God and His Word.

⁵ Evil men do not understand justice,
but those who seek the LORD understand it completely.

With this proverb the sage understood that basic justice and fair play are not inherently human qualities. Due to man's fallen nature, evil men think of justice in terms of what benefits them. Only when an individual understands the holiness of God and the justice that proceeds from His nature, will that individual practice the justice that God demands of His creatures in their treatment of one another. This proverb teaches that justice apart from God will be perverted and inconsistent. Jesus' parable of the persistent widow in Luke 18:1–8 touches on the interplay between one's fear of God and the practice of justice.

⁶ Better is a poor man who walks in his integrity
than a rich man who is crooked in his ways.

Using the "better than" formula, the sage used an economic difference to contrast an ethical difference. We have seen this contrast in an earlier proverb (19:1). If one had to make a choice, it is better to be poor, but principled, than to be prosperous and unprincipled. Perhaps implied in the comparison is the observation that riches and unethical behavior unfortunately often go together. While there are exceptions to the rule, a person's wealth often negatively influences a person's walk.

> For the love of money is a root of all kinds of evils. It is through this craving that some have wandered away from the faith and pierced themselves with many pangs. (1 Timothy 6:10)

> [7] The one who keeps the law is a son with understanding,
>   but a companion of gluttons shames his father.

The sage made an interesting contrast between the individual who obeyed the Mosaic Law and the one who kept the company of gluttons. It is interesting that the sage would cite gluttony as the behavior that reflected a rejection of parental instruction. Elsewhere in the book of Proverbs, the sin of gluttony was singled out by the sage as an indication of an undisciplined life (23:20–21). The thinking is that if an individual is undisciplined in the diet, he or she will also be undisciplined in the larger decisions of life. The early church fathers considered gluttony to be one of the gateway sins. Obeying the Mosaic Law helped an individual discipline those areas of life that were prone to abuse. Keeping the company of gluttons encouraged an individual to extend that lack of discipline to other areas of life. Included in both lines was the impact the behavior of the child had on the parents (see Deuteronomy 21:18–21).

> [8] Whoever multiplies his wealth by interest and profit
>   gathers it for him who is generous to the poor.

With this proverb, the sage became an economic adviser. He advised his students to invest in people instead of investing in merely financial profits. The Mosaic Law forbade the charging of interest to a fellow Israelite (Exodus 22:25; Deuteronomy 23:19–20). The concern was that the wealthy would ruthlessly take advantage of the poor during their time of distress. The sage warned that any profit that was made at the expense of someone else would be lost in the end, and be given to those who properly knew how to invest in people. According to the psalmist, we are to help others in need without benefitting ourselves and we are not to change our ethics for financial gain.

Who does not put out his money at interest and does not take a bribe against the innocent. He who does these things shall never be moved. (Psalm 15:5)

⁹ If one turns away his ear from hearing the law,
even his prayer is an abomination.

With this proverb the sage made a dramatic statement about the topic of prayer. Detestable behaviors that are particularly offensive to a holy God have been listed in earlier proverbs (6:16–19; 11:1; 15:8). Added to the despicable list is an individual who uses the mouth to offer up prayers to God, while at the same time, the ears are actively rejecting God's instruction. The psalmist understood the connection between obedience and answered prayer (Psalm 6:18-20). God will not listen to us in our prayers if we are not listening to Him.

¹⁰ Whoever misleads the upright into an evil way will fall into his own pit,
but the blameless will have a goodly inheritance.

The sage realized he lived in a fallen world where the wicked were not content merely to pursue their sinful ways. The wicked also wanted to corrupt those who were trying to live righteously. He warned the wicked that their guile would not go unpunished.

And he said to his disciples, "Temptations to sin are sure to come, but woe to the one through whom they come! It would be better for him if a millstone were hung around his neck and he were cast into the sea than that he should cause one of these little ones to sin." (Luke 17:1–2)

In the second line, the sage encouraged the righteous to remain steadfast in the face of temptation with the promise of divine reward.

¹¹ A rich man is wise in his own eyes,
but a poor man who has understanding will find him out.

This proverb contrasts individuals on opposite ends of the economic spectrum and it shows that appearances can be deceptive. Speaking in general terms that allowed for exceptions, the sage saw that wealthy people generally have a high opinion of their intelligence, motivated in part by their riches. Their large income gave them an equally large ego. On the other hand, an individual who was poor financially, but who possessed a wealth of wisdom, was able to see through the façade of the rich person. The sage believed it was better to have wisdom than to merely have wealth. This proverb is a word to the wise when we find ourselves enviously looking at a person who is better off financially.

> 12 When the righteous triumph, there is great glory,
> but when the wicked rise, people hide themselves.

The sage recognized that the stakes were high for society in the battle between good and evil, between wisdom and folly. The lives of many people are negatively affected when the wicked rise to power for they must abuse people to maintain their power. That was true of rulers in the sage's day, and we saw it on a great scale throughout Europe in particular during the Second World War when Adolph Hitler came to power with the Nazi party. But when the righteous are victorious, and we must think of righteousness in biblical terms, people have reason to rejoice. Biblical righteousness takes place when a leader is in a right relationship with God and the leader and the administration is patterning their rule after God's righteous standards. The sage will repeat this proverb at the end of the chapter.

> 13 Whoever conceals his transgressions will not prosper,
> but he who confesses and forsakes them will obtain mercy.

With this proverb the sage advocated for transparency with God and with people when dealing with sin. While human nature tells you to hide your sin, like Adam and Eve did (Genesis 3:8), the sage knew that nothing good comes from a cover-up. True restoration requires repentance and the renunciation of sin. Instead of concealment, the first step in restoration is confession where the sinner admits the transgression and stops making excuses for the sinful behavior. The second necessary step is the abandonment of sin. The individual needs to take the necessary steps to eliminate the sinful behavior so it is not repeated. The sage advocated for transparency with God because he knew God was a merciful Being. The New Testament version of this proverb was written by the apostle John.

If we confess our sins, he is faithful and just to forgive us our
sins and to cleanse us from all unrighteousness. (1 John 1:9)

Read David's psalms of confession (Psalms 32 and 51) where human
repentance resulted in divine mercy.

> ¹⁴ Blessed is the one who fears the LORD always,
> but whoever hardens his heart will fall into calamity.

The sage did not explicitly mention Yahweh in the opening line (the
Hebrew reads "blessed is the one who trembles continually"). But he did
advocate for a fearful attitude which may be shorthand for "the fear of the
LORD" which is the theme of the entire book (1:7). The wise individual who
maintains a reverential attitude toward God will enjoy divine blessing. But
the foolish individual who rejects divine authority will experience the negative
consequences that come with rebellion. Like Pharaoh who hardened his
heart (Exodus 7:13), the fool's rebellion will bring down disaster on himself
or herself.

> ¹⁵ Like a roaring lion or a charging bear
> is a wicked ruler over a poor people.

The sage turned to the animal world to illustrate the damage a ruthless
tyrant could wreak on his poor subjects if he abused his authority. The poor
are already at a disadvantage due to their economic status of having no
political power. Their situation is even more terrifying when the king who
rules over them is not guided by any ethical standards. It is fitting that the
roaring lion and the charging bear were two of the four future kingdoms
featured in the vision of Daniel 7. These were also the two animals David
talked about killing as he talked with King Saul before his contest with
Goliath (1 Samuel 17:34).

> ¹⁶ A ruler who lacks understanding is a cruel oppressor,
> but he who hates unjust gain will prolong his days.

The sage continued his commentary on leadership by noting how the
ethics of the ruler will impact both the quality and the quantity of his reign.
Leadership that is void of wisdom will lead to the oppression of those who are

governed. But a ruler who is motivated by ethics over economics will enjoy a long reign.

> ¹⁷ If one is burdened with the blood of another,
> he will be a fugitive until death; let no one help him.

The first line of the Hebrew literally reads "A man tormented by the blood of a life." The ESV translation interprets the phrase to be addressing the topic of murder. The sage shared a similar viewpoint on the sanctity of life that was expressed in the Mosaic Law (Exodus 21:12–14). God first expressed the dignity of human life when Noah exited the ark (Genesis 9:5–6). The taking of human life was a serious offense, especially if the homicide was premeditated. The sage agreed that the taking of human life should result in punishment in the form of the murderer living the rest of his life as a fugitive. He further instructed his readers not to aid such a person who was tormented by the crime and the punishment.

> ¹⁸ Whoever walks in integrity will be delivered,
> but he who is crooked in his ways will suddenly fall.

Life is comprised of choices and the consequences that come with those choices. The way an individual walks describes the manner of life. According to the sage, there are two ways from which to choose, and each choice comes with attending consequences. If the individual chooses to live a blameless life characterized by honesty and transparency, the person will avoid many painful situations because he or she will not get into a compromising position. On the other hand, if the individual is dishonest, the deceit will bring about his or her own downfall.

> ¹⁹ Whoever works his land will have plenty of bread,
> but he who follows worthless pursuits will have plenty of poverty.

One of the reoccurring themes of the book of Proverbs is the promotion of a good work ethic, with the promise of reward for the industrious worker. This saying which addressed the farmer who works his plot of ground can be added to the list. The sage made a promise, that all things being equal, the individual who labors hard will experience prosperity. But he can also guarantee poverty for the lazy individual who wastes time and energy on meaningless activities.

²⁰ A faithful man will abound with blessings,
but whoever hastens to be rich will not go unpunished.

The individual who faithfully fulfills his or her obligations will be rewarded for the reliability. Faithfulness is demonstrated by a commitment to God and to one's fellow man, as defined by Jesus in his answer to the scribe (Mark 12:28–31). On the other hand, the individual who is only committed to his or her own financial welfare, perhaps at the expense of others and by means of deceitful and unethical shortcuts, will not escape the punishment that is associated with shortsighted thinking (Proverbs 13:11). Instead of long-term commitments that are rewarded, the desire for a quick financial reward will lead to ruin.

²¹ To show partiality is not good,
but for a piece of bread a man will do wrong.

The first line of the saying condemns the showing of favoritism, while the second line reveals the sinful motivation behind the unjust discrimination. The context of the favoritism could be in a courtroom setting (Deuteronomy 1:16–17) or between individuals in a community (Proverbs 18:5). Showing partiality is usually based on the personal gain that the discriminating individual can receive for the unjust favoritism. The sage understood human depravity noting that some individuals are easily motivated to show favoritism. In the New Testament James condemned the showing partiality in the church because God does not show partiality to His creatures (James 2:1–7).

> For the LORD your God is God of gods and Lord of lords, the great, the mighty, and the awesome God, who is not partial and takes no bribe. He executes justice for the fatherless and the widow, and loves the sojourner, giving him food and clothing. (Deuteronomy 10:17–18)

²² A stingy man hastens after wealth
and does not know that poverty will come upon him.

This saying makes some interesting observations concerning the acquisition of wealth. Wealth management is determined by how one looks at money. The "stingy man" in Hebrew literally has an "evil eye" in that he looks at money with the wrong perspective (see Proverbs 23:6). Instead of viewing money as a means of investing in others, he views it merely as a commodity to be accumulated. Read the parable of the rich fool in Luke 12:13–21 which makes the same point. The individual who is driven to acquire wealth, but who lacks a generous spirit, will actually become impoverished. The key to true wealth, as defined by the Bible, is to be generous, not greedy. The individual who possesses a generous spirit will experience true prosperity. This is the point of Proverbs 22:9 that speaks of the "bountiful eye" who shares his prosperity with the poor.

> ²³ Whoever rebukes a man will afterward find more favor
>   than he who flatters with his tongue.

This proverb addresses the moral decision to either tell people what they need to hear (rebuke) or to tell them what they want to hear (flattery). A sign of genuine friendship is the willingness to give reproof when it is needed, even if the criticism is painful at first. A previous proverb stated, "Faithful are the wounds of a friend; profuse are the kisses of an enemy" (27:6). In the long run, honesty will serve a relationship better than the dishonesty of false flattery. Flattery is used, either in the mistaken effort to maintain a friendship, or in an effort to manipulate people, which is not the definition of friendship.

> ²⁴ Whoever robs his father or his mother and
>   says, "That is no transgression,"
>   is a companion to a man who destroys.

With the fifth commandment of the Decalogue God legislated the proper treatment of parents.

> "Honor your father and your mother, that your days may
> be long in the land that the LORD your God is giving you.
> (Exodus 20:12)

The individual who callously violates this commandment by stealing from the parents, and then protests his or her innocence, is no different than the stranger who would attack them. To rob one's parents is to destroy one of the basic foundations of a stable society. Jesus addressed this problem when he condemned the Pharisees for their circumvention of "the (written) commands of God" in favor of "the (oral) traditions of men" (Mark 7:9–13). By declaring that one's offering was "Corban," that is, reserved for sacred use and withdrawn from common use, an adult child could "make void the word of God" and not care for their parents.

> ²⁵ A greedy man stirs up strife,
>   but the one who trusts in the Lord will be enriched.

This proverb expresses two opposing philosophies of life that are expressed by the object of one's faith. The "greedy man" believes that having more things will enrich his life. On the opposite spectrum, the "one who trusts in the Lord" finds contentment in God. The second individual believes in the promise Jesus made in the Sermon on the Mount.

> Seek first the kingdom of God and his righteousness, and all
>   these things will be added to you. (Matthew 6:33)

The value of these two belief systems is determined by the end product. The "greedy man," while he may accumulate more things, will also create conflict because his selfishness and unethical conduct will violate the rights of others. On the other hand, the individual who finds his or her contentment in God will experience true prosperity (1 Timothy 6:6–10).

> ²⁶ Whoever trusts in his own mind is a fool,
>   but he who walks in wisdom will be delivered.

The book of Proverbs is a collection of addresses and individual sayings that provide wise advice on the important matters of life. This particular saying declares the foolishness of self-reliance when the counsel of others is available. To keep one's own counsel is to look at a matter from only one limited perspective. The wise individual will follow the advice of the second line of the previous proverb which states, "the one who trusts in the Lord will be enriched."

> ²⁷ Whoever gives to the poor will not want,
>   but he who hides his eyes will get many a curse.

One of the characteristics of a wise life is the demonstration of generosity toward others, especially toward the poor. Several earlier proverbs made the connection between generosity and godliness (14:21, 31). The sage knew that true joy came through generosity, while a miserly spirit would be cursed by God and mankind. One of the main obstacles to generosity is the selfish fear of not having enough for ourselves. This fear is overcome when the giver has faith in God to provide as he or she provides for the needs of others. Another proverb promises blessing on the one who chooses to be a blessing to others.

> Whoever has a bountiful eye will be blessed, for he shares
> his bread with the poor. (Proverbs 22:9)

> [28] When the wicked rise, people hide themselves,
>   but when they perish, the righteous increase.

The sage returned to a proverb on human government that was similar to one he issued in Proverbs 28:12, except the order is reversed. The people hiding from the wicked is seen in the Gideon narrative during the days of the judges (Judges 6).

> [29:1] He who is often reproved, yet stiffens his neck,
>   will suddenly be broken beyond healing.

Everyone needs friends and counselors in their lives to bring constructive criticism to correct bad behavior and to point out faulty thinking. The wise individual will receive and respond to this reproof, but the fool will repeatedly reject the correction that is offered. This saying warns the fool that repeated rejection of reproof will result in unexpected and permanent harm. The nation of Israel was often characterized as a stiff-necked people (Exodus 32:9; Acts 7:51), which is why its repeated rejection of the prophets sent to warn them resulted in such painful consequences (2 Chronicles 36:13–16).

> [2] When the righteous increase, the people rejoice,
>   but when the wicked rule, the people groan.

This saying that connects the quality of human government to the quality of life of the governed people is similar to Proverbs 28:12 and 28. Righteous rulers will cause the people to rejoice, but wicked leaders bring misery to their people. This saying was true when Israel was a theocracy with a king as God's representative. But it is also true when people live in a democracy or under a dictatorship. If the ruler serves God, he or she will also serve the people well. But if the ruler rejects God and His righteous statutes, the leader will serve self and the people will suffer.

> ³ He who loves wisdom makes his father glad,
> but a companion of prostitutes squanders his wealth.

This proverb could be a commentary on the parable of the prodigal son (Luke 15:11–31). The younger son left the safety of his father's house, and, in the words of the older brother, "devoured the father's property with prostitutes." The two lines of the saying teach that a positive response to wisdom will enrich the lives of those who care about the morals of the young person. But a rejection of wisdom will enrich the lives of strangers who only care about the young person's money. A young person who embraces wisdom will bring joy to his or her parents who have invested in that life. But if the counsel of the parents is rejected, it will lead to moral and financial ruin.

> ⁴ By justice a king builds up the land,
> but he who exacts gifts tears it down.

This proverb describes the impact the ethics of a leader will have on the people. If the leader pursues justice, the leader will enhance the lives of the people that are governed. But if the leader uses the office for personal gain, the leader will wreak havoc on the very people he or she is supposed to lead. The word that is translated "gifts" makes us think of bribes, but in this case, it refers to unjust taxes. The ten tribe's rejection of King Rehoboam because of his father Solomon's heavy taxation is an illustration of this proverb (1 Kings 12:1–15). Serving others selflessly brings security, while serving self brings strife.

> ⁵ A man who flatters his neighbor
> spreads a net for his feet.

Genuine compliments can be used to build a great friendship, but this proverb examines the manipulative nature of false flattery (5:3–6; 26:28). Calculated compliments appeal to the vanity of an individual with the purpose of creating an advantage for the one who offers the flattery.

> ⁶ An evil man is ensnared in his transgression,
> but a righteous man sings and rejoices.

The first line of this proverb is similar to a warning Moses gave the tribes of Reuben and Gad as they settled in the land of Gilead. The latter part of Numbers 32:23 states, "be sure your sin will find you out." The sage spoke of sin as a rebellion against God's moral standards. As a result of the evil man's sin, he will step unsuspectingly into a trap. The contrast in the second line has an interesting emphasis on the righteous man who breaks out into singing as he rejoices in God's blessing on his obedience.

> ⁷ A righteous man knows the rights of the poor;
> a wicked man does not understand such knowledge.

This proverb addresses the matter of social justice and the believer's responsibility toward the poor and the oppressed in this world. The saying draws a connection between a person's relationship with God and a person's relationship with other people. A righteous individual understands that God is holy and that God requires us to treat other people with respect, whether they are rich or poor, since they are also made in the image of God. A wicked individual does not think of God in this way. With no consideration for God, the wicked also is insensitive to the needs of the poor (Luke 18:1–4). The following proverbs detail one's responsibility for the poor (14:21, 31; 16:19; 17:5; 19:17; 21:13; 22:2, 9, 22; 28:27).

> ⁸ Scoffers set a city aflame,
> but the wise turn away wrath.

Scoffers are the worst kind of fools because they mock divine truth and human authority. Because these fools reject the wisdom that is handed down by parents (Proverbs 13:1) and teachers (Proverbs 15:12), long-term damage is done to a society. This damage is implied by the image of a city set aflame. The wise on the other hand, because they accept the advice of respected authority figures will turn away wrath in the sense that they will avoid the painful consequences that come from making foolish choices. Ultimately the wise will turn away the wrath of God, while fools will incur God's wrath.

9 If a wise man has an argument with a fool,
the fool only rages and laughs, and there is no quiet.

This proverb is the Old Testament version of one of Jesus' commands in the Sermon on the Mount.

> Do not give dogs what is holy, and do not throw your pearls before pigs, lest they trample them underfoot and turn to attack you. (Matthew 7:6)

The sage warns individuals not to get into an argument with a fool for it will not accomplish anything constructive (Proverbs 26:4). Because a fool does not know what he or she does not know, the fool will leave the conversation thinking the wise person is the real fool and it will only lead to further conflict.

10 Bloodthirsty men hate one who is blameless
and seek the life of the upright.

The sage believed in the doctrine of human depravity and he cited an extreme example of its manifestation. Evil individuals not only live unrighteous lives, but they are also antagonistic toward those who do strive to live with integrity. The presence of righteousness irritates and convicts them to the point that they try to eliminate it. The supreme example of this hatred was directed toward Jesus Christ.

11 A fool gives full vent to his spirit,
but a wise man quietly holds it back.

This proverb returns to the familiar topic of the fool with the sage focusing on the emotions that reveal the difference between the fool and the wise person. The fool has no emotional control but freely speaks his or her mind with no regard for the damage their words will cause. On the other hand, the wise person has emotional controls and carefully chooses their words so he or she inflicts no harm. The second line of the proverb can also be understood to say that the wise person can hold back the anger of the fool. While self-control is not our natural response (Galatians 5:16–24), it is a necessary response when dealing with the emotions that are natural to us.

¹² If a ruler listens to falsehood,
all his officials will be wicked.

In the 1980s the American president Ronald Reagan promoted economic policies that were described by his opponents as trickle-down economics. The theory believed that taxes on businesses and the wealthy in society should be reduced as a means to stimulate business investment in the short term and benefit society at large in the long term. While this policy is still debated, the sage believed in trickle-down leadership where an unethical leader would produce an equally corrupt court. If a ruler was known to only hear what he or she wanted to hear, the court would adjust to this dishonesty and corruption would reign throughout the palace. The antidote to this corruption is David's pledge.

> No one who practices deceit shall dwell in my house; no one who utters lies shall continue before my eyes. (Psalm 101:7)

¹³ The poor man and the oppressor meet together;
the LORD gives light to the eyes of both.

With this proverb the sage reminds us that despite our differences with other people, we have one significant thing in common, namely, the LORD as the source of our existence. In this particular proverb the sage focused on the economic difference that separated the oppressed poor person and the creditor who was exploiting him or her. But despite being on opposite ends of the economic spectrum, both individuals were dependent on the LORD for their very existence (see Proverbs 22:2). With this proverb the sage wanted to encourage the poor person that the LORD had not abandoned him or her, and at the same time he issued a warning to the rich person that the LORD would bring punishment for the abuse of the poor.

¹⁴ If a king faithfully judges the poor,
his throne will be established forever.

This proverb is connected to the two previous sayings in that it combines the two subjects of the king and his reign and the lives of the poor people who live in his kingdom. The sage believed that how a ruler treated the most vulnerable subjects in the kingdom was the clearest indicator of the quality of that ruler. If the king was not influenced by money and power, but cared for the poor, the sage wanted the reign of this ruler to be blessed by God with many years on the throne. Because proverbs are general statements of truth and not promises, the second line should be viewed as the sage's wish that this righteous ruler would reign for many years (Proverbs 20:28; 25:5). What king ever judged the poor so well as Christ? His throne is truly established forever.

> ¹⁵ The rod and reproof give wisdom,
> but a child left to himself brings shame to his mother.

This proverb on child discipline was written for the instruction of the parents. The sage promoted both the corporal and verbal correction of the child, with the warning to the parents that to neglect their primary parental responsibility would one day bring them sorrow. In today's culture with its emphasis on child abuse, the reference to the "rod" can cause an unfortunate negative reaction. But the failure to discipline a child is another form of child abuse. Because the sage believed in the doctrine of human depravity (Proverbs 22:15), he knew that leaving a child to his or her own devices would result in the corruption of the child. His emphasis on the mother was probably done for emotional reasons.

> ¹⁶ When the wicked increase, transgression increases,
> but the righteous will look upon their downfall.

In wisdom literature, there are only two choices in life, wickedness and righteousness. Living in a fallen world that is antagonistic to a holy God, wickedness thrives and mankind's ability to violate God's standards is ever increasing. With this proverb, the sage wanted to encourage the righteous that God will be ultimately victorious. It also served as a warning to the wicked that his or her days were numbered. Every wicked person will eventually face the judgment of a righteous God. This was the theology of the poet in the Civil War poem "Christmas Bell."

> Then pealed the bells more loud and deep: God is not dead,
> nor does he sleep, the wrong shall fail, the right prevail, with
> peace on earth, good will to men. (Henry W. Longfellow)

> ¹⁷ Discipline your son, and he will give you rest;
> he will give delight to your heart.

The sage returned to the important topic of child rearing with a positive motivation for the parents to make the needed effort. While the daily task of consistent discipline can be frustrating and emotionally and physically exhausting, the effort is worth it because of the long-term rewards. The rewards of biblical parenting are twofold in this proverb. The first reward is the peace of mind that comes from knowing you did not shirk from your responsibilities to your children when they were young. The second reward is the joy of watching your children grow into maturity.

> [18] Where there is no prophetic vision the people cast off restraint,
> but blessed is he who keeps the law.

This proverb is a commentary on the history of the nation of Israel in the Old Testament. When God was actively revealing His holy nature to the nation, the people more closely watched their behavior. But when the nation ignored God and indulged in sin, God at times would choose to go silent. As the period of the judges came to an end during the days of Eli the high priest, the narrator made this comment about the lack of divine revelation.

> And the word of the LORD was rare in those days; there was
> no frequent vision. (1 Samuel 3:1a)

Exodus 32:25 and the incident with the golden calf define the meaning of casting off restraint. The second stanza of the proverb recognized the Mosaic Law was the primary revelation from God to His people as to His holy nature and the holy behavior He expected from them (see Deuteronomy 4:6–8).

> [19] By mere words a servant is not disciplined,
> for though he understands, he will not respond.

This proverb addresses the most effective methods for discipline. The sage recognized that when it came to effective discipline that would change the behavior of a stubborn servant, a word to the wise would be insufficient. While corrective words in the form of a verbal rebuke are a good start, most people need negative reinforcement to really get one's attention. There must be a certain amount of pain to get the point across, whether it is corporal or financial or social pain.

²⁰ Do you see a man who is hasty in his words?
There is more hope for a fool than for him.

If this proverb sounds familiar, that is because the second stanza is identical to an earlier proverb.

> Do you see a man who is wise in his own eyes? There is more
> hope for a fool than for him. (Proverbs 26:12)

The fool is a common foil for the sage and with these sayings he is describing the worst kind of fool. When the two proverbs are combined, they described two common character flaws among fools. A fool thinks he or she is the smartest person in the room, and because of that, the fool thinks he or she has something worthwhile to say. The sage would be in agreement with the New Testament author James.

> Know this, my beloved brothers: let every person be quick to
> hear, slow to speak, slow to anger. (James 1:19)

God gave us twice as many ears as he gave us mouths. Commonsense tells us to listen twice as much as we speak.

²¹ Whoever pampers his servant from childhood
will in the end find him his heir.

Just as a child who grows up without discipline brings grief to his parents (Proverbs 29:17), so too will a servant who is not disciplined bring grief to his master (Proverbs 29:19). The precise meaning of the second line of the proverb is uncertain because the Hebrew word *manon* is used only this time in the Old Testament, known as a *hapax legomenon*, and its etymology is uncertain. What is certain about this proverb is that the sage denounced the thought of a pampered life. Every person who wants to amount to something in life needs discipline.

²² A man of wrath stirs up strife,
and one given to anger causes much transgression.

The person who cannot control the temper is going to irritate other people when he or she gets irritated. Giving in to one's sin nature will result in angry outbursts, which in turn, will cause more sin. The apostle Paul understood the connection between anger and sin when he wrote his list of the works of the flesh (Galatians 5:18–21). The first three sins are associated with sensuality, or matters of morality (sexual immorality, impurity, sensuality). The next two sins are associated with pagan religions (idolatry, sorcery). The next eight sins describe fractured fellowship which is the focus of this proverb (enmity, strife, jealousy, fits of anger, rivalries, dissensions, divisions, envy).

> **²³** One's pride will bring him low,
> but he who is lowly in spirit will obtain honor.

In a memorable statement back in chapter 6, the sage listed human pride as one of the sins that God finds most offensive to His sovereign nature. Notice that pride is first on the list.

> There are six things that the LORD hates, seven that are an abomination to him: haughty eyes. (Proverbs 6:16–17a)

Because God is offended by human pride, He will humiliate the proud, and He will elevate the humble.

> **²⁴** The partner of a thief hates his own life;
> he hears the curse, but discloses nothing.

For the sage, to join forces with a thief is to live a wasted life. Stealing from others is no way to make a living and it usually does not end well. This was the father's warning to his son back in Proverbs 1:8-19 about the danger of joining in with thieves. The second line of the proverb is a little more difficult to interpret. If the curse is understood in a legal setting, and the accomplice remains silent in a court of law, he or she is just as guilty as the thief. The Mosaic Law had the following legislation.

> If anyone sins in that he hears a public adjuration to testify, and though he is a witness, whether he has seen or come to know the matter, yet does not speak, he shall bear his iniquity. (Leviticus 5:1)

Knowing about a theft and remaining silent makes an individual just as guilty as the thief who committed the crime.

> ²⁵ The fear of man lays a snare,
> but whoever trusts in the LORD is safe.

The "fear of the LORD" is a reoccurring theme that opens the book of Proverbs and it is an emotion and a mentality that is to be pursued in one's relationship with God (1:7). Therefore, the "fear of man" is a negative emotion and mentality that should be avoided. In this proverb, fear is the opposite of trust and a mere mortal is the opposite of the eternal LORD. The two combinations do not mix. When we allow the opinions of people to intimidate us, it is impossible to be intimate with the LORD and trust Him. The third set of opposites are a snare and safety. Trusting in the LORD leads to protection, while fearing people leads to peril. The psalmist asked the question, "in God I trust; I shall not be afraid. What can man do to me?" (Psalm 56:11).

> ²⁶ Many seek the face of a ruler,
> but it is from the LORD that a man gets justice.

It is human nature for human beings to look to another human being who is in a position of power to present their case and to take their side. In the days of the sage, people looked to their king for his favor in a dispute. The sage recognized that if someone is looking for true justice, only the LORD can grant that. While the focus of this proverb makes us think of justice between human beings, the ultimate matter of justice is with a holy God. Justice with a holy God is never based on human merit, but is always based always on divine mercy.

> ²⁷ An unjust man is an abomination to the righteous,
> but one whose way is straight is an abomination to the wicked.

With this proverb the sage recognized that in the moral realm, opposites do not attract. The righteous and the wicked actually repel one another and create feelings of disgust. A dishonest person will be offensive to people who are striving to live a righteous life. But the same thing is true in the opposite direction. An individual who is living a godly life will irritate those who want to live a wicked life.

The Words of Agur (30:1-33)

³⁰:¹ The words of Agur son of Jakeh. The oracle.
The man declares, I am weary, O God;
I am weary, O God, and worn out.

There is much uncertainty and speculation as to the identity of the author of this section and the correct translation of his opening words. The only thing we know for certain about the anonymous sage Agur was that he was the son of Jakeh. The next word rendered "oracle" (*massa*) is understood by some scholars as the place name Massa, identifying Agur as being from the tribe of the Massaites, an Arab tribe associated with the Ishmaelites (Genesis 25:14). But how the sayings of a non-Israelite sage were included in the collection of proverbs has no valid explanation either. Some translations render the next line as "The man declares to Ithiel, to Ithiel and Ucal," taking the difficult words as personal names.

² Surely I am too stupid to be a man.
I have not the understanding of a man.
³ I have not learned wisdom,
nor have I knowledge of the Holy One.

There are two ways to understanding the opening statement of Agur's oracle. Either he was offering a sincere confession of his own shortcomings concerning his knowledge of the holy ways of God. Or, he was being sarcastic toward those individuals who claimed that they did have a good knowledge of the ways of God. Even though Agur claimed that he did not know wisdom, and that he did not have a proper understanding of God's unique nature, the fact that he realized his deficiencies was a good starting point. The fool does not know what he does not know. At least Agur knew that "the fear of the LORD is the beginning of knowledge" (Proverbs 1:7).

⁴ Who has ascended to heaven and come down?
Who has gathered the wind in his fists?
Who has wrapped up the waters in a garment?
Who has established all the ends of the earth?
What is his name, and what is his son's name? Surely you know!

The series of rhetorical questions that Agur asked sound similar to the questions that God asked of Job. The frustrated patriarch had demanded an audience with God to get his questions answered as to the cause of his suffering. Instead of answering Job's questions, God posed His own questions.

> Where were you when I laid the foundation of the earth? Tell me, if you have understanding. Who determined its measurements—surely you know! Or who stretched the line upon it? On what were its bases sunk, or who laid its cornerstone, when the morning stars sang together and all the sons of God shouted for joy?" (Job 38:4–7)

A similar series of rhetorical questions were voiced by Isaiah where the prophet demonstrated to Israel its ignorance of God.

> Who has measured the waters in the hollow of his hand and marked off the heavens with a span, enclosed the dust of the earth in a measure and weighed the mountains in scales and the hills in a balance? Who has measured the Spirit of the LORD, or what man shows him his counsel? Whom did he consult, and who made him understand? Who taught him the path of justice, and taught him knowledge, and showed him the way of understanding? (Isaiah 40:12–14)

The purpose of these questions is to prove that the only source of true knowledge is God in the form of His self-revelation known as the scriptures, and not man.

> ⁵ Every word of God proves true;
> he is a shield to those who take refuge in him.
> ⁶ Do not add to his words,
> lest he rebuke you and you be found a liar.

This section deals with words, divine and human, and whose words can be counted on, especially during difficult times. Agur came to the conclusion that only the statements of God as contained in the scriptures are the trustworthy declarations on which an individual can rely. In fact, so precise are God's statements that they are not to be tampered with. Because the statements of God are perfectly reliable, any human addition would actually be a serious detraction, and punishable by divine rebuke. Agur's confidence in the words of God is reminiscent of the psalmist's declaration of divine truth.

> The law of the LORD is perfect, reviving the soul; the testimony of the LORD is sure, making wise the simple; the precepts of the LORD are right, rejoicing the heart; the commandment of the LORD is pure, enlightening the eyes; the fear of the LORD is clean, enduring forever; the rules of the LORD are true, and righteous altogether. (Psalm 19:7–9)

And, his warning not to add to God's Word is similar to Moses' warning to Israel before the nation entered the Promised Land.

> And now, O Israel, listen to the statutes and the rules that I am teaching you, and do them, that you may live, and go in and take possession of the land that the LORD, the God of your fathers, is giving you. You shall not add to the word that I command you, nor take from it, that you may keep the commandments of the LORD your God that I command you. (Deuteronomy 4:1–2)

> 7 Two things I ask of you; deny them not to me before I die:
> 8 Remove far from me falsehood and lying;
> give me neither poverty nor riches;
> feed me with the food that is needful for me,
> 9 lest I be full and deny you and say, "Who is the LORD?"
> or lest I be poor and steal and profane the name of my God.

This section offers a fascinating look into the prayer life of Agur. And what is notable about his prayer list are the two areas of life that the sage chose to focus on. First, he prayed about his integrity for he realized that a life of dishonesty would contaminate every relationship that he had. Honesty and integrity are common themes in the book of Proverbs (12:17, 19; 23:23). Second, he prayed about his income, and wisely, he wanted to be somewhere in the middle. Jesus picked up on this theme with his reference to a person's "daily bread" in the Sermon on the Mount (Matthew 6:11). The apostle Paul also promoted a life of contentment when it came to the material things.

> But if we have food and clothing, with these we will be content. (1 Timothy 6:8)

Agur had learned from the experiences of other people and he realized that the two extremes of prosperity and poverty came with their own set of problems. He saw the human tendency to ignore God spiritually when a person has everything financially. This was God's concern for the nation of Israel in Deuteronomy 8:11–14. He also saw the temptation to steal with the excuse that God was not meeting my needs. This proverb on the basic necessities of life reminds me of one of my favorite memories of my father. I went with him to the bank when I was a young boy to cash a check. After the teller had counted out his cash, he proceeded to count it out again in front of her. This made the teller nervous and she asked my father, "Did I give you enough money?" His humorous answer was, "Just barely."

> [10] Do not slander a servant to his master,
> lest he curse you, and you be held guilty.

After wading through the cultural matters, Agur's advice is to mind your own business, for if you do not, you will regret it. If you use your tongue in private to make false accusations against someone who has less social standing than you, they will use their tongue in public to pronounce your guilt in the matter.

> [11] There are those who curse their fathers
> and do not bless their mothers.
> [12] There are those who are clean in their own eyes
> but are not washed of their filth.
> [13] There are those—how lofty are their eyes,
> how high their eyelids lift!
> [14] There are those whose teeth are swords,
> whose fangs are knives,
> to devour the poor from off the earth,
> the needy from among mankind.

In this numerical set of proverbs Agur begins each line with the same expression (literally "a generation") as he describes a certain type of person. He lists four groups of people whose behavior he finds particularly offensive. The first group of offenders are people who dishonor their parents in violation of the fifth commandment (Exodus 20:12). The Mosaic Law required an extreme form of punishment for this offense because of its attack on the social order of the family (Exodus 21:17). The second group of offenders are people who are self-righteous, and because of their distorted perception, they are ignorant of the moral filth that covers their lives. Jesus condemned the religious self-righteous in his day (Matthew 23:25–27). The third group of offenders are the arrogant who think highly of themselves. Feelings of superiority toward self always result in attitudes of inferiority toward others. The fourth group of offenders use their words as weapons to destroy vulnerable people who cannot defend themselves. Agur's list of offensive behaviors is very similar to an earlier numerical list of behaviors that are particularly offensive to a holy God (Proverbs 6:16–19).

> 15 The leech has two daughters: Give and Give.
> Three things are never satisfied;
> four never say, "Enough":
> 16 Sheol, the barren womb,
> the land never satisfied with water,
> and the fire that never says, "Enough.

Agur's reference to the leech takes my mind in a pleasant direction to fishing in the Canadian province of Ontario. One of the benefits of fishing with leeches is that you don't have to hold on to them when you are trying to bait your hook on a cold morning. A leech will always hold on to you. Agur understood the anatomy of a leech in that it has two suckers, hence the "two daughters." They have a distinct head end with a mouth consisting of sharp cutting beaks located within the head sucker. Their rear sucker is larger and is used to anchor the leech in place. As Agur considered the leech, it caused his mind to wander as he thought about other things in life that are never satisfied. He had lived long enough to realize the harsh reality of life that death would never end (Proverbs 27:20). Think about the Sunday paper and the endless columns of obituaries week after week. He must have known some childless women in his clan whose lifelong desire for a child never ended. Read 1 Samuel 1:10 about Hannah who "was deeply distressed and prayed to the

Lord and wept bitterly." The grave wants to end life and the womb wants to create life. Because he lived in the land of Palestine with its minimal rainfall, he knew the land would never have a surplus of water. And, as he sat around his camp fire, he knew the fire would continue to burn until it ran out of fuel. Fire and water are also opposite elements. It seems that the overriding thought of this numerical proverb is a warning against the dangers of greed which is never satisfied.

> ¹⁷ The eye that mocks a father
> and scorns to obey a mother
> will be picked out by the ravens of the valley
> and eaten by the vultures.

Agur had briefly addressed the problem of parental disrespect earlier in his collection (30:11). He returned to the important topic and used some shocking imagery to get the reader's attention. A child who grows into adulthood and who displays a contempt for parents is accursed in life because the child fails to show the proper respect for the two people who gave him or her life. Agur imagined a painful end to that life because the child's contempt for the parents bodes ill for later generations. When the family structure breaks down, the ruin of the society is not far behind. In two of the apostle Paul's sin lists, he listed "disobedient to parents" as a sign of human depravity (Romans 1:30; 2 Timothy 3:2).

> ¹⁸ Three things are too wonderful for me;
> four I do not understand:
> ¹⁹ the way of an eagle in the sky,
> the way of a serpent on a rock,
> the way of a ship on the high seas,
> and the way of a man with a virgin.

In addition to being a keen observer of human behavior, Agur also enjoyed observing the natural world. This is his numerical list of the natural wonders that he found most fascinating. The common denominator in the four items is the aspect of movement. Being earthbound, he marveled at the sight of an eagle soaring overhead in the sky. Walking through the Judean wilderness, he was intrigued when he saw a snake use the motion of its body to slither across a rock. Visiting the coastal plain, he watched with fascination as a cargo ship plowed through the Mediterranean Sea. And then, returning to the world of human behavior, he was captivated by the sexual intimacy that took place between a man and his wife. Agur's celebration of God-sanctioned intimacy within the bounds of marriage is contrasted with his condemnation of marital infidelity in the next proverb. Since Agur had the chance to write his list of fascinating things, now you get the chance. What natural wonders fascinate you?

> ²⁰ This is the way of an adulteress:
> she eats and wipes her mouth and says, "I have done no wrong."

Having marveled at the joys of marital intimacy in the previous proverb, Agur turned his attention to the callous nature of an adulterous woman. An ad popped up on my laptop the other day with the slogan, "Life is short. Have an affair." This vulgar attack on the sanctity of marriage represents the hardened nature of the adulterous woman who engaged in illicit sexual activity and then denied any wrongdoing. She viewed her appetite for sex as no different than what she would do to satisfy her appetite for food.

> ²¹ Under three things the earth trembles;
> under four it cannot bear up:
> ²² a slave when he becomes king,
> and a fool when he is filled with food;
> ²³ an unloved woman when she gets a husband,
> and a maidservant when she displaces her mistress.

Agur was an observer of human behavior and he composed a list of individuals, who, when they attained a position of power, would most likely abuse that power and upset the social order. An elevation in social status, without a change in character will reveal their lack of character. An individual who was raised as a slave, but who becomes a king will most likely rule his subjects with the same cruelty with which he was treated when he was a slave (see Proverbs 19:10). The second individual on the list is the fool, a reoccurring character in Proverbs. A fool with a full stomach will have even less motivation to work. The next two abusive individuals are women which demonstrates that the potential to abuse power is not limited to the male gender. A woman who goes through life and has not experienced affection will become bitter when a man finally does marry her. Her bitterness is fed by the knowledge that the marriage is based on need and not on love. And finally, a slave woman who once served her mistress, but then replaces her in the affections of the master of the house, will become vindictive when the tables are turned. The narrative of Sarah and Hagar is a biblical illustration of this observation (Genesis 16:1–5).

> ²⁴ Four things on earth are small,
> but they are exceedingly wise:
> ²⁵ the ants are a people not strong,
> yet they provide their food in the summer;
> ²⁶ the rock badgers are a people not mighty,
> yet they make their homes in the cliffs;
> ²⁷ the locusts have no king,
> yet all of them march in rank;
> ²⁸ the lizard you can take in your hands,
> yet it is in kings' palaces.

Agur turned his attention back to the natural world and he made a list of four small creatures, that despite their diminutive size, display great wisdom. In contrast to the four human beings who lived chaotic lives in the previous section, these creatures survive because of their skillful instincts. Ants, who have appeared earlier in the collection of wise sayings (6:6–11), are moved by instinct to collect their food as a colony despite their small frame. Science has discovered that a common field ant can carry up to fifty times its body weight. The rock badger (Syrian coney) wisely makes its home high in the cliffs for security from predators. Better known as a hyrax, this rodent-like creature is the size of a rabbit with a squat body and a plump head. The neck, ears, and tail are short, as are the slender legs. The rock hyrax is a terrestrial animal that lives in groups among rocks and is active by day. Agur marveled as he watched an invasion of locusts descend on the land and consume all the vegetation (read Joel 1:1–4). Finally, the sage was amused to see a small lizard, that he could hold in his hands, creeping around the palace of the king. By citing these creatures, Agur was telling human beings to live skillful lives and that brains are better than brawn.

> ²⁹ Three things are stately in their tread;
> four are stately in their stride:
> ³⁰ the lion, which is mightiest among beasts

and does not turn back before any;
    ³¹ the strutting rooster, the he-goat,
    and a king whose army is with him.

From a group of insignificant creatures that survive by means of stealth, Agur turned his attention to four impressive creatures that convey a sense of majesty and power in their bearing. The lion was a universal symbol of strength and majesty in many of the cultures of the ancient Middle East. The strength of the lion was cited by Samson in the riddle that he put to his Philistine wedding guests (Judges 14). Solomon had an impressive ivory throne that was overlaid with gold. There were six steps that led up to the throne which was guarded by twelve lions (2 Chronicles 9:17–19). The next creature, the strutting rooster, although it is not impressive in size, has a large personality. If you grew up on a farm that raised chickens, you would appreciate the image of a strutting rooster amidst the laying hens. The third creature was a male mountain goat that due to its unique hooves could climb high into the hills. The prophet Daniel described the power of the male mountain goat in one of his visions (Daniel 8:1–8). The last majestic creature on the list was human. A king backed by a powerful army can be bold and majestic in his bearing when he confronts his enemies. Two earlier proverbs compared the anger of a king to a growling lion (19:12; 20:2).

    ³² If you have been foolish, exalting yourself,
        or if you have been devising evil,
        put your hand on your mouth.
    ³³ For pressing milk produces curds,
        pressing the nose produces blood,
        and pressing anger produces strife.

In his final set of proverbs Agur warned against irritating people because the speaker talked too much. Two ways of irritating others with too much talk are highlighted. People who talk too much about themselves are irritating because no one likes a braggart. Equally irritating are people who like to talk out loud about the evil plans they have for their enemies. Agur's advice for people who have a tendency to talk too much is simply to stop talking. The expression "put your hand to your mouth" is a polite way of saying "shut up." Agur used two similes to describe the natural consequences of talking too much. Just as milk turns into butter curds when it is churned, and the nose starts to bleed when it is punched or twisted, so too the irritation of others will occur when their anger is pressed when someone talks too much.

The Words of King Lemuel (31:1–9)

¹ The words of King Lemuel. An oracle that his mother taught him:
² What are you doing, my son? What are you doing, son of my womb?
What are you doing, son of my vows?
³ Do not give your strength to women,
your ways to those who destroy kings.

Most of the book of Proverbs was written from a male perspective ("Hear, my son, your father's instruction"). This chapter is unique in that it was written from the female perspective (31:1–9) or was written to describe the ideal woman (31:10–31). While Jewish legend identified Lemuel as Solomon, and the advice to be from Bathsheba, his identity remains a mystery. The recipient is identified as a king and the advice came from the queen mother. Being a woman who was familiar with life in the royal court, she warned her son not to engage in sexual gratification with women who were attracted to power. An immoral king could use women for his sensual pleasure, but in the end, these women would destroy him. While Solomon was not the recipient of the advice, his ruined reign provides an apt object lesson of its truth (1 Kings 11:1–8).

⁴ It is not for kings, O Lemuel,
it is not for kings to drink wine,
or for rulers to take strong drink,
⁵ lest they drink and forget what has been decreed
and pervert the rights of all the afflicted.
⁶ Give strong drink to the one who is perishing,
and wine to those in bitter distress;
⁷ let them drink and forget their poverty
and remember their misery no more.

Having warned her son about the dangers of immoral women in the palace, Lemuel's mother turned her attention to another potential area of abuse for a king. A king needed a clear head to rule his realm and to judge his people with justice. The abuse of wine and strong drink would negatively affect his mood and his memory. The queen mother's advice on the consumption of alcohol is in agreement with the other sages (Proverbs 20:1; 23:19–21, 29–35). If Lemuel was a king in Israel, "what has been decreed" would be a reference to the Mosaic Law which established justice for God's people. If the king had a drinking problem, the people most negatively affected by his abuse of alcohol would be the most vulnerable in his kingdom. The Mosaic Law specifically highlighted the poor, widows and orphans, and strangers as the most vulnerable people in Israeli society (Deuteronomy 24:17; 27:19). Because drinking does lead to forgetfulness, Lemuel's mother did recommend the appropriate use of alcohol to relieve the pain of those who were truly suffering. Much like the administration of morphine to those in hospice, the queen mother approved the alleviation of physical and mental pain for those who were perishing. Some commentators take the second proverb as sarcasm in an effort on the part of the mother to shame her son. Don't abuse alcohol and thus act like those miserable poor people in your kingdom who drink to forget their misery.

> [8] Open your mouth for the mute,
> for the rights of all who are destitute.
> [9] Open your mouth, judge righteously,
> defend the rights of the poor and needy.

Having warned her son about the dangers of being king (women and wine), the queen mother concluded her advice by directing him to what issues he should focus on as ruler. He should use his mouth, not for kissing immoral women or for consuming large amounts of wine, but for speaking on behalf of those citizens in his kingdom who had no voice. The queen mother knew there were people in her son's kingdom whose poverty and destitution rendered them invisible and voiceless to those in power. She wanted her son to speak up for the rights of people who carried no influence and to render justice on their behalf. She rightly knew that how he cared for the poor would ultimately define his reign. The narrative of Solomon and his dealings with the two prostitutes is an illustration of this kingly care (1 Kings 3:1–28). A royal psalm composed by the sons of Korah to commemorate Israel's king on his wedding day speaks to this type of justice.

> Gird your sword on your thigh, O mighty one, in your splendor and majesty! In your majesty ride out victoriously

for the cause of truth and meekness and righteousness; let your right hand teach you awesome deeds! (Psalm 45:3–4)

Another royal psalm prayed that the king would take his cue from God's justice so that the most vulnerable people in the kingdom would be protected.

For he delivers the needy when he calls, the poor and him who has no helper. He has pity on the weak and the needy, and saves the lives of the needy. From oppression and violence he redeems their life, and precious is their blood in his sight. (Psalm 72:12–14)

The Ideal Woman (31:10–31)

It is important to remember that the book of Proverbs was written from a male perspective. It was intended as a book of wisdom written by older men, fathers and teachers, to give advice to younger men, their sons and students. Because of this male authorship and audience, women have been featured prominently in the book, beginning with Lady Wisdom who called out to naïve young men to listen to her advice.

Wisdom cries aloud in the street, in the markets she raises her voice; at the head of the noisy streets she cries out; at the entrance of the city gates she speaks: "How long, O simple ones, will you love being simple? How long will scoffers delight in their scoffing and fools hate knowledge? If you turn at my reproof, behold, I will pour out my spirit to you; I will make my words known to you. (Proverbs 1:20–23)

And the reason why Lady Wisdom is so vocal is because of the presence of the other woman, known as the forbidden or foreign woman who is wandering the same streets calling out to the same young men.

So you will be delivered from the forbidden woman, from the adulteress with her smooth words, who forsakes the companion of her youth and forgets the covenant of her God; for her house sinks down to death, and her paths to the departed; none who go to her come back, nor do they regain the paths of life. (Proverbs 2:16–19)

Since the poem was written from the male perspective, the author was describing the ideal woman who did not exist, except in his imagination. But because he was writing to his son, he wanted his son to marry a woman who met as many of the qualities that he was describing. The poem falls into the category of the heroic hymn, normally used to celebrate the victory of soldiers. With this in mind, it is interesting to note how often the author cited the physical vigor of the ideal woman. There are several words of caution when it comes to this passage.

> This passage cannot be read as a kind of blueprint of the ideal Israelite housewife, either for men to measure their wives against or for their wives to try to live up to. (Kenneth Aitken)

To be fair, the poem describes a relatively wealthy woman who managed a large household estate that consisted of children and servants. This woman was involved in buying real estate, cultivating vineyards, and engaging in commerce. She was also involved in charity work within her community.

Also, because the poem was written from the male perspective, it is interesting to note what the male writer found laudable in the ideal woman. He was particularly impressed with her business acumen as her commerce brought income to the household. Instead of costing her husband money, she was contributing money to the household income. The author described a woman who was industrious and independent, so her husband could take his rightful place in the community. He wanted a woman who had a confident attitude, and who cared not only about the betterment of her family, but also the welfare of the poor in the community. But what is probably most notable about this poem, written from the male perspective, is the absence of physical traits and matters of sexual intimacy, like the Song of Solomon. And while it is only mentioned at the end of the poem, the author also commented on the woman's relationship with God.

The poem is an acrostic that uses the 22 letters of the Hebrew alphabet to describe the ideal woman. The poem begins with *Aleph, Beth, Gimel, Daleth,* and ends with *Resh, Shin, and Taw.* Due to the alphabetical constraints, the poem is somewhat random in its organization. The male counterpart to this poem is Psalm 112 which is also an acrostic poem.

The Ideal Woman: Her Rhetorical Rarity (31:10).

> ¹⁰ An excellent wife who can find?
> She is far more precious than jewels.

The acrostic poem begins with a rhetorical question whose answer is obvious. By asking the question, the sage wanted to awaken a desire on the part of his male audience to find such a woman to marry. A secondary goal on the part of his female audience was to become such a woman. Finding a "excellent" woman, that is, a woman of valor, a woman of strength, to marry is easier said than done (Proverbs 12:4). In fact, this strong woman is so rare that her value is compared to precious stones (Proverbs 3:13–15). In one sense, the author was putting a price on this woman, which is interesting, because in the ancient world, a marriage was more of an economic transaction than it was about romantic love. Think of the price Jacob had to pay Laban in order to marry Rachel and Leah (Genesis 29:20, 30). Ruth was the one woman in the Old Testament who was described by Boaz with the same adjective "excellent" used by the sage.

> And now, my daughter, do not fear. I will do for you all that you ask, for all my fellow townsmen know that you are a worthy woman. (Ruth 3:11)

And from the Ruth narrative, she demonstrated her worth to Boaz by her commitment to Naomi and her willingness to work hard in the fields.

The Ideal Woman: Her Impact on Her Husband (31:11–12, 23).

> ¹¹ The heart of her husband trusts in her,
> and he will have no lack of gain.
> ¹² She does him good, and not harm,
> all the days of her life.

The first category that defines an excellent woman is her primary role as a wife. The sage described the intimate relationship that exists between a husband and his wife. A wife who can be trusted completely is a great asset to her husband. A negative example of this would be the unhealthy marriage of Isaac and Rebekah and the narrative of her deception of her elderly husband in the case of the stolen birthright (Genesis 27). The statement "the heart of her husband trusts in her" is remarkable because the Old Testament consistently tells us not to trust in man, but to only trust in the Lord (Psalm 118:8–9). But in this instance, the excellent wife can be completely trusted because she also trusts in the Lord (31:30). The husband and wife share a special spiritual relationship. She shares the same values as her husband, which will be detailed in the poem. Because this married couple values the same things, the wife brings value to the husband's life for the duration of their marriage.

> [23] Her husband is known in the gates
> when he sits among the elders of the land.

The sage once again returned to the impact an excellent wife has on the reputation of her husband. The city gate was the place of commerce, counsel, and business in the ancient world (Ruth 4:1–12). A man who married well was highly respected by the other elders in the community. If he showed that much wisdom in his choice of a wife, he was thought to be equally wise in other areas of life. The godly wife wants her husband to be well-respected in the community because then he will be respected in the home by his wife and children. The apostle Paul also wrote about the respect a wife has for her husband.

> However, let each one of you love his wife as himself, and let the wife see that she respects her husband. (Ephesians 5:33)

The Ideal Woman: Her Impact on Her Family (31:13–27).

> [13] She seeks wool and flax,
> and works with willing hands.
> [14] She is like the ships of the merchant;
> she brings her food from afar.
> [15] She rises while it is yet night

and provides food for her household
and portions for her maidens.
¹⁶ She considers a field and buys it;
with the fruit of her hands she plants a vineyard.
¹⁷ She dresses herself with strength
and makes her arms strong.
¹⁸ She perceives that her merchandise is profitable.
Her lamp does not go out at night.
¹⁹ She puts her hands to the distaff,
and her hands hold the spindle.
²⁰ She opens her hand to the poor
and reaches out her hands to the needy.

Notice the references to the hands of this ideal woman in this section of the acrostic poem. She willingly works with her hands in the domestic areas that were common to women of this time period. She goes to the marketplace to purchase the wool and flax that she will spin into thread to turn into garments for her large household. As an accomplished business woman, she uses her earnings to purchase a vineyard and then she plants the vines with her own hands. Isaiah 5:2 describes the hard work that goes into creating a productive vineyard. In addition to caring for her household, she is also generous with the poor in her community by giving away food with an open hand. The overall image is that of a woman who is capable in her home and compassionate in her community. She is industrious, disciplined, discerning, strong, and generous. To accomplish everything, the woman does not sleep much as she rises early in the morning to begin her day's work (v. 15), and stays up late to complete her tasks (v. 18).

²¹ She is not afraid of snow for her household,
for all her household are clothed in scarlet.
²² She makes bed coverings for herself;
her clothing is fine linen and purple.
²⁴ She makes linen garments and sells them;
she delivers sashes to the merchant.
²⁵ Strength and dignity are her clothing,
and she laughs at the time to come.
²⁶ She opens her mouth with wisdom,
and the teaching of kindness is on her tongue.

²⁷ She looks well to the ways of her household
and does not eat the bread of idleness.

In these verses the sage continued to rehearse the industry of this excellent woman by focusing on her skill as a weaver of fine linens. She skillfully uses her hands to make clothing for her home and for the marketplace. And finally, she is also skillful when it comes to the wisdom that flows from her lips (v. 26).

The Ideal Woman: Words of Praise (31:28-30).

²⁸ Her children rise up and call her blessed;
her husband also, and he praises her:
²⁹ "Many women have done excellently,
but you surpass them all."

Speaking on behalf of her family, the sage envisioned what the children and husband will say about their ideal mother and wife. Praise from people who only know you casually can be suspect because they don't truly know you. But praise from the individuals who see you day in and day out, and throughout the day is what matters. Because she rose up early to care for the needs of her family (31:15), her grown children will rise up and praise her dedication to them. Knowing that children will rise up and say something about their mother, it is wise on the part of mothers to sacrificially invest in the lives of their children so that what they say about their mother is praiseworthy. The sage then put words of praise on the lips of her husband. While he was well respected in the city gate because of his wife's character (31:23), she was respected in the home, and that is no secondary position. While the husband acknowledged the existence of other excellent women, he married the best of the best.

³⁰ Charm is deceitful, and beauty is vain,
but a woman who fears the LORD is to be praised.

The typical man focuses on the physical attributes of a woman first, and often neglects her spiritual qualities. Therefore, it is significant what the sage had to say about these two categories as he concluded his poem. Only a lying man will say that the physical appearance of his wife is not important to him. Read Proverbs 5 for the celebration of feminine beauty and the joys of marital intimacy. A woman's physical appearance is important, but it is not the most important factor. Physical beauty can mask an unattractive personality. Do you remember the memorable statement about a beautiful woman earlier in the book?

> Like a gold ring in a pig's snout is a beautiful woman without discretion. (Proverbs 11:22)

It was at the end of the acrostic poem that the sage commented on the ideal woman's relationship with God. The book of Proverbs opened with the statement, "The fear of the LORD is the beginning of knowledge" (1:7a), and it is fitting that it concludes with this theme. That she has a great relationship with God is implied by her excellent relationship with her husband, her children, and her community. The reason she is so highly thought of in these relationships is because she thinks so highly of God.

> [31] Give her of the fruit of her hands,
> and let her works praise her in the gates.

Having focused on the industry produced by the hands of the ideal woman (31:13–20), the sage concluded his acrostic poem with a command that she would be generously rewarded for her labor. While there is an element of financial reward in the poem (31:18, 24), for the ideal woman the principal reward would be the praise of her grown children and her husband (31:28–29). And, because of her sacrificial labor on behalf of her husband and the household, which brought him praise in the gates of the city (31:23), the sage commanded the elders of the city to give this woman the same praise that they had given her husband.

PROVERBS INDEX

10:1	89		10:27	128
10:2	91		10:28	94
10:3	93		10:29	130
10:4	94		10:30	132
10:5	95		10:31	119
10:6	96		10:32	109
10:7	98			
10:8	100		11:1	134
10:9	102		11:2	136
10:10	100		11:3	102
10:11	104		11:4	137
10:12	105		11:5	138
10:13	107		11:6	139
10:14	107		11:7	139
10:15	109		11:8	94
10:16	111		11:9	141
10:17	113		11:10	139
10:18	114		11:11	142
10:19	116		11:12	143
10:20	118		11:13	115
10:21	108		11:14	145
10:22	120		11:15	144
10:23	122		11:16	147
10:24	93		11:17	149
10:25	124		11:18	111
10:26	126		11:19	132

11:20	134		12:23	174
11:21	151		12:24	95
11:22	152		12:25	180
11:23	94		12:26	113
11:24	154		12:27	95
11:25	155		12:28	113
11:26	97			
11:27	156		13:1	89
11:28	120		13:2	150
11:29	158		13:3	117
11:30	160		13:4	126
11:31	140		13:5	182
			13:6	133
12:1	162		13:7	183
12:2	164		13:8	184
12:3	125		13:9	138
12:4	153		13:10	185
12:5	166		13:11	184
12:6	142		13:12	161
12:7	133		13:13	187
12:8	168		13:14	105
12:9	170		13:15	168
12:10	149		13:16	175
12:11	143		13:17	189
12:12	161		13:18	162
12:13	151		13:19	190
12:14	157		13:20	169
12:15	172		13:21	112
12:16	174		13:22	159
12:17	176		13:23	192
12:18	119		13:24	162
12:19	177		13:25	141
12:20	178			
12:21	140		14:1	153
12:22	134		14:2	130

14:3	101		15:1	189
14:4	194		15:2	101
14:5	177		15:3	164
14:6	169		15:4	189
14:7	101		15:5	175
14:8	175		15:6	92
14:9	191		15:7	101
14:10	196		15:8	135
14:11	133		15:9	131
14:12	172		15:10	163
14:13	197		15:11	197
14:14	157		15:12	203
14:15	198		15:13	180
14:16	191		15:14	14
14:17	179		15:15	181
14:18	199		15:16	170
14:19	191		15:17	171
14:20	109		15:18	186
14:21	98		15:19	127
14:22	158		15:20	89
14:23	96		15:21	123
14:24	92		15:22	188
14:25	177		15:23	190
14:26	160		15:24	114
14:27	128		15:25	165
14:28	145		15:26	166
14:29	200		15:27	112
14:30	180		15:28	142
14:31	193		15:29	165
14:32	152		15:30	181
14:33	202		15:31	162
14:34	146		15:32	162
14:35	182		15:33	147

16:1	205
16:2	173
16:3	125
16:4	206
16:5	136
16:6	128
16:7	131
16:8	92
16:9	125
16:10	207
16:11	209
16:12	208
16:13	208
16:14	208
16:15	209
16:16	202
16:17	130
16:18	136
16:19	171
16:20	97
16:21	190
16:22	105
16:23	203
16:24	190
16:25	172
16:26	195
16:27	179
16:28	186
16:29	150
16:30	179
16:31	161
16:32	201
16:33	206

17:1	171
17:2	183
17:3	207
17:4	211
17:5	193
17:6	213
17:7	101
17:8	215
17:9	106
17:10	191
17:11	150
17:12	192
17:13	211
17:14	186
17:15	217
17:16	144
17:17	219
17:18	144
17:19	187
17:20	119
17:21	90
17:22	198
17:23	215
17:24	173
17:25	90
17:26	217
17:27	117
17:28	117
18:1	220
18:2	101
18:3	183
18:4	221
18:5	217
18:6	101

18:7	101
18:8	116
18:9	95
18:10	165
18:11	121
18:12	137
18:13	183
18:14	197
18:15	203
18:16	216
18:17	222
18:18	223
18:19	224
18:20	195
18:21	120
18:22	154
18:23	110
18:24	220
19:1	103
19:2	201
19:3	224
19:4	110
19:5	177
19:6	216
19:7	110
19:8	169
19:9	178
19:10	224
19:11	106
19:12	226
19:13	154
19:14	154
19:15	95
19:16	130

19:17	155
19:18	163
19:19	201
19:20	188
19:21	206
19:22	194
19:23	128
19:24	127
19:25	204
19:26	90
19:27	188
19:28	143
19:29	205
20:1	226
20:2	227
20:3	148
20:4	127
20:5	221
20:6	220
20:7	103
20:8	227
20:9	210
20:10	134
20:11	213
20:12	174
20:13	96
20:14	211
20:15	202
20:16	144
20:17	112
20:18	125
20:19	116
20:20	213
20:21	196

20:22	218
20:23	134
20:24	207
20:25	119
20:26	227
20:27	207
20:28	227
20:29	214
20:30	212
21:1	228
21:2	173
21:3	218
21:4	137
21:5	96
21:6	92
21:7	150
21:8	131
21:9	154
21:10	167
21:11	204
21:12	152
21:13	156
21:14	216
21:15	152
21:16	144
21:17	123
21:18	212
21:19	154
21:20	192
21:21	148
21:22	203
21:23	118
21:24	204
21:25	127

21:26	127
21:27	135
21:28	177
21:29	212
21:30	168
21:31	207
22:1	99
22:2	121
22:3	200
22:4	121, 129
22:5	212
22:6	214
22:7	184
22:8	219
22:9	97
22:10	205
22:11	228
22:12	165
22:13	194
22:14	222
22:15	163
22:16	185